Management Accounting: Costing

Tutorial

David Cox

Published by Osborne Books Limited
Tel 01905 748071
Email books@osbornebooks.co.uk
Website www.osbornebooks.co.uk

Design by Laura Ingham

Printed by CPI Group (UK) Limited, Croydon, CR0 4YY, on environmentally friendly, acid-free paper from managed forests.

British Library Cataloguing in Publication Data
A catalogue record for this book is available from the British Library

ISBN 978 1909173 750

Contents

Introduction

Qualifications covered

This book has been written specifically to cover the Unit 'Management Accounting: Costing' which is a mandatory Unit for the following qualifications:

AAT Advanced Diploma in Accounting – Level 3

AAT Advanced Diploma in Accounting at SCQF – Level 6

The book contains a clear text with worked examples and case studies, chapter summaries and key terms to help with revision. Each chapter concludes with a wide range of activities, many in the style of AAT computer based assessments.

Osborne Study and Revision Materials

The materials featured on the previous page are tailored to the needs of students studying this Unit and revising for the assessment. They include:

- **Workbooks:** paperback books with practice activities and exams
- **Wise Guides:** pocket-sized spiral bound revision cards
- **Student Zone:** access to Osborne Books online resources
- **Osborne Books App:** Osborne Books ebooks for mobiles and tablets

Visit www.osbornebooks.co.uk for details of study and revision resources and access to online material.

1 An introduction to cost accounting

this chapter covers...

- *This first chapter examines the purpose of cost accounting (which is often referred to as management accounting) and its role in providing information to the managers of a business. In particular we see how the role of cost accounting provides information to assist managers with:*
  - *decision-making*
  - *planning for the future*
  - *control of expenditure*

  These themes will be developed in later chapters.
- *We then identify cost units and see how responsibility centres, cost centres, profit centres, investment centres and revenue centres are used to monitor the performance of sections of a business.*
- *We see how costs can be grouped together or classified in different ways:*
  - *by element*
  - *by nature*
  - *by function*
  - *by behaviour*

  Each of these ways enables us to see the same business from a different viewpoint, which will help managers to run the business better.
- *After studying this chapter you should have a clear idea of the role of costing and appreciate some of the ideas that it uses.*

PURPOSE OF COST ACCOUNTING

Cost accounting, as its name implies, enables the managers of a business to know the cost of the firm's output – whether a product or a service – and the revenues from sales. Once costing information is available, managers can use it to assist with

- decision-making
- planning for the future
- control of expenditure

Cost accounting (which is also often referred to as management accounting) is widely used by all types of businesses and organisations – whether they provide a service or make a product. Businesses and organisations need to keep their costs under review and in order to do this, they need accurate cost information. Thus a cost accounting system will provide answers to questions such as:

What does it cost us to provide a student with a day's accountancy course?

What does it cost us to carry out a hip replacement operation?

What does it cost us to make a pair of trainers?

What does it cost us to serve a cheeseburger and fries?

What is the cost of a passenger-mile on a bus journey?

What does it cost us to provide a week's holiday in the Canaries?

The cost accounting system helps managers with production planning and decision-making, such as:

- short-term decisions, eg "how many do we need to make and sell in order to break-even?"; "shall we increase production of Aye or Bee, bearing in mind that shortages of skilled labour mean that we can't do both?"
- long-term decisions, eg "we need to buy a new machine for the factory – shall we buy Machine Exe or Machine Wye?"

COST ACCOUNTING AND FINANCIAL ACCOUNTING

These two types of accounting, although they produce different reports and statements, obtain their data from the same set of transactions carried out by the business or organisation over a given period. This is illustrated in the diagram on the next page.

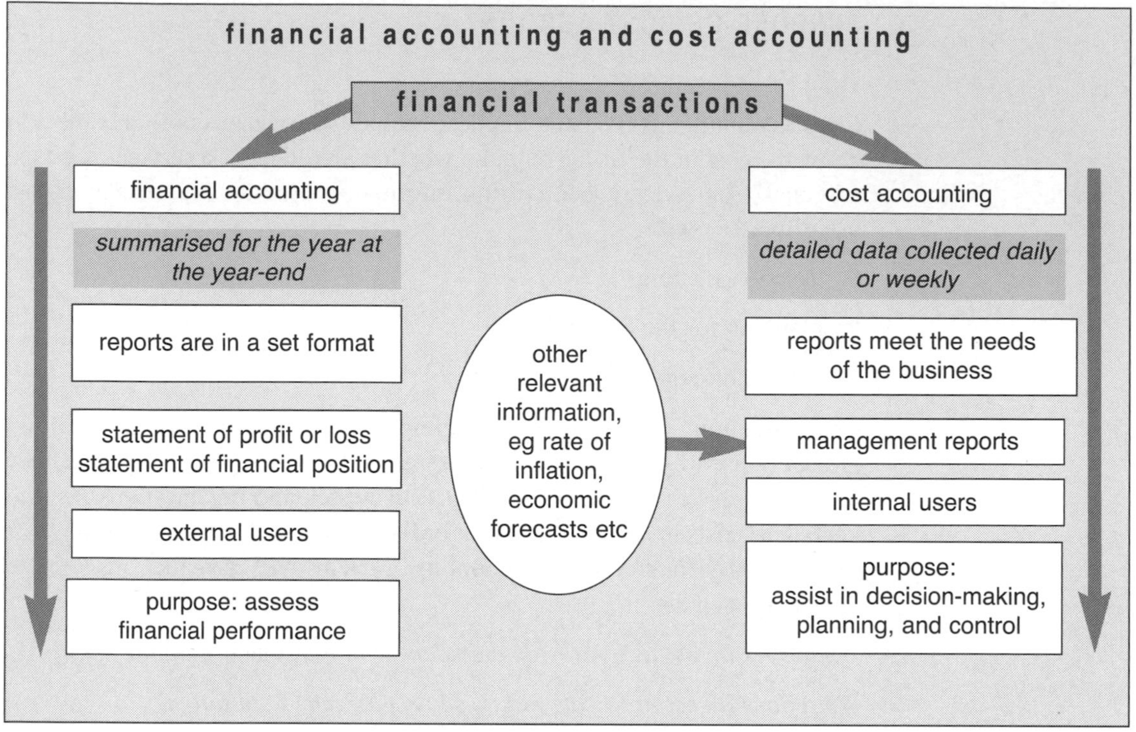

Financial accounting uses the financial data relating to transactions carried out over a period of time. The information is processed through the accounting records and extracted in the form of financial statements – the statement of profit or loss and the statement of financial position. The statements are often required to be produced by law, eg the Companies Act, and are available to external users such as shareholders, suppliers, bank, HM Revenue & Customs, Companies House.

Cost accounting uses the same data to produce reports containing financial information on the recent past and projections for the future. The reports are available to internal users, such as managers, directors, and owners (but not to shareholders generally), and may also be made available to third parties (such as banks). There is no legal requirement to produce this information and the content of the report and the principles used can be suited to the activities of the business or organisation and the requirements of its managers. The information is prepared as frequently as it is required, and speed is often vital as the information may go out-of-date very quickly. It is important that the information is prepared accurately and in line with the **ethical principle of integrity** – accounting staff are straightforward and honest in all professional and business relationships.

COST UNITS AND COMPOSITE COST UNITS

Cost units are units of output to which costs can be charged.

A cost unit can be:

- a unit of production from a factory such as a car, a television, an item of furniture
- a unit of service, such as a passenger on a bus, an attendance at a swimming pool

Composite cost units are units of output which comprise two variables.

Examples of composite cost units:

- the cost of a bus passenger, per mile/kilometre
- the cost of a hospital patient, per day

Note that composite cost units are common in service sector businesses.

RESPONSIBILITY CENTRES

Within a business different managers will have responsibilities at different levels, eg

- a responsibility for controlling costs
- a responsibility to achieve a particular level of profit
- a responsibility to achieve a particular return on money invested
- a responsibility to achieve a level of sales revenue

Responsibility centres are segments of a business for which a manager is accountable.

Examples of responsibility centres are:

- cost centres
- profit centres
- investment centres
- revenue centres

COST CENTRES

As well as charging costs to cost units they also need to be charged to a specific part of a business – a **cost centre.**

Cost centres are segments of a business to which costs can be charged.

A cost centre in a manufacturing business, for example, is a department of a factory, a particular stage in the production process, or even a whole factory. In a college, examples of cost centres are the teaching departments, or particular sections of departments such as the college's administrative office.

Cost centres enable segmented costs – which relate to a centre – to be identified, and this assists with control of the business.

PROFIT CENTRES

For some sections of businesses the cost centre approach of analysing costs is taken to a further level by also analysing sales revenue to centres. As revenue less costs equals profit, such centres are called profit centres.

Profit centres are segments of a business to which costs can be charged, revenue can be identified, and profit can be calculated.

From the definition we can see that profit centres have both costs and revenue. For example, a garden centre has conservatory plants as a profit centre as shown in the following diagram:

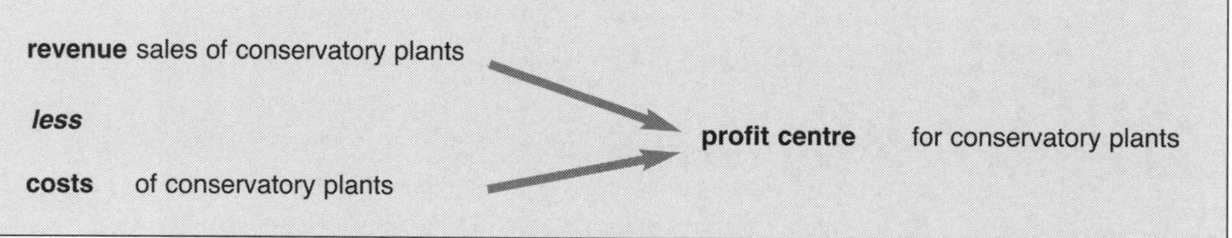

Note that many cost centres provide support services within a business or organisation and, so, cannot become profit centres because they do not have any significant revenue, for example, the administration department of a business.

The management of a profit centre has control over the centre's costs – both variable and fixed – and its revenues. By deducting costs from revenue the centre's management can quantify the profit made and can make comparisons with previous periods (eg last month, last quarter, last year, etc), with profit targets set for the current period (eg 'our profit is 10 per cent above target'), and also with other profit centres (eg 'our profit last month was higher than the other profit centres').

INVESTMENT CENTRES

For **investment centres** the profit of the centre is compared with how much money the business has put in to earn that profit.

Investment centres are segments of a business where profit is compared with the amount of money invested in the centre.

Profit is compared with money invested by means of a percentage as shown in the following diagram for a garden centre's conservatory plants investment centre.

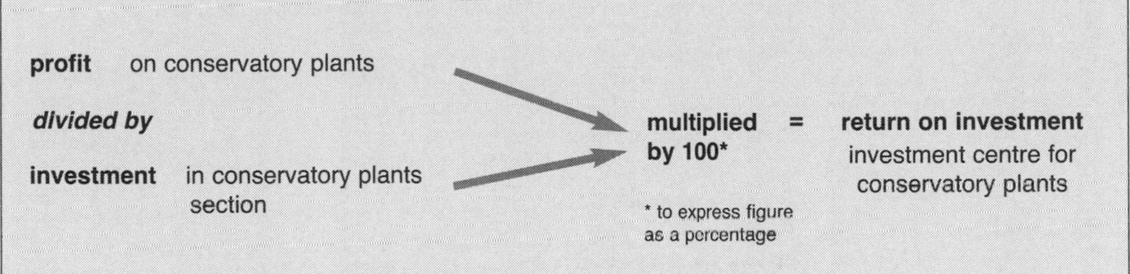

The management of an investment centre has control over the centre's costs – both variable and fixed – and its revenues, assets and liabilities. By calculating the return on investment, the centre's management will wish to make comparisons of the return for the current period with that of previous periods (eg 'have we done better than last year?') against targets set for the current period (eg 'are we on target for the current period?'), and also with the other investment centres of the business (eg 'how do we compare with the other investment centres?').

REVENUE CENTRES

In a revenue centre, the responsibility of the manager is for the sales revenue generated.

Revenue centres are segments of a business where sales revenue from the product sold or service provided is measured.

Examples of revenue centres include shop departments, restaurants, coffee shops – where the manager is responsible for generating sales revenue.

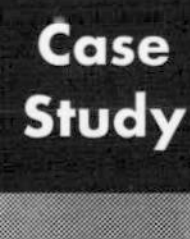

PROVIDING INFORMATION FOR MANAGEMENT

situation

You are an Accounts Assistant at Severnvale Garden Centre.

The Managing Director, Charlie Rimmack, has asked you for accounting information that is needed for a meeting with the managers of two sections of the garden centre – the manager for conservatory plants and the manager for shrubs. Charlie wants the information in order to see which department is performing better; she requests details for each section of costs and revenue for last year, and the amount of money invested in each section at the end of the year. (She says that all figures can be to the nearest £000.)

solution

You go to the accounts which have been set up to show segmented costs, revenue and money invested, and extract the following information for last year:

		Conservatory plants	Shrubs
		£000	*£000*
Costs:	materials	137	151
	labour	93	134
	expenses	45	70
Revenue		425	555
Money invested		450	400

In order to help the Managing Director you decide to present the management information for each section in the following way:

	Conservatory plants	Shrubs
	£000	*£000*
Cost Centre		
Materials	137	151
Labour	93	134
Expenses	45	70
Total	275	355

Here the cost centre for conservatory plants has the lower costs.

Profit Centre		
Revenue	425	555
less Costs (see above)	275	355
Profit	150	200

These figures show that shrubs is the better profit centre.

Investment Centre

$\frac{\text{Profit (see above)}}{\text{Investment}}$	$\frac{150}{450}$	$\frac{200}{400}$
Expressed as a percentage (multiplied by 100)	33%	50%

These figures show that shrubs is the better investment centre.

Revenue Centre		
Revenue	425	555

These figures show that shrubs is the better revenue centre.

Conclusion

You complete a comparison table to summarise the results you have calculated:

Responsibility centre	Criteria	Conservatory plants	Shrubs
Cost centre	Low cost	£275,000 ✓	£355,000 x
Profit centre	High profit	£150,000 x	£200,000 ✓
Investment centre	High %	33% x	50% ✓
Revenue centre	High sales	£425,000 x	£555,000 ✓

Advice to Charlie Rimmack:

The shrubs department is performing better than the conservatory plants department for three of the four criteria. However, both sections are earning profits which contribute to the overheads of the business, so both should continue to trade.

Note that further use of cost accounting techniques such as contribution and break-even (covered in later chapters) – can be used to provide additional management information.

CLASSIFICATION OF COSTS

Within any business, whether it manufactures a product or provides a service, there are certain costs involved at various stages to produce the units of output. The diagram on the next page shows the costs of a manufacturing business which are incurred by the three main sections or 'areas' of a manufacturing business.

These three separate sections are:

- **factory** – where production takes place and the product is 'finished' and made ready for selling
- **warehouse** – where finished goods are stored and from where they are despatched when they are sold
- **office** – where the support functions take place – marketing, sales, administration, finance and so on

Note that while the diagram on the next page shows the costs of a manufacturing business, it can be adapted easily to fit non-manufacturing organisations, such as a shop, a hospital, a school or college, a church, a club. While the units of output of these organisations differ from those of a manufacturer, nevertheless they still incur costs at various stages of the 'production' process.

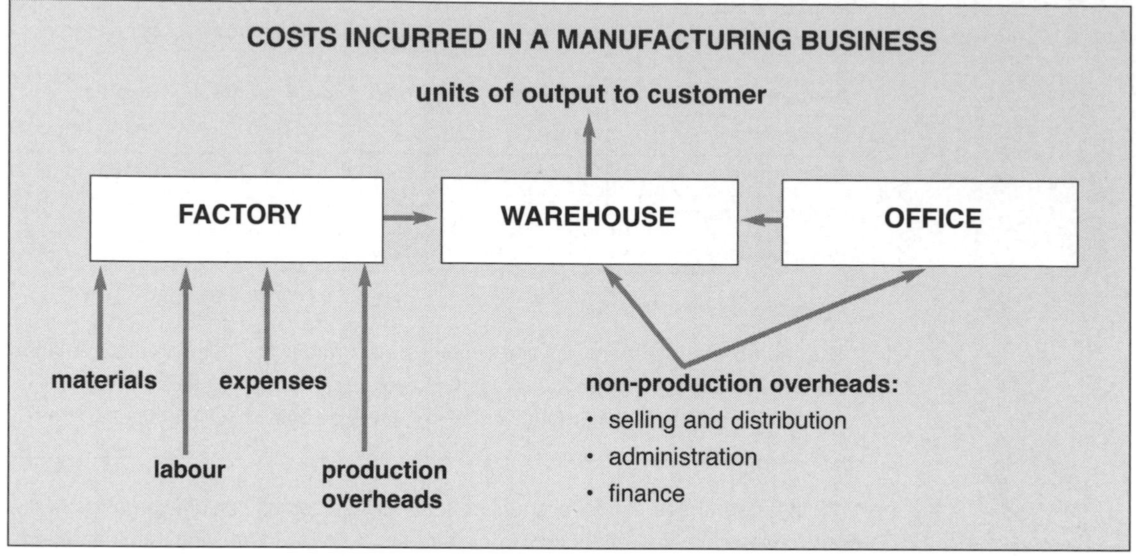

In order to prepare information for the managers of a business, costs must be classified, ie organised into sets in a way which the managers will find useful.

This can be done in four ways:

- by element
- by nature
- by function
- by behaviour

classification of costs by element

Businesses incur many different kinds of cost in the production of goods or 'output', including costs of the warehouse and the office. The most basic way of splitting up costs is according to the type of expenditure under the headings:

- materials, eg the components to make a car
- labour, eg wages of an employee
- expenses, eg rent and rates, telephone charges, insurance

Note: material, labour, and expenses are often referred to as the three elements of cost.

Materials costs (physical items which you can see and touch) are the costs of raw materials, components and other goods used.

Labour costs are the costs of employees' wages and salaries.

Expenses are other costs, which cannot be included in 'materials' or 'labour'.

Splitting costs into these three elements applies to both manufacturing and service businesses. The classification provides important information to managers as they can see the breakdown of the total into different kinds of cost.

classification of costs by nature

Within each of the three elements of materials, labour and expenses, some costs can be identified directly with each unit of output. For example:

- the cost of components used in making cars
- the wages of workers on a production line in a factory

These are termed **direct costs**. In manufacturing, the total of all the direct costs is called the **prime cost** of the output.

A direct cost is a cost that can be identified directly with each unit of output.

Prime cost is the total of all direct costs.

Costs which cannot be identified directly with each unit of output are **indirect costs** or overheads.

Indirect costs (overheads) are all costs, other than those identified as 'direct costs', and they cannot be identified directly with each unit of output.

There are many examples of overheads, including:

- telephone charges
- insurance premiums
- cost of wages of non-production staff, such as managers, office staff, cost accountants and so on
- running costs of delivery vehicles
- depreciation charge for non-current assets

Note particularly the last two examples. In cost accounting, as in financial accounting, we distinguish between capital and revenue expenditure. In our analysis of costs we are referring to revenue expenditure, and therefore include the running costs and depreciation of non-current assets, rather than the capital cost of their purchase.

We now have six possible classifications for costs, each of the three elements of materials, labour and expenses being split by their nature into direct and indirect costs. These are illustrated for a manufacturing business in the table on the next page.

Classification of costs by element and by nature		
nature / element	Direct Costs	Indirect Costs (Overheads)
Materials	The cost of raw materials from which the finished product is made.	The cost of all other materials, eg grease for machines, cleaning materials.
Labour	Wages paid to those who work the machinery on the production line or who are involved in assembly or finishing of the product.	Wages and salaries paid to all other employees, eg managers and supervisors, maintenance staff, administration staff.
Expenses	Any expenses which can be identified with particular units of output, eg royalties payable to the designer of a product, fees linked directly to specific output and paid to people who are not employees.	All other expenses, eg rent, rates, telephone, lighting and heating costs, depreciation of non-current assets, insurance, advertising, etc. These are costs which cannot be identified directly with units of output.
Total	**TOTAL DIRECT COST = PRIME COST**	**TOTAL INDIRECT COST = TOTAL OVERHEADS**

classification of costs by function

Another method of classifying costs is to look at the costs incurred in different sections of the organisation, according to their 'function', or the kind of work being done.

In manufacturing, the main function is production of the goods. The business could not be run, however, without administrators, accountants, sales and delivery staff and so on – these are examples of non-production costs.

When costs are classified by function, the main headings generally used are:

production

administration
selling and distribution — non-production costs (administration, selling and distribution, finance)
finance

Other functions can be added to suit the needs of a particular business. For example, a 'Research and Development' heading could be used if a company spent large sums of money in researching and developing new products.

Non-manufacturing organisations – such as a hospital or a college – may use other 'function' headings, according to the kind of work each section of the organisation carries out.

Please note that, in classifying costs by their function, we are looking at the same set of costs for the business or organisation as before. We are simply presenting them in different groupings.

It is an important function of accounting that information should be presented in the form most suitable for the purpose for which it is required. For some management purposes, classification of costs by function provides better information.

classification of costs by behaviour

In cost accounting, it is important to appreciate the behaviour of costs – in particular to understand that not all costs increase or decrease directly in line with increases or decreases in output. By behaviour, costs in the short-term are:

- fixed, or
- semi-variable, or
- variable

We shall be studying the relationship between fixed and variable costs and output in detail later in the book (Chapter 8). In particular, we will be looking at the technique of break-even analysis – the point at which costs are exactly equal to income.

fixed costs

Fixed costs remain constant over a range of output levels, despite other changes – for example, insurance, rent, rates. In the form of a graph, they appear as follows (note that money amounts are shown on the vertical axis and units of output on the horizontal axis):

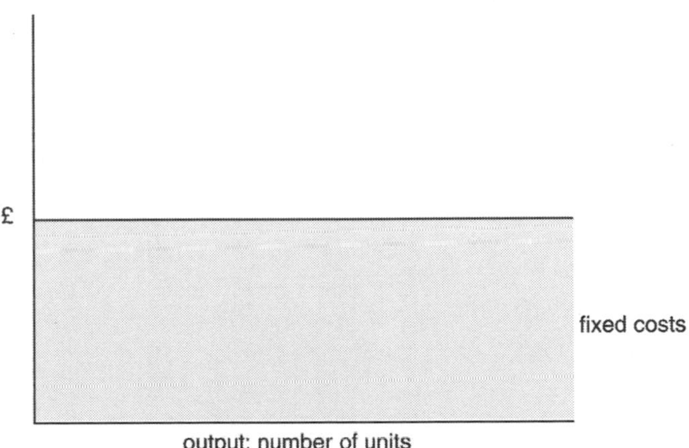

For fixed costs the **cost remains the same** at different levels of output.

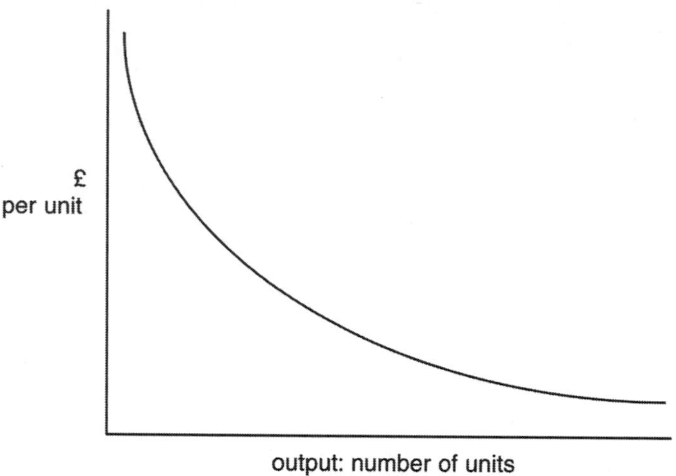

For fixed costs, the **cost per unit** falls as output increases, as follows:

For example, with rent of £40,000 per year:

- at output of 4,000 units, equals £10 per unit
- at output of 10,000 units, equals £4 per unit

Whilst it is sensible to seek to achieve maximum output in order to reduce the cost per unit, fixed costs do not remain fixed at all levels of production. For example, a decision to double production is likely to increase the fixed costs – an increase in factory rent, for example, because an additional factory may need to be rented. Fixed costs are described as **stepped fixed costs**, because they increase by a large amount all at once; graphically, the cost behaviour is shown as a step:

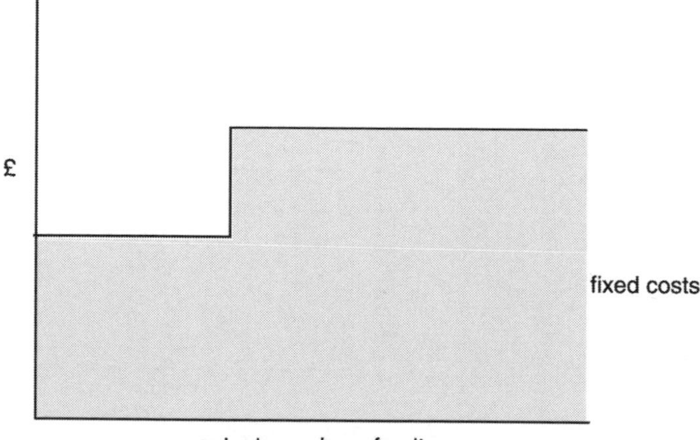

semi-variable costs

These combine both a fixed and a variable cost. For example, a telephone bill comprises the fixed rental for the line, together with the variable amount for each call made. Such a **mixed cost** is expressed graphically as:

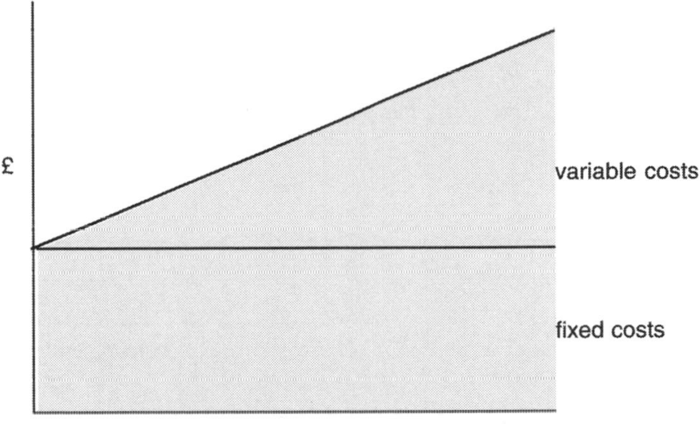

variable costs

Variable costs alter directly with changes in output levels, ie as activity increases, then the cost increases. Examples include direct materials, direct labour, direct expenses such as royalties. Graphically, variable costs appear as follows:

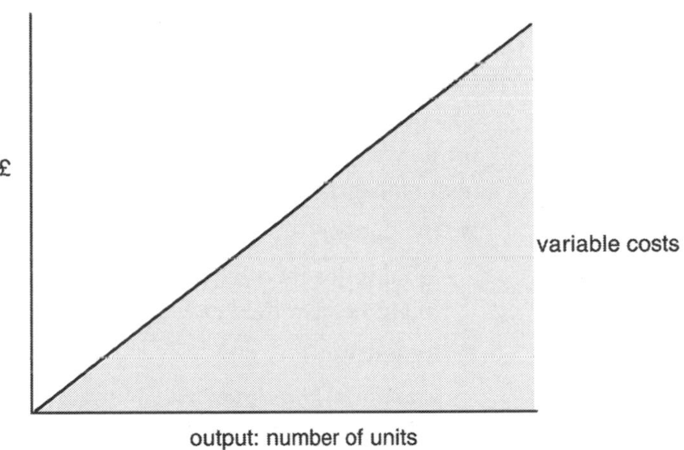

For example, a publishing company paying a royalty of £1 to an author for each book sold:

- at sales of 1,000 books, equals variable cost of £1,000 royalties
- at sales of 10,000 books, equals variable cost of £10,000 royalties

The cost per unit remains the same at different levels of output (unless there are economies of scale, eg bulk discount), as follows:

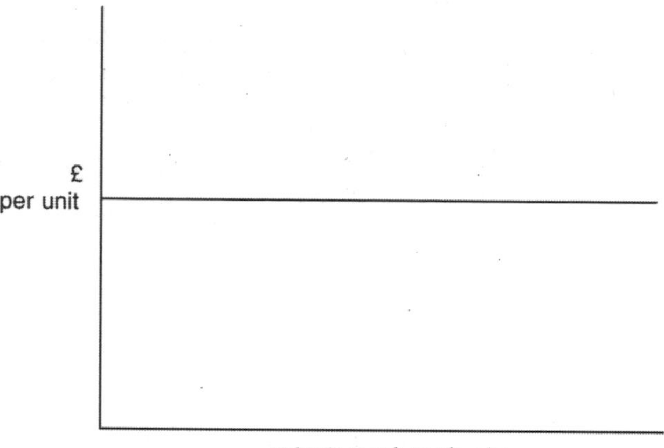

all costs are variable

Whilst we have made the distinction between fixed and variable costs, it is important to appreciate that these cost behaviours hold only in the short term – in the long term, all costs are variable. The example we have seen earlier is of factory rent as a fixed cost but, if production increases, it may result in a larger, or another, factory being rented at an additional cost.

REASONS FOR CLASSIFYING COSTS

The question might be asked, "Why classify costs in four ways?" The answer is that we can see the same business from four different viewpoints – this will help managers to run the business better:

- **by element**

  looking for the high cost elements in order to make savings, eg labour might be identified as being too high

- **by nature**

  looking at the direct and indirect costs to see where savings could be made – eg the business might be able to reduce the cost of direct labour

- **by function**

  looking at the different departments to see which are the high-spending departments – perhaps savings can be made

- **by behaviour**

  identifying the costs as being fixed, semi-variable, or variable – the business might be able to make savings by altering the balance between fixed and variable costs

Thus classifying costs helps management with:

- decision-making, when implementing changes
- planning, when preparing forecasts and budgets
- control, when checking results against what was planned

CALCULATING THE COST OF GOODS AND SERVICES

Using the principles of costing will help to calculate the cost of a product – whether goods or services. Only when the cost of producing each unit of output is known, can a business make decisions about the selling price.

The steps towards calculating the cost of goods and services are:

identify the unit of output

The cost units for a particular business or organisation must be identified. As we have seen earlier, these are the units of output to which costs can be charged. Only by recovering costs through the sales of output can a business make a profit.

Examples of units of output include:

- cars
- meals
- passenger-miles
- hair cuts
- books printed

calculate the number of units of output for a particular time period

Once the unit of output is identified, the business is then able to calculate how many units can be produced or provided in a given time period, such as a day, week, month, quarter or year. For example, a garage will work out how many hours of mechanics' time are available, or a car manufacturer will calculate how many cars it can produce in a year.

calculate the direct costs

Having established the number of units of output for a particular time period, the next task is to calculate the direct costs, or prime cost, for that time period. As we have seen earlier in this chapter, the direct costs comprise:

direct materials	identifiable with the product
direct labour	the wages paid to those who make the product
direct expenses	identifiable with the product
Total direct costs or Prime costs	

calculate the indirect costs

The indirect costs, or overheads, of the production or service must be calculated for the particular time period. Indirect costs comprise:

indirect materials	materials used that are not identified directly with production
indirect labour	wages and salaries paid to those who are not directly involved in production
indirect expenses	expenses of the business not identified directly with production
Total indirect costs or Overheads	

Once the indirect costs have been calculated, we must then ensure that their total cost is charged to the cost units for a particular time period. Only by including indirect costs in the total cost of the output can a business recover their cost from the sales made.

calculate the total cost of a unit of output

Once the direct and indirect costs for a time period are known, the total cost of a unit of output can be calculated, as follows:

$$\frac{\textit{direct costs + indirect costs (overheads)}}{\textit{number of units of output}} = \textit{total cost of a unit of output}$$

The total cost is also known as the absorption cost – because it absorbs (includes) both the direct costs and the indirect costs. Once total cost is known, the business can use the information to help it make pricing and other decisions. Note that, for inventory valuation purposes, only those indirect costs which relate to production are to be included in total cost (see page 56).

calculating the cost – a summary

The process of calculating the cost of output is illustrated in the diagram shown below.

costs for a service business

While the units of 'output' of businesses or organisations that produce a service are not manufactured products, they still incur the costs of:

- materials
- labour
- expenses

Some of the costs of a service business can be linked directly to the 'output' or the cost units of the organisation, but others are classified as overheads.

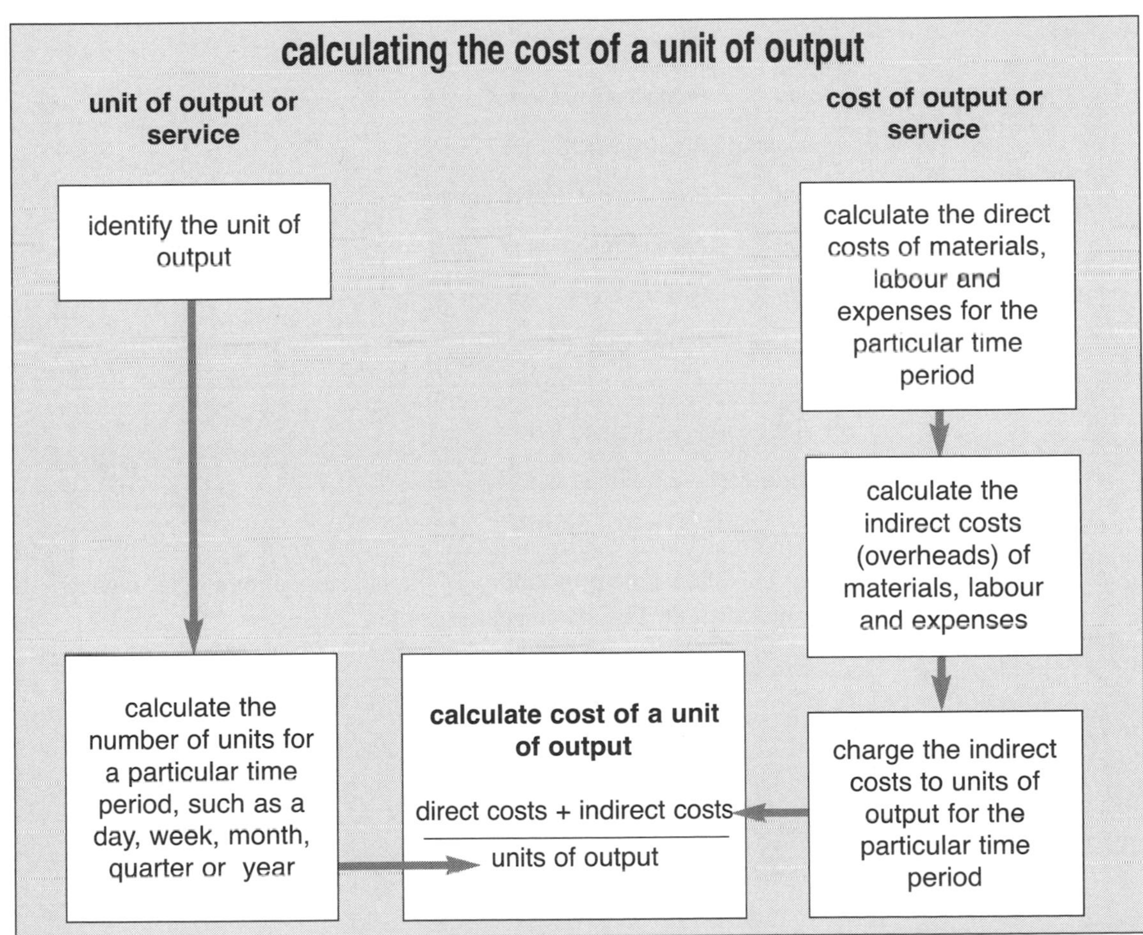

TOTAL COST STATEMENT

The total cost statement brings together all the costs involved in producing the output of a business. It can be prepared on the basis of:

- a single cost unit, eg the cost of making one car in a car factory
- a batch, eg the cost of making 1,000 'special edition' cars
- the whole factory, eg the cost of all the car factory's output for a given time period

The total cost statement is prepared using the following layout:

TOTAL COST STATEMENT

			£
	Direct materials		x
add	Direct labour		x
add	Direct expenses		x
equals	PRIME COST		x
add	Production overheads		x
equals	PRODUCTION COST*		x
add	Selling and distribution costs	non-production overheads**	x
add	Administration costs		x
add	Finance costs		x
equals	TOTAL COST		x

* product cost – explained below

** period cost – explained below

By taking total cost away from revenue we can create a statement of profit or loss. This shows the profitability of the business after all costs have been taken into account. The statement of profit or loss is:

STATEMENT OF PROFIT OR LOSS

		£
	Revenue	x
less	Total cost	x
equals	PROFIT	x

From the total cost statement note the difference between **product cost** and **period cost**:

Product cost

The costs that become part of the manufactured product, that is, direct materials, direct labour, direct expenses (if any), and production overheads. Product costs are included in the closing inventory of the product at the year end and are carried forward to the next financial year.

Period cost

The costs that are not part of the manufactured product and cannot be assigned to products or closing inventory. Period costs – which are incurred in a period of time, eg monthly – are expensed to the statement of profit or loss in the accounting period in which they are incurred.

Chapter Summary

- Cost accounting (also often referred to as management accounting) is essential to provide information for managers of businesses in order to assist with decision-making, planning and control.
- Responsibility centres are segments of a business and include cost centres, profit centres, investment centres and revenue centres.
- Costs may be charged directly to cost units or to specific parts of a business called cost centres.
- Profit centres analyse costs and revenue to show profit (revenue less costs).
- Investment centres compare profit with the amount of money invested in the centre.
- Revenue centres measure sales revenue from the product sold or service provided.
- Costs may be classified by element, by nature, by function, or by behaviour, depending on the purpose for which the information is required.
- Classifying costs by element and by nature gives a six-way split:

DIRECT MATERIALS DIRECT LABOUR DIRECT EXPENSES	INDIRECT MATERIALS INDIRECT LABOUR INDIRECT EXPENSES
TOTAL DIRECT COSTS or PRIME COST	TOTAL INDIRECT COSTS or OVERHEADS

- Overheads may be classified by dividing them amongst the functions or sections of the business:
  - factory (or production)
  - selling and distribution
  - administration
  - finance
  - other section headings as appropriate to the organisation
- By behaviour, costs are fixed, or semi-variable, or variable, in relation to output.
- Total cost of a unit of output $= \dfrac{\text{direct costs + indirect costs (overheads)}}{\text{number of units of output}}$
- A total cost statement lists the total of the direct costs and the overheads. A statement of profit or loss shows revenue minus total cost equals profit.

Key Terms

integrity	ethical principle requiring accounting staff to be straightforward and honest in all professional and business relationships
cost unit	unit of output to which costs can be charged
composite cost unit	unit of output which comprises two variables
responsibility centre	segment of a business for which a manager is accountable
cost centre	segment of a business to which costs can be charged
profit centre	segment of a business to which costs can be charged, revenue can be identified, and profit can be calculated
investment centre	segment of a business where profit is compared with the amount of money invested in the centre
revenue centre	segment of a business where sales revenue from the product sold or service provided is measured
materials costs	the costs of raw materials, components and other goods used
labour costs	the costs of employees' wages and salaries
expenses	other costs, which cannot be included in 'materials' or 'labour'
direct cost	a cost that can be identified directly with each unit of output

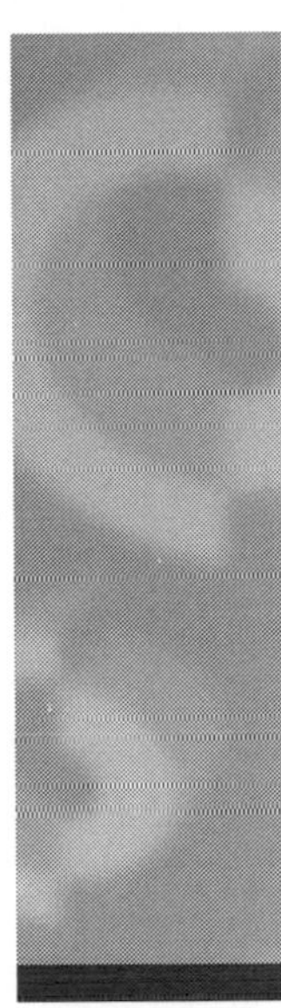

indirect cost (overhead)	a cost that cannot be identified directly with each unit of output
prime cost (direct cost)	the total of all direct costs
fixed costs	costs which remain fixed over a range of output levels
semi-variable costs	costs which combine a fixed and variable element
variable costs	costs which vary directly with output
total cost statement	list of the total of the direct costs and the overheads
product cost	costs that become part of the manufactured product
period cost	costs that cannot be assigned to the manufactured product and are incurred in a period of time, eg monthly

Activities

1.1 Which **one** of these is an example of an accounting technician applying the ethical principle of integrity?

(a) Preparation of cost accounting information that is inaccurate	
(b) Making estimates of cost accounting information in order to get the job done quickly	
(c) Preparation of cost accounting information without reference to source data	
(d) Preparation of cost accounting information in a straightforward and honest way	

1.2 **(a)** Explain the difference between:

- cost centre
- profit centre
- investment centre
- revenue centre

(b) The owner of a business with two departments – Cee and Dee – wishes to know which is performing better. The cost accountant has produced the following results (shown on the next page) and the owner now seeks your advice.

Complete the comparison table (on the next page) and advise the owner – in a sentence – which department is performing better.

Responsibility centre	Criteria	Department Cee	Department Dee
Cost centre	Low cost	£10,000	£12,000
Profit centre	High profit	£5,000	£4,000
Investment centre	High %	20%	15%
Revenue centre	High sales	£55,000	£35,000
Advice to the owner:			

1.3 You work as an Accounts Assistant at City News and Books, a company which owns a group of shops selling newspapers and magazines, books and stationery. The accounting system has been set up to show costs, revenue and money invested for each of these three sections of the business: newspapers and magazines, books, stationery, as separate segments.

The Finance Director has requested details for each segment of costs and revenue for last year, and the amount of money invested in each segment at the end of the year. (She says that all figures can be to the nearest £000.)

The Accounts Supervisor asks you to deal with this request and you go to the accounts and extract the following information for last year:

	Newspapers and magazines	Books	Stationery
	£000	*£000*	*£000*
Costs: materials	155	246	122
labour	65	93	58
expenses	27	35	25
Revenue	352	544	230
Money invested	420	850	250

The Accounts Supervisor asks you to present the information for the Finance Director in the form of a report which shows the costs, profit, return on investment (to the nearest percentage point), and revenue for each segment of the business.

1.4 **(a)** Why is it important to analyse costs in different ways, eg by element, by nature, by function and by behaviour?

(b) Classify each of the following costs by behaviour (ie fixed, or semi-variable, or variable):

- raw materials
- factory rent
- telephone
- direct labour, eg production workers paid on the basis of work done
- indirect labour, eg supervisors' salaries
- commission paid to sales staff

Taking the costs in turn, explain to a friend, who is about to set up a furniture manufacturing business, why you have classified each as fixed, or semi-variable, or variable. Answer the comment, 'What difference does it make anyway, they are all costs that have to be paid.'

1.5 Classify the following costs (tick the appropriate column):

	Fixed	**Semi-variable**	**Variable**
(a) Rates of business premises			
(b) Royalty paid to designer for each unit of output			
(c) Car hire with fixed rental and charge per mile			
(d) Employees paid on piecework basis			
(e) Straight-line depreciation			
(f) Units of output depreciation			
(g) Direct materials			
(h) Telephone bill with fixed rental and a charge for each call made			
(i) Office salaries			

1.6 Severn Manufacturing Limited makes chairs for school and college use. The chairs have plastic seats, and tubular steel legs. **You are to** classify the company's costs into:

- direct materials
- indirect materials
- direct labour
- indirect labour
- direct expenses
- indirect expenses

The cost items to be classified are:

Cost item	**Classification (write your answer)**
Tubular steel	
Factory supervisor's salary	
Wages of employee operating the moulding machine which produces the chair seats	
Works canteen assistant's wages	
Rates of factory	
Power to operate machines	
Factory heating and lighting	
Plastic for making chair seats	
Hire of special machinery for one particular order	
Grease for the moulding machine	
Depreciation of factory machinery	
Depreciation of office equipment	

If you believe alternative classifications exist, argue the case and state if you need further information from the company.

1.7 Betterwell NHS Trust is a large hospital with many departments. Costs of the general operating theatre have been identified and you are to classify them into:

- direct materials
- indirect materials
- direct labour
- indirect labour
- direct expenses
- indirect expenses

The cost items to be classified are:

Cost item	Classification (write your answer)
Dressings	
Disposable scalpels	
Surgeon's salary	
Floor cleaning materials	
Laundry	
Depreciation of staff drinks machine	
Theatre heat and light	
Porter's wages	
Anaesthetic gas	
Depreciation of theatre equipment	
Maintenance of theatre equipment	
CDs for music in theatre	
Anaesthetist's salary	

If you believe alternative classifications exist, argue the case and state if you need further information.

1.8 Wyvern Water Limited bottles natural spring water at its plant at Walcoll at the base of the Wyvern Hills. The natural spring is on land owned by a local farmer to whom a royalty is paid for each bottle of water produced.

You are working in the costing section of Wyvern Water and are asked to analyse the following cost items into the appropriate columns and to agree the totals:

Cost item	**Total cost** £	**Prime cost** £	**Production overheads** £	**Admin-istration costs** £	**Selling and distribution costs** £
Wages of employees working on the bottling line	6,025				
Wages of employees in the stores department	2,750				
Bottles	4,050				
Safety goggles for bottling line employees	240				
Advertisement for new employees	125				
Depreciation of bottling machinery	500				
Depreciation of sales staff's cars	1,000				
Royalty paid to local farmer	750				
Trade exhibition fees	1,500				
Computer stationery	210				
Sales staff salaries	4,095				
TOTALS	21,245				

1.9 Which **one** of the following is normally classed as a fixed cost for a manufacturing business?

(a) Raw materials to make the product	
(b) Salaries of maintenance staff	
(c) Production workers paid on the basis of work done	
(d) Royalties paid to the designer of the product	

1.10 Which **one** of the following is normally classed as a variable cost for a 'high street' printing shop?

(a) Supervisor's salary	
(b) Rent of shop	
(c) Electricity used	
(d) Cost of paper	

1.11 Which **one** of these is a product cost?

(a) Production overheads	
(b) Selling and distribution costs	
(c) Finance costs	
(d) Administration costs	

1.12 Which **one** of these is a period cost?

(a) Direct labour	
(b) Direct materials	
(c) Administration costs	
(d) Production overheads	

1.13 Which **one** of the following statements is correct?

(a) A period cost is included in inventory valuation	
(b) Only direct costs are included in inventory valuation	
(c) A product cost is included in inventory valuation	
(d) Both product and period costs are included in inventory valuation	

2 Materials costs

this chapter covers...

In Chapter 1 we saw how costs can be classified by element as materials, labour and expenses. In this chapter we focus on materials – or inventory – costs. Inventory is the word used for stock.

Businesses and other organisations hold materials inventory in the form of raw materials and components, products bought for resale, and service items. Often the value of such materials is high, representing a considerable investment of money. In this chapter we explain:

- *purchasing and control of materials*
- *re-ordering procedures*
- *records that are kept for materials*
- *valuation of inventory*
- *use of inventory records*
- *bookkeeping entries for materials costs*

TYPES OF MATERIALS INVENTORY

Materials inventory is the cost of:

- raw materials and components bought for use by a manufacturing business
- products bought for resale by a shop or a wholesaler
- service or consumable items, such as stationery, bought for use within a business or organisation

In costing we need to distinguish between direct materials and indirect materials. Thus a manufacturer classifies the cost of materials from which the finished product is made as direct materials; other materials used – grease for machines, cleaning materials, etc – are classified as indirect materials, and form part of the overheads of the business.

The buying of materials is normally undertaken by a firm's Purchasing Department, although in smaller businesses the responsibility will be carried out by an individual or the owner. The job of the buyer(s) is to ensure that the purchases made by the business are bought in compliance with the inventory control policies of the business and at the lowest possible cost, consistent with quality and quantity.

At any time, most businesses will hold materials ready to use or for resale. The diagram shown on the next page examines the materials held by three types of business: a manufacturing business which makes products, a trading business such as a shop, which buys and sells goods, and a service business or organisation, which holds consumable materials.

PLANNING OF PURCHASES AND CONTROL OF MATERIALS

Planning for the purchase of materials and the control of materials inventory is critical to the efficiency of a business. However, holding materials is expensive:

- they have to be financed, possibly by using borrowed money (on which interest is payable)
- there are storage costs, including rent and rates, security, insurance

Within a business there are conflicting demands on its policy for materials. On the one hand, the finance department will want to minimise materials inventory levels to keep costs as low as possible; on the other hand, production and marketing departments will be anxious to keep materials inventory high so that output can be maintained and new orders satisfied speedily before customers decide to buy elsewhere.

MATERIALS HELD BY BUSINESSES

Manufacturing Business	Trading Business	Service Business
Raw materials and components These inventories are held by a manufacturer to reduce the risk of production delays if a supplier fails to deliver on time. A vehicle manufacturer may hold components ready to use, for example. **Work-in-progress** These are part- finished goods on the production line. In a car factory these would be cars partly assembled, for example. **Finished goods** These are goods that have been completed and are ready for sale to customers. A vehicle manufacturer would have completed cars ready for sale, for example.	**Goods for sale** These are items the retailer or wholesaler has bought in (eg from the manufacturer) and has available for sale to the customer. For example: ■ *retailers* a supermarket will have cans of orange drink ready for sale ■ *wholesalers* a timber merchant will have quantities of wood for sale to customers	**Consumable materials** These are materials that are either for use in the organisation or for sale to the customer as part of the service provided. For example: ■ *for use in the organisation* in a college there will be paper ready for use in the photocopiers ■ *items for sale* an optician will sell reading glasses as part of the service provided

There are a number of methods of planning purchases and of inventory control. Which is adopted will depend on the size and sophistication of the business. It is important that a business knows how much inventory it has at any time – either by making a physical count, or by keeping computer records (which need physical verification at regular intervals) – and it must know when it will have to re-order more inventory. The business then needs to know the quantity that needs to be re-ordered. The main methods are:

perpetual inventory

This system records receipt and issue of inventory as the items pass in and out of the business, and re-orders are made accordingly. Inventory records are often kept on computer file activated by the reading of bar codes. Many supermarkets work on this basis.

just in time (JIT)

A method favoured by manufacturing businesses where supplies of components are delivered to the production line just as they are needed. For JIT to operate effectively, quality suppliers are needed who can be contracted to deliver goods in accordance with manufacturing schedules. In this way inventory levels are kept very low.

formulas

Businesses need to calculate when to order inventory, and how much to order; formulas can be used to help with this. These are explained in the sections which follow.

MATERIALS PURCHASES: FIXED QUANTITY METHOD

Using the fixed quantity method of re-ordering, materials are ordered in set amounts, eg 750 reams of photocopying paper (a ream is 500 sheets). For such a system to operate, the business should know:

- the **maximum inventory level** that can be held – this can be calculated, but may well be determined by the amount of storage space available in the warehouse, shop or office stationery 'cupboard'
- the **inventory buffer,** ie the minimum level that inventory should fall to before the new order from the supplier is delivered
- the **lead time**, ie how long it takes for new inventory to be delivered after being ordered
- the **re-order level**, ie the point at which a new order is to be placed – this is often the most critical factor to determine
- the appropriate **re-order quantity,** including the maximum order quantity and the minimum order quantity

Many businesses use manual or computer inventory control systems to keep a running record of the amount of each material held, the lead time for re-ordering, and the inventory buffer. The fixed quantity method of re-ordering is illustrated as follows:

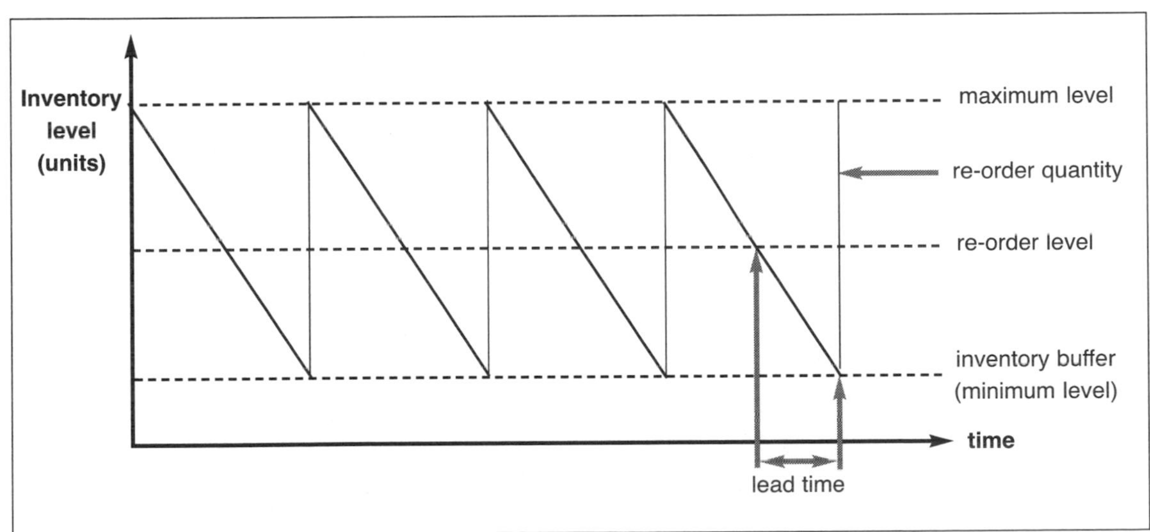

inventory buffer

This is the minimum inventory level to be held in order to meet unexpected emergencies and will be set by the purchasing or the stores department. The calculation of inventory buffer is:

re-order level – (average usage x average lead time)*

* per day/week/month

Note: the lead time for different items of inventory will be known by the purchasing department.

re-order level

The re-order level is calculated so that replacement materials will be delivered just as the inventory level reaches the level of the inventory buffer. The calculation of re-order level is:

(average usage x average lead time) + inventory buffer

Note: the inventory buffer is the minimum inventory level, and will be set by the management of the business.

re-order quantity

At the re-order level, a purchase order for new inventory is forwarded to the supplier.

Maximum order quantity is calculated as:

maximum inventory level – inventory buffer

Note: the maximum order quantity will, when delivered, restore inventory to the maximum level.

Minimum order quantity is calculated as:

re-order level – inventory buffer

Note: the minimum order quantity will, when delivered, restore inventory to the re-order level (which means that a further order will have to be placed).

worked example

A4, white photocopying paper

average daily usage	30 reams (a ream is 500 sheets)
average lead time	5 days
inventory buffer	100 reams
maximum inventory level	900 reams

Calculations

Re-order level

= (30 reams usage x 5 days' lead time)
+ 100 reams inventory buffer

= (30 x 5) + 100

= 250 reams (re-order level)

Maximum order quantity

= 900 reams maximum inventory level – 100 reams inventory buffer

= 800 reams maximum order quantity

Minimum order quantity

= 250 reams re-order level – 100 reams inventory buffer

= 150 reams minimum order quantity

Note: by the time this order is delivered – in five days' time – inventory will have fallen to 100 reams; the order will restore the inventory to 250 reams (which is the re-order quantity), so another order will have to be placed immediately.

It is important not to treat inventory calculations in isolation – there does need to be consideration of wider issues which may affect the business or organisation. Such issues include:

- needs of the business – for example, if an inventory item is being used less frequently than before, the calculations will need to be revised to suit current and future needs
- obsolescence of inventory – for example, if spare parts are kept for a particular make and model of vehicle, inventory levels will need to be run down when the vehicles are being replaced by those of a different make and model
- seasonal variations affecting usage and inventory levels – for example, a business using oil for heating may be offered a cheaper price when usage is low in the summer which may make it worthwhile to buy; by contrast, when usage is high in the winter, the supplier's price and lead times may increase

MATERIALS PURCHASES: ECONOMIC ORDER QUANTITY (EOQ)

It is clear that the re-order quantity is critical to the efficiency of inventory holding:

- if re-order amounts are **too large**, too much inventory will be held, which will be an expense to the business

- if re-order amounts are **too small**, the expense of constantly re-ordering will outweigh any cost savings of lower inventory levels, and there will be the danger that the item might 'run out'

The most economic re-order quantity – **the economic order quantity (EOQ)** – can be calculated by a mathematical formula which involves a number of different costs and other figures:

- **ordering cost** – the administration cost of placing each order, eg stationery, postage, wages, telephone
- **inventory holding cost** – the cost of keeping the inventory on the shelves expressed as the cost of holding one unit of inventory per year; examples of inventory holding costs include rent and rates, insurance, wages, deterioration, obsolescence, security
- **annual usage** – the number of inventory units used per year

The formula is:

$$\textbf{Economic Order Quantity (EOQ)} = \sqrt{\frac{2 \text{ x annual usage x ordering cost}}{\text{inventory holding cost}}}$$

On a calculator with a square root function, this formula can be worked out easily. Calculate the figures in the formula first, and then press the square root button (√).

For example, for a particular inventory item, the ordering cost of each order is £30, the inventory holding cost is £2 per unit per year, and annual usage is 2,000 units. The EOQ formula is applied as follows:

$$\textbf{Economic Order Quantity (EOQ)} = \sqrt{\frac{2 \text{ x } 2{,}000 \text{ x £}30}{\text{£}2}}$$

$$= \sqrt{\frac{120{,}000}{2}}$$

$$= \sqrt{60{,}000}$$

$$= \underline{245 \text{ units}}$$

As a result of using EOQ, a balance is struck between the cost of placing an order and the cost of holding inventory; EOQ represents the most efficient level of order to place because it minimises the total cost of ordering and storage.

Once the EOQ has been calculated, it is used as the quantity of inventory to be ordered each time an order is placed. This principle is illustrated in the Case Study on page 45.

INVENTORY RECORDS

Most businesses will have records of their inventories. Such records may be kept either by using a computer inventory control system, or manually on individual inventory records. Under both methods – computer and manual – a separate record is maintained for each type of inventory. The system is used whether the materials are held for resale by a retailer, or for use in production by a manufacturer. When supplies of the material are received they are entered in the inventory record, and when items are sold (or issued to production) they are shown as issues on the inventory record.

A typical inventory record is shown below. Note that:

- a separate inventory record is used for each type of inventory
- the 'quantity' column can be expressed in units, kg, litres, metres, etc – whatever is suitable for the inventory item
- the 'cost per unit' and 'total cost' columns are always the cost price of the inventory

INVENTORY RECORD

Date	Receipts			Issues			Balance		
	Quantity (units)	Cost per unit	Total Cost	Quantity (units)	Cost per unit	Total Cost	Quantity (units)	Cost per unit	Total Cost
		£	£		£	£		£	£

The layout of the inventory record may vary slightly from one business to another.

The way in which inventory records are used is shown in the Case Study on page 40.

VALUATION OF INVENTORY

The amount of materials inventory held by a business or organisation invariably has considerable value and ties up a lot of money. At the end of the financial year, it is essential to value the inventory for use in the calculation of profit in the financial statements. A process of inventory taking is used to make a physical check of the inventory held, which is then compared with the inventory records. The inventory held is then valued as follows:

number of items held x cost per item = inventory value at cost

The auditors may make random checks to ensure that the inventory value is correct.

The general rule is that inventory can be valued at *either*:

- what it cost the business to buy (including additional costs to bring the product or service to its present location or condition, such as delivery charges), *or*
- the net realisable value – which is the actual or estimated selling price (less any extra costs, such as selling and distribution) – ie what you would get for it

Inventory valuation is normally made at the **lower of cost and net realisable value**. This valuation is taken from International Accounting Standard (IAS) No 2, entitled *Inventories*. This method of valuation is illustrated as follows:

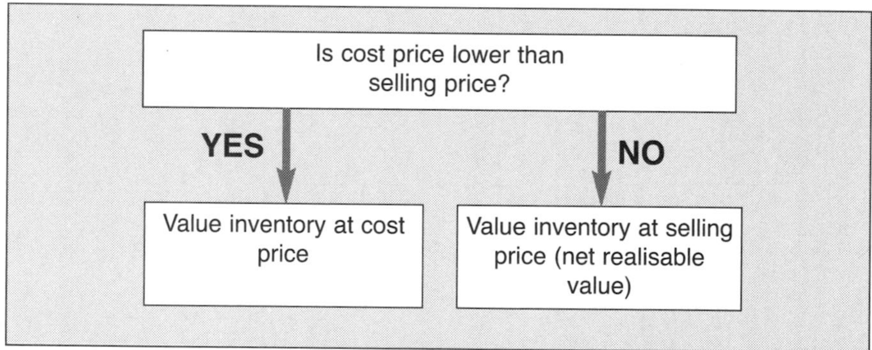

The difficulty with inventory valuation is in finding out the cost price of inventory – this is not easy when quantities of a particular item are continually being bought in – often at different prices – and then sold. Some organisations have inventory in a number of different forms, eg manufacturing businesses have raw materials, work-in-progress and finished goods.

METHODS OF INVENTORY VALUATION

issuing of materials and goods

The costing process requires that a value is given to raw materials (for a manufacturer) and goods (for a shop) when they are 'issued'. This means the point at which they are handed over to the production line or placed on the shop shelves. Traditionally the materials and goods were issued from 'stores' – a storage area – where they had been kept by the business since delivery from the supplier. The phrase 'issued from stores' is still used, although nowadays materials and goods are often delivered just before they are needed – this saves on storage and finance costs.

The cost of the materials or goods at the time of issue is normally the purchase cost – ie the price the business paid the supplier. But purchase costs do vary – so which cost do you take and what valuation do you give the materials or goods?

The two most commonly used methods for deciding which 'cost' to use for raw materials used in the production process or sold from shop shelves are either FIFO (first in, first out) or AVCO (weighted average cost). A third method, LIFO (last in, first out), is sometimes used for cost accounting purposes but is not permitted by IAS 2 for financial accounting. The methods work as follows:

FIFO (First In, First Out)

In this method, the first (oldest) cost prices are used first when goods are issued from stores. This means that the remaining inventory is valued at the most recent cost prices.

AVCO (Weighted Average Cost)

In this method, a weighted average cost is calculated for the inventory held at a given time, using the formula:

$$\text{weighted average cost} = \frac{\text{total cost of inventory held}}{\text{number of items held}}$$

The weighted average cost is then used to attach a value to issues from stores. A new weighted average must be calculated each time that further purchases are made.

LIFO (Last In, First Out)

In this method, the most recent (last) cost prices are used first when goods are issued from stores. This means that the remaining inventory is valued at older cost prices.

which method to use?

The use of a particular method of inventory valuation does not necessarily correspond with the method of physical distribution adopted in a firm's stores. For example, in a car factory one car battery of type X is the same as another, and no-one will be concerned if the issue is one from the last batch received, even if the FIFO system has been adopted. However, perishable goods are always physically handled on the basis of first in, first out, even if the accounting inventory records use another method.

Having chosen a suitable inventory valuation method, a business will continue to use that method unless there are good reasons for making the change.

Case Study

H RASHID COMPUTER SUPPLIES: INVENTORY RECORDS

situation

H Rashid runs a computer supplies company. One of the items he sells is the 'Zap' data disk.

To show how the inventory records would appear under FIFO, LIFO and AVCO, and the closing inventory valuation at 31 May 20-4, the following data is used for each method:

January	Opening inventory of 40 units at a cost of £3.00 each
February	Bought 20 units at a cost of £3.60 each
March	Sold 36 units for £6 each
April	Bought 20 units at a cost of £3.75 each
May	Sold 25 units for £6 each

Note: show the cost per unit to two decimal places.

What will be the profit for the period using each inventory valuation method?

Tutorial notes:

- This Case Study shows the inventory records using the three methods: FIFO, LIFO and AVCO. AAT Assessments will usually ask for either FIFO or AVCO – this is because LIFO is not permitted under IAS 2 and, therefore, is not used for external reporting purposes, but can be used for internal reporting. For Assessments you need to be able to identify and explain the principles behind all three methods.
- The inventory records in this Case Study include, under the 'balance' heading, a column for 'cost per unit'. This column is not always given in AAT Assessments (see Case Study on page 45) but is included here to show the workings clearly.

- In the solution which follows there are often several calculations in the issues and balance columns – these are given to show clearly the calculations. However, in the AAT Assessment, you will only be able to record one entry in each inventory record cell: what you will record is the total of each cell, eg for February, below, you will record 60 in the quantity cell and 192.00 in the total cost cell.
- In AAT Assessments you must read the task instructions to see how many decimal places you should work to.

solution

Note: In the first two methods – FIFO and LIFO – units issued at the same time may be valued at different costs. This is because the quantities received, with their costs, are listed separately and used in a specific order. There may be insufficient units at one cost, eg see the May issue using both FIFO and LIFO methods.

FIFO

For FIFO, in the 'Balance' columns, a new list of inventory quantities and costs is started after each receipt or issue. When inventory is issued, costs are used from the **top** of the list downwards.

INVENTORY RECORD

Date	Receipts			Issues			Balance		
	Quantity (units)	Cost per unit	Total Cost	Quantity (units)	Cost per unit	Total Cost	Quantity (units)	Cost per unit	Total Cost
20-4 Jan	Balance	£	£		£	£	40	£ 3.00	£ 120.00
Feb	20	3.60	72.00				40 20 60	3.00 3.60	120.00 72.00 192.00
March				36	3.00	108.00	4 20 24	3.00 3.60	12.00 72.00 84.00
April	20	3.75	75.00				4 20 20 44	3.00 3.60 3.75	12.00 72.00 75.00 159.00
May				4 20 1 25	3.00 3.60 3.75	12.00 72.00 3.75 87.75	19	3.75	71.25

LIFO

For LIFO, in the 'Balance' columns, a new list of inventory quantities and costs is started after each receipt or issue. When inventory is issued, costs are used from the **bottom** of the list upwards. However, the new balance list each time must be kept in date order.

INVENTORY RECORD

Date	Receipts			Issues			Balance		
	Quantity (units)	Cost per unit	Total Cost	Quantity (units)	Cost per unit	Total Cost	Quantity (units)	Cost per unit	Total Cost
20-4		£	£		£	£		£	£
Jan	Balance						40	3.00	120.00
Feb	20	3.60	72.00				40	3.00	120.00
							20	3.60	72.00
							60		192.00
March				20	3.60	72.00			
				16	3.00	48.00			
				36		120.00	24	3.00	72.00
April	20	3.75	75.00				24	3.00	72.00
							20	3.75	75.00
							44		147.00
May				20	3.75	75.00			
				5	3.00	15.00			
				25		90.00	19	3.00	57.00

AVCO

For AVCO, each quantity issued is valued at the weighted average cost per unit, and so is the balance of inventory. The complete list of different costs does not have to be re-written each time.

INVENTORY RECORD

Date	Receipts			Issues			Balance		
	Quantity (units)	Cost per unit	Total Cost	Quantity (units)	Cost per unit	Total Cost	Quantity (units)	Cost per unit	Total Cost
20-4		£	£		£	£		£	£
Jan	Balance						40	3.00	120.00
Feb	20	3.60	72.00				40	3.00	120.00
							20	3.60	72.00
							60	3.20	192.00
March				36	3.20	115.20	24	3.20	76.80
April	20	3.75	75.00				24	3.20	76.80
							20	3.75	75.00
							44	3.45	151.80
May				25	3.45	86.25	19	3.45	65.55

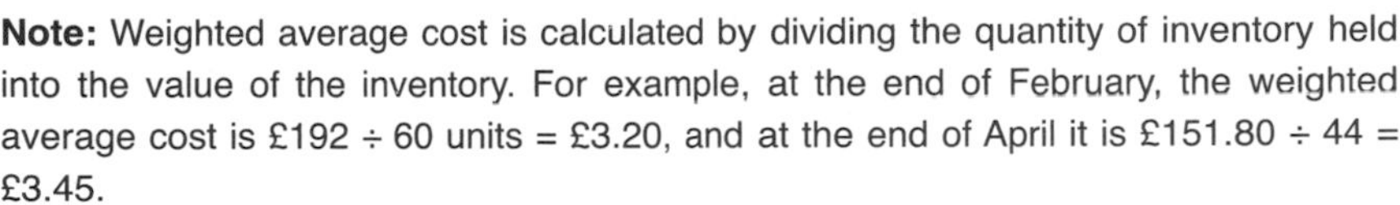

Note: Weighted average cost is calculated by dividing the quantity of inventory held into the value of the inventory. For example, at the end of February, the weighted average cost is £192 ÷ 60 units = £3.20, and at the end of April it is £151.80 ÷ 44 = £3.45.

Each time a new receipt of inventory is recorded, a new weighted average cost is calculated. When inventory is issued, the cost is at the last calculated weighted average cost.

The closing inventory valuations at the end of May 20-4 under each method show total cost prices of:

FIFO	£71.25
LIFO	£57.00
AVCO	£65.55

There is quite a difference, and this has come about because different inventory valuation methods have been used.

effect on profit

In the example above, the selling price was £6 per unit. The effect on gross profit of using different inventory valuations is shown below.

		FIFO	LIFO	AVCO
		£	£	£
Revenue: 61 units at £6		366.00	366.00	366.00
Opening inventory:	40 units at £3	120.00	120.00	120.00
Purchases:	20 units at £3.60 and 20 units at £3.75	147.00	147.00	147.00
		267.00	267.00	267.00
Less Closing inventory: 19 units		71.25	57.00	65.55
Cost of sales		195.75	210.00	201.45
Gross profit = Revenue – Cost of sales		170.25	156.00	164.55

Notice that the cost of sales figure in each case is also obtainable by adding up the values in the 'Issues' column. You can also check in each case that, both in Units and in Values:

opening inventory + receipts – issues = closing inventory

This Case Study shows that in times of rising prices, FIFO produces the highest reported profit, LIFO the lowest, and AVCO between the other two. However, over the life of a business, total profit is the same in total, whichever method is chosen: the profit is allocated to different years depending on which method is used.

Accounting staff must resist being pressured into using different inventory valuations in order to manipulate profits. The application of **ethical considerations** in accounting must ensure that information is prepared with **objectivity** – that is without manipulation or bias.

COMPARISON OF FIFO, LIFO AND AVCO

The table on the next page compares the three inventory techniques and consolidates what you have learned so far.

It is important to note that a business must adopt a consistent inventory valuation policy, ie it should choose one method of finding the cost price, and not change it without good reason. FIFO and AVCO are more commonly used than LIFO; in particular, LIFO usually results in an inventory valuation for the final accounts which bears little relationship to recent costs – for this reason it is not permitted by IAS 2. However, LIFO has the advantage that it gives a more realistic production cost – this is because materials are issued at more up-to-date prices. It is also appropriate to apply LIFO principles when costing materials in a quotation to be given to a potential customer: in times of rising prices you wouldn't want to quote old prices – for example, under FIFO – and then, when the quotation is accepted, find that there is no more of the older-priced materials left. Thus LIFO is often used for internal reporting purposes.

Comparison of the methods of inventory valuation			
	FIFO	**LIFO**	**AVCO**
Method	The costs used for goods sold or issued follow the order in which the goods were received.	The costs used for goods sold or issued are opposite to the order in which the goods were received.	Does not relate issues to any particular batch of goods received, but uses a weighted average cost.
Calculation	It is easy to calculate costs because they relate to specific receipts of materials or goods.	It is easy to calculate costs because they relate to specific receipts of materials or goods.	More complex because of the need to calculate weighted average costs after each receipt of goods.
Inventory valuation	Inventory valuations are based on the most recent costs of materials or goods received.	Inventory valuations are based on older costs of materials or goods received.	Weighted average costs are used to value closing inventory.
Profits and taxation	In times of rising prices this method will result in higher reported profits than the other methods, resulting in more tax being payable. This method is acceptable for tax purposes and is permitted under IAS 2, *Inventories*.	In times of rising prices this method will result in lower reported profits than the other methods. This is not usually acceptable for tax purposes and is not permitted under IAS 2, *Inventories*.	The weighted average method will smooth out some of the peaks and troughs of profit and loss. This method is acceptable for tax purposes and is permitted under IAS 2, *Inventories*.
Administration	Use of this method will mean keeping track of each receipt until the goods are issued or sold.	Use of this method will mean keeping track of each receipt until the goods are issued or sold.	There is no need to track each receipt as a weighted average cost is used. This also means it is easier to computerise the inventory records.
Cost of sales	In a time of rising prices this method will use older, out of date prices for cost of sales or goods issued.	In a time of rising prices this method will use more up-to-date prices for cost of sales or goods issued.	This method will give an average price for the cost of sales.

Case Study

USING ECONOMIC ORDER QUANTITY AND INVENTORY RECORDS

Tutorial note: This Case Study is based on AAT Assessments – note that the inventory record does not give a 'cost per unit' under the 'balance' heading.

situation

You are an Accounts Assistant at Stoke Park Limited and have been asked to help with the inventory records.

The cost accountant has given you the following information for metal grade FE4.

- Annual demand – 28,125 kilograms
- Annual holding cost per kilogram – £0.50
- Fixed ordering cost – £20

(a) **You are to** calculate the Economic Order Quantity (EOQ) for FE4.

The inventory record shown below for metal grade FE4 for the month of September has only been fully completed for the first three weeks of the month.

(b) **You are to** complete the entries in the inventory record for the two receipts on 25 and 29 September that were ordered using the EOQ method.

(c) **You are to** complete all entries in the inventory record for the two issues in the month and for the closing balance at the end of September using the FIFO method of issuing inventory.

Note: show the cost per kilogram (kg) to two decimal places.

Inventory record for metal grade FE4

Date	**Receipts**			**Issues**			**Balance**	
	Quantity (kg)	Cost per kg	Total Cost	Quantity (kg)	Cost per kg	Total Cost	Quantity (kg)	Total Cost
		£	£		£	£		£
Balance as at 23 September							740	814
25 September		1.20						
27 September				850				
29 September		1.25						
30 September				1,630				

solution

(a) Economic Order Quantity (EOQ) $= \sqrt{\frac{2 \times 28{,}125 \text{ kg} \times £20}{£0.50}}$

$$= \sqrt{\frac{1{,}125{,}000}{0.50}}$$

$$= \sqrt{2{,}250{,}000}$$

$$= 1{,}500 \text{ kg}$$

(b) and **(c)**

Inventory record for metal grade FE4

Date	Receipts			Issues			Balance	
	Quantity (kg)	Cost per kg	Total Cost	Quantity (kg)	Cost per kg	Total Cost	Quantity (kg)	Total Cost
		£	£		£	£		£
Balance as at 23 September							740	814
25 September	1,500	1.20	1,800				740 1,500 2,240	814 1,800 2,614
27 September				740 110 850	1.10 1.20	814 132 946	1,390	1,668
29 September	1,500	1.25	1,875				1,390 1,500 2,890	1,668 1,875 3,543
30 September				1,390 240 1,630	1.20 1.25	1,668 300 1,968	1,260	1,575

Tutorial notes:

- This Case Study uses the FIFO method of issuing inventory – AAT Assessments will usually ask for either FIFO or AVCO. As LIFO is not permitted under IAS 2 it is, therefore, not used for external reporting purposes, but can be useful for internal reporting. For Assessments you need to be able to identify and explain the principles behind the three methods.
- With the FIFO method you will note that issues may be valued at different costs – as here on 27 and 30 September. This is because the quantities received, with their costs, are listed separately and used in a specific order.

CATEGORIES OF INVENTORY

International Accounting Standard No 2, *Inventories*, requires that, in calculating the lower of cost and net realisable value, note should be taken of:

- separate items of inventory, or
- groups of similar items

This means that the inventory valuation 'rule' must be applied to each separate item of inventory, or each group or category of similar inventory. The total cost cannot be compared with the total net realisable value.

INVENTORY VALUATION FOR MANUFACTURING BUSINESSES

The principle of inventory valuation, as set out in International Accounting Standard No 2, *Inventories*, is that inventories should be valued at **'the lower of cost and net realisable value'.** This principle applies to a manufacturer for the three types of inventory that may be held at the year-end:

- raw materials
- part-finished goods or work-in-progress
- finished goods

For raw materials, the comparison is made between cost (which can be found using techniques such as FIFO, LIFO, or AVCO) and net realisable value.

For part-finished and finished goods, IAS 2 requires that the cost valuation includes expenditure not only on direct materials but also on direct labour, direct expenses and production overheads. Thus for part-finished and finished goods, 'cost' means 'production cost', ie the total of:

- direct materials
- direct labour
- direct expenses
- production overheads (to bring the product to its present location or condition)

Such 'cost' is then compared with net realisable value – less any further costs necessary to complete the item or get it in a condition to be sold – and the lower figure is taken as the inventory valuation. (Remember that different items or groups of inventory are compared separately.)

Case Study

ABC MANUFACTURING: INVENTORIES VALUATION

situation

ABC Manufacturing started in business on 1 July 20-3 producing security devices for doors and windows. During the first year 2,000 units were sold and, at the end of the year, on 30 June 20-4, there were 200 units which were finished and 20 units which were exactly half-finished as regards direct materials, direct labour and production overheads.

Costs for the first year were:

	£
Direct materials used	18,785
Direct labour	13,260
Production overheads	8,840
Non-production overheads	4,420
Total cost for year	45,305

At 30 June 20-4 it was estimated that the net realisable value of each completed security device was £35. At the same date, the company holds raw materials as follows:

	Cost	**Net realisable value**
	£	£
Material A	1,400	1,480
Material B	400	360
Material C	260	280

Calculate the inventories valuation at 30 June 20-4 for:

- raw materials
- work-in-progress
- finished goods

solution

RAW MATERIALS

Using the IAS 2 rule of the 'lower of cost and net realisable value', and applying it to each group or category of inventory, the total value is:

	£	
Material A	1,400	(cost)
Material B	360	(net realisable value)
Material C	260	(cost)
	2,020	

WORK-IN-PROGRESS

To calculate the value of both work-in-progress and finished goods we need to know the production cost, ie direct materials, direct labour and production overheads. This is:

	£
Direct materials used	18,785
Direct labour	13,260
Production overheads	8,840
Production cost for year	**40,885**

All these costs are included because they have been incurred in bringing the product to its present location or condition. Non-production overheads are not included because they are not directly related to production.

Thus, a production cost of £40,885 has produced:

Units sold	2,000
Closing inventory of completed units	200
Closing inventory of work-in-progress –	
20 units exactly half-finished equals 10 completed units	10
Production for year	**2,210**

The **cost per unit** is:

$$\frac{\pounds 40{,}885}{2{,}210} = \textbf{£18.50 per unit}$$

The 20 half-finished units have a cost of (20 ÷ 2) x £18.50 = **£185**.

They have a net realisable value of (20 ÷ 2) x £35 = £350.

The value of work-in-progress will, therefore, be shown in the financial statements as £185, which is the lower of cost and net realisable value.

FINISHED GOODS

The completed units held at the end of the year have a production cost of 200 x £18.50 = £3,700, compared with a net realisable value of 200 x £35 = £7,000. Applying the rule of lower of cost and net realisable value, finished goods inventory will be valued at the cost price, **£3,700**.

BOOKKEEPING FOR MATERIALS COSTS

In this section we look at the cost bookkeeping entries to record inventory transactions – the purchase of materials either on credit from suppliers or on cash terms, and the issue or return of inventory to production. These entries form part of the bookkeeping system for costing.

When making cost bookkeeping entries, remember to use the principles of double-entry bookkeeping:

- a debit entry records a gain in value, an asset or an expense
- a credit entry records the giving of value, a liability or an income item

With direct materials, the general ledger entries are:

- **purchase of materials on credit from a supplier**
  - debit inventory (asset gained)
  - credit trade payables control (liability incurred)
- **purchase of materials on cash terms** (ie immediate payment from bank)
  - debit inventory (asset gained)
  - credit bank (value given by bank)
- **issue of materials to production**
  - debit production (asset of materials gained)
  - credit inventory (value of materials given to production)
- **return of materials from production to inventory**
  - debit inventory (asset gained)
  - credit production (value given by production)

Four accounts are involved in these transactions

- inventory account
- production account
- trade payables control account
- bank account

The cost bookkeeping entries for direct materials are shown diagrammatically at the top of the next page.

With indirect materials (such as grease used to lubricate factory machinery) the general ledger entries for the issue of materials are:

– debit production overheads

– credit inventory

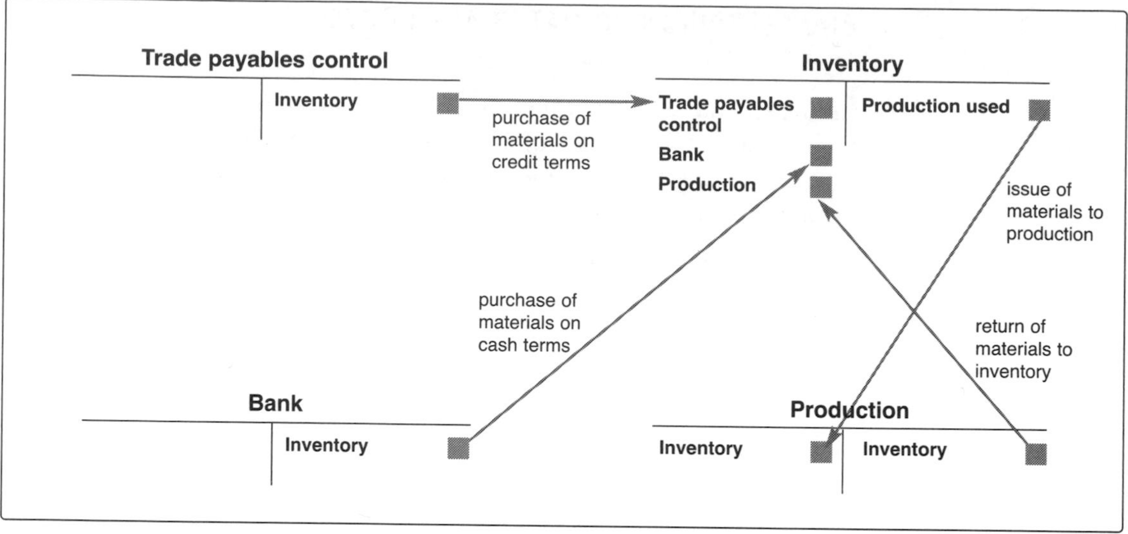

Case Study

BLUE JEANS LIMITED: BOOKKEEPING FOR MATERIALS COSTS

situation

Blue Jeans Limited manufactures and sells denim jeans and jackets. The company uses the first in, first out (FIFO) method for valuing issues of materials to production and for valuing inventory.

The company has been very busy in recent weeks and, as a consequence, some of the accounting records are not up-to-date. The inventory record shown at the top of the next page has not been completed.

All issues of blue denim are for the manufacture of blue jeans. The following cost accounting codes are used to record material costs:

Code number	Description
2000	inventory – blue denim
2200	production – blue jeans
4000	trade payables control

As an Accounts Assistant at Blue Jeans Limited, you are asked to complete the inventory record (showing the cost per metre to two decimal places) and to fill in the table opposite to record the journal entries for the two purchases and two issues of blue denim in the cost accounting records.

INVENTORY RECORD

Product: Blue denim

Date	**Receipts**			**Issues**			**Balance**	
	Quantity (metres)	Cost per metre	Total Cost	Quantity (metres)	Cost per metre	Total Cost	Quantity (metres)	Total Cost
20-4		£	£		£	£		£
Balance at 1 Oct							20,000	10,000
11 Oct	10,000	0.60	6,000				30,000	16,000
14 Oct				25,000				
19 Oct	20,000	0.70	14,000					
25 Oct				20,000				

20-4	**Code number**	**Debit £**	**Credit £**
11 October	2000		
11 October	4000		
14 October	2000		
14 October	2200		
19 October	2000		
19 October	4000		
25 October	2000		
25 October	2200		

solution

The inventory record is completed as shown below.

Note that there may be a need to calculate the balance from more than one receipt cost. For example, on 11 October, the balance is made up of:

			£
20,000	metres at £0.50 per metre	=	10,000
10,000	metres at £0.60 per metre	=	6,000
30,000	metres	=	16,000

Similarly, on 19 October, the balance is made up of:

			£
5,000	metres at £0.60 per metre	=	3,000
20,000	metres at £0.70 per metre	=	14,000
25,000		=	17,000

INVENTORY RECORD

Product: Blue denim

Date	Receipts			Issues			Balance	
	Quantity (metres)	Cost per metre	Total Cost	Quantity (metres)	Cost per metre	Total Cost	Quantity (metres)	Total Cost
20-4		£	£		£	£		£
Balance at 1 Oct							20,000	10,000
11 Oct	10,000	0.60	6,000				20,000 10,000 30,000	10,000 6,000 16,000
14 Oct				20,000 5,000 25,000	0.50 0.60	10,000 3,000 13,000	5,000	3,000
19 Oct	20,000	0.70	14,000				5,000 20,000 25,000	3,000 14,000 17,000
25 Oct				5,000 15,000 20,000	0.60 0.70	3,000 10,500 13,500	5,000	3,500

The cost bookkeeping entries are:

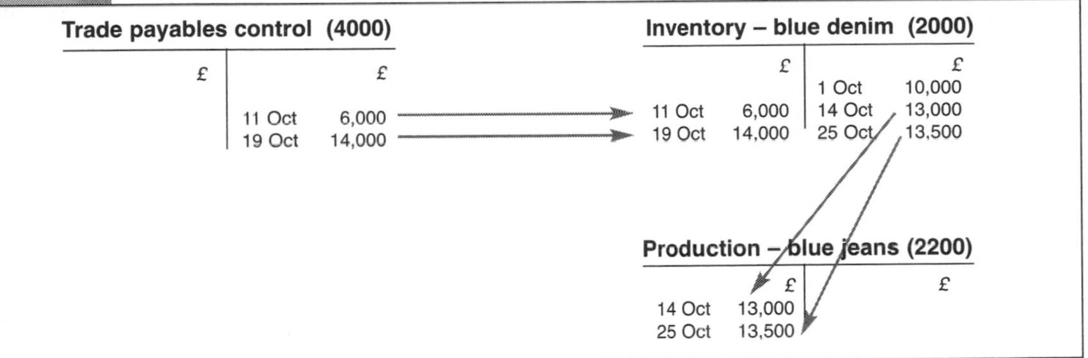

The cost bookkeeping transactions are recorded as journal entries in the following way:

20-4	Code number	Debit £	Credit £
11 October	2000	£6,000	
11 October	4000		£6,000
14 October	2000		£13,000
14 October	2200	£13,000	
19 October	2000	£14,000	
19 October	4000		£14,000
25 October	2000		£13,500
25 October	2200	£13,500	

Chapter Summary

- Businesses and other organisations hold materials inventory in the form of raw materials and components bought for production, products bought for resale, and service items bought for use within the business.
- Two important inventory costs are the ordering cost and the inventory holding cost.
- Materials purchases can be made using:
  - the fixed quantity method
  - Economic Order Quantity (EOQ)
- The quantity of inventory is recorded on an inventory record, which also indicates:
  - the level at which inventory should be ordered
  - the quantity of inventory that should be re-ordered
- Inventory valuation is normally made **at the lower of cost and net realisable value** (IAS 2).
- Inventory valuation methods include:
  - FIFO (first in, first out)
  - LIFO (last in, first out)
  - AVCO (weighted average cost)

  LIFO is not permitted under IAS 2 and is, therefore, not used for external reporting purposes
- For a manufacturer, cost comprises the direct manufacturing costs of materials, labour and expenses, together with the production overheads which bring the product to its present location or condition.
- Cost bookkeeping entries are made to record inventory transactions such as:
  - purchase of materials on credit from suppliers or on cash terms
  - issue of materials to production
  - return of materials from production to inventory

Key Terms

materials	the cost of: – raw materials and components used in production – products bought for resale – service items bought for use within the business
fixed quantity method	the re-ordering of materials in set amounts
Economic Order Quantity (EOQ)	a method of minimising ordering costs and inventory holding costs; calculated by the formula: $\sqrt{\dfrac{2 \times \text{annual usage} \times \text{ordering cost}}{\text{inventory holding cost}}}$
inventory record	record held for each inventory item which shows receipts of supplies and sales (or issues to production)
inventory value	number of items held x inventory valuation per item
cost	the amount it cost to buy the inventory (including additional costs to bring the product to its present location or condition)
net realisable value	selling price (less any extra costs, such as selling and distribution)
FIFO	'First in, first out' method of attaching a value to each issue of materials or goods from stores, using the oldest cost prices first
LIFO	'Last in, first out' method of attaching a value to each issue of materials or goods from stores, using most recent cost prices first
AVCO	'Average cost' method of attaching a value to each issue of materials or goods from stores, using a weighted average of the cost prices of all items in inventory at the date of issue
inventory record	method of recording inventory data in order to ascertain the cost at which materials are issued, and to ascertain a valuation of closing inventory
cost bookkeeping	double-entry system to record costing transactions; uses the principles of double-entry bookkeeping

Activities

2.1 Calculate, for inventory items D and E, the re-order level and the maximum order quantity from the following information:

- average daily usage of D = 3 units, of E = 4 units
- total inventory should never exceed 95 days' usage
- 10 days' inventory should always be held
- there is space available in the store for 350 units of each item of inventory
- average lead time is 7 days

2.2 The following information is available for material XX5:

- annual demand – 72,000 kilograms
- annual holding cost per kilogram – £2
- fixed ordering cost – £20

You are to calculate the Economic Order Quantity (EOQ) for material XX5.

2.3 From the following information prepare inventory records for product X using:

(a) FIFO

(b) LIFO

(c) AVCO

- 20 units of the product are bought in January 20-4 at a cost of £3 each
- 10 units are bought in February at a cost of £3.60 each
- 8 units are sold in March
- 10 units are bought in April at a cost of £4.00 each
- 16 units are sold in May

Notes:

- a blank inventory record, which may be photocopied, is provided in the Appendix
- where appropriate, work to the nearest penny

2.4 XY Limited is formed on 1 January 20-4 and, at the end of its first half-year of trading, the inventory records show the following:

20-4	TYPE X		TYPE Y	
	Receipts (units)	**Issues (units)**	**Receipts (units)**	**Issues (units)**
January	100 at £4.00		200 at £10.00	
February		80	100 at £9.50	
March	140 at £4.20			240
April	100 at £3.80		100 at £10.50	
May		140	140 at £10.00	
June	80 at £4.50			100

You are to complete inventory records for products X and Y using **(a)** FIFO, **(b)** LIFO, **(c)** AVCO.

Notes:

- a blank inventory record, which may be photocopied, is provided in the Appendix
- where appropriate, work to the nearest penny, ie to two decimal places

2.5 Breeden Bakery Limited makes 'homestyle' cakes which are sold to supermarket chains.

The company uses the first in, first out (FIFO) method of issuing inventory.

As an Accounts Assistant at Breeden Bakery you have been given the following tasks.

Task 1

Complete the following inventory record for wholewheat flour for May 20-4 (showing the cost per kilogram to two decimal places):

INVENTORY RECORD

Product: Wholewheat flour

Date	**Receipts**			**Issues**			**Balance**	
	Quantity (kgs)	Cost per kg	Total Cost	Quantity (kgs)	Cost per kg	Total Cost	Quantity (kgs)	Total Cost
20-4		£	£		£	£		£
Balance at 1 May							10,000	2,500
6 May	20,000	0.30	6,000				30,000	8,500
10 May				20,000				
17 May	10,000	0.35	3,500					
20 May				15,000				

Task 2

All issues of wholewheat flour are for the manufacture of fruit cakes. The following cost accounting codes are used to record materials costs:

Code number	**Description**
3000	inventory – wholewheat flour
3300	production – fruit cakes
5000	purchases ledger control

Complete the table below to record the journal entries for the two purchases and two issues of wholewheat flour in the cost accounting records.

20-4	Code number	Debit £	Credit £
6 May			
6 May			
10 May			
10 May			
17 May			
17 May			
20 May			
20 May			

2.6 The following information is available for plastic grade P5:

- Annual demand – 57,600 kilograms
- Annual holding cost per kilogram – £2
- Fixed ordering cost – £25

(a) You are to calculate the Economic Order Quantity (EOQ) for P5.

EOQ = [ ] kg

The inventory record shown on the next page for plastic grade P5 for the month of June has only been fully completed for the first three weeks of the month.

(b) Complete the entries in the inventory record for the two receipts on 23 and 26 June that were ordered using the EOQ method.

(c) Complete ALL entries in the inventory record for the two issues in the month and for the closing balance at the end of June using the AVCO method of issuing inventory.

Show the costs per kilogram (kg) in £ to three decimal places, and the total costs in whole £.

INVENTORY RECORD

Product: Plastic grade P5

Date	**Receipts**			**Issues**			**Balance**	
	Quantity (kg)	Cost per kg	Total Cost	Quantity (kg)	Cost per kg	Total Cost	Quantity (kg)	Total Cost
		£	£		£	£		£
Balance as at 22 June							4,400	10,560
23 June		2.634						
25 June				1,000				
26 June		2.745						
29 June				1,500				

2.7 Crossways Limited uses the following accounts to record inventory transactions in its cost bookkeeping system:

- inventory account
- trade payables control account
- bank account
- production account

For each of the four transactions in the following table show the account which will be debited and the account which will be credited.

Transaction	**Account debited**	**Account credited**
1 Receipt of materials into inventory, paying on credit		
2 Issue of materials from inventory to production		
3 Receipt of materials into inventory, paying immediately by BACS		
4 Return of materials from production to inventory		

2.8 Which **one** of these is an example of unethical behaviour by an accounting technician?

(a)	Valuing inventory in an objective way	
(b)	Valuing inventory in accordance with IAS 2, *Inventories*	
(c)	Valuing inventory without being influenced by the business owner	
(d)	Valuing inventory in order to maximise profit	

3 Labour costs

this chapter covers...

In Chapter 1 we saw how costs can be classified by element as materials, labour and expenses. In this chapter we focus on labour costs and explain:

- *the factors that affect labour costs*
- *the methods by which the direct labour employees of a business can be paid*
- *how payroll information is gathered*
- *overtime, idle time and equivalent units*
- *the use of a time sheet to calculate gross wages*
- *the bookkeeping entries for labour costs*

ACCOUNTING FOR LABOUR COSTS

Labour cost is one of the elements of costs – all businesses incur labour costs which are the costs of wages and salaries of all their employees.

factors that affect labour costs

There are many factors that need to be considered by a business when deciding how much to pay employees. The starting point will always be the amount that is paid by other businesses in the area for similar grades of employees but, at the same time, the wider economic implications of supply and demand will affect wage rates.

The factors to consider include:

- wage rates paid by other local businesses
- comparisons with national average wage rates
- the national living wage rate imposed by government
- any government incentives to take on additional employees, such as young people or the long-term unemployed
- local employment conditions – high unemployment in the area will drive down wage rates; conversely low unemployment, and especially a shortage of skilled labour, will increase wage rates
- housing and transport costs in the locality
- the impact of interest rate changes, and exchange rates (eg against the euro) on business confidence
- for a new business, it might be prudent to choose to locate in an area of high unemployment – in addition to lower wage rates, there may be government incentives in the form of reduced rents and rates, training and other grants

Before taking on labour, a business must decide how to calculate gross pay for its employees. Labour payment methods are looked at in detail on the next page. Wages are usually calculated according to time worked or work done, or a combination of both.

LABOUR PAYMENT METHODS

Direct labour cost is the wages paid to those who work on a production line, are involved in assembly, or are involved in the output of a service business.

The three main payment methods for direct labour are:

time rate Time rate, or basic pay, is where the employee is paid on the basis of time spent at work. Overtime is often paid for hours worked beyond a standard number of hours, or for work carried out on days which are not part of the working week, eg Saturdays or Sundays. Overtime is often paid at rates such as 'time-and-a-quarter', 'time-and-a-half', or 'double-time'. 'Time-and-a-half', for example, means that 1.5 times the basic hourly rate is paid.

Time rate is often referred to as a 'day rate'.

piecework rate The employee is paid an agreed sum for each task carried out or for each unit of output completed. Units of output can be based on an agreed output per hour, which is referred to as 'standard hour produced'.

In some cases, employees may have a guaranteed minimum wage.

bonus system The employee is paid a time rate and then receives a bonus if output is better than expected when comparing the time allowed with the time taken. The bonus is calculated as an agreed percentage of the time saved multiplied by the time rate.

Bonus systems base employees' earnings on a combination of time taken and work done.

Most other employees, eg factory supervisors, sales staff, office staff, are usually paid on a weekly or monthly basis. Such wages and salaries – classed as indirect labour costs – may be increased by bonus payments; for example, a production bonus for factory supervisors, commissions for sales staff, a profit-sharing scheme for all employees.

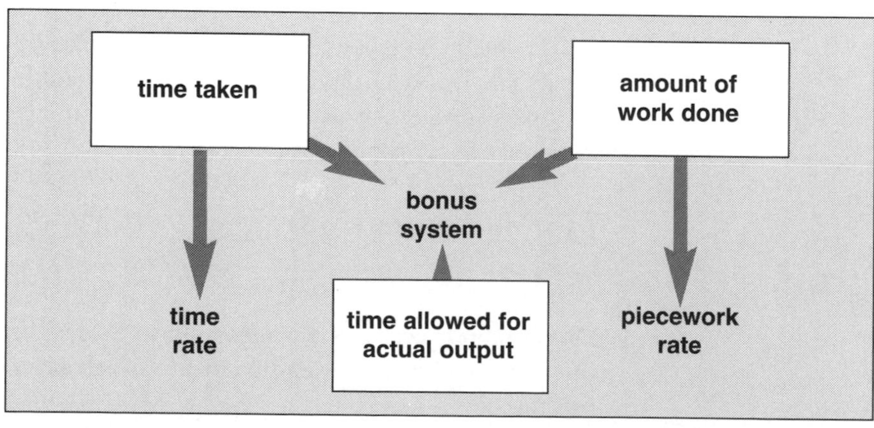

There are many variations on the three methods outlined above and, indeed, changing patterns of employment create different payment methods from those that would have been the norm just a few years ago. For example, the contracting out of many business support services – such as cleaning, security, computers – means that the costing of such services by the provider may incorporate time rates and bonus systems whereas previously the employees would have been paid on a weekly or monthly basis.

In order to calculate gross wages, information about hours worked and/or work done must be recorded. The documents used include:

- **time sheets,** where employees record the hours they have worked
- **clock cards**, where employees 'clock in' at the start of work, and 'clock out' at the end – these are often computerised
- **piecework tickets,** completed by employees who work on a batch of output
- **job cards,** where each employee records the amount of time spent on each job
- **route cards** – which are used to follow a product through the production process – on which employees record the amount of time they spend working on the product
- **computer cards** – 'swipe' cards which link direct into the computerised payroll are increasingly being used by employers to record attendance

qualities of a good labour payment method

These include:

- reward should be related to effort and fair to all staff
- the method should be easy to manage and administer, and cheap and efficient to run
- it should be easy for employees to understand how pay is calculated
- payment should be made at regular intervals and soon after the event, eg employees on piecework should be paid in the week after the production has been achieved
- the principles of the scheme should remain constant, but there should be flexibility to deal with changes in production techniques

summary

The three main labour payment methods, together with some alternative systems, are summarised in the table on the next page.

As an Accounts Assistant, always remember that payroll information is confidential and any queries should be referred to the appropriate person – for example, the Payroll Manager, or the Accounts Supervisor.

Labour payment methods – a summary			
	Time rate	**Piecework rate**	**Bonus system**
Situation	This method is used where it is difficult to measure the quantity of output and where quality is more important than volume of output.	This method is used where the work is repetitive and quantity of output is more important than quality.	This method is used to motivate employees, where the work is not so repetitive as in piecework but is measurable.
Gross Pay Calculation	*Hours worked x rate per hour = basic pay.* This is easy to calculate and understand. Overtime often paid for extra hours worked	*Number of items produced x rate per item.* This is easy to calculate and understand.	*Basic pay + proportion of the time saved.* Time saved is the difference between time allowed and time taken to do a task. More complex to calculate and understand.
Motivation	Pay is not linked to output and therefore there is no incentive to work hard. Slower workers may get paid overtime at higher rates.	Pay is related directly to output. There is a direct incentive to work as the amount of output determines the amount paid.	There is some incentive to work in order to earn a bonus as well as basic pay.
Quality Of Output	There is no pressure on time and so quality should be maintained.	The fact that pay is related to output means it is important that quality standards of output are met.	The link between pay and output means that the quality of output needs to be checked.
Control	It is important that the volume and quality of output is maintained.	It is important that the volume and quality of output is maintained.	It is important that the volume and quality of output is maintained.
Administration	There is no need to set time allowances for output.	There is a need to set time allowances for work done and to keep these up to date.	There is a need to set time allowances for work done and to keep these up to date.
Payment to Employees	A regular amount is earned by the employee.	The amount earned by the employee varies with the output the employee produces.	There is some regular income but pay can be increased by additional effort.
Alternative Systems	**High day rate** – employees are paid a higher than average rate per hour but agree to produce a given amount of output at a given quality.	**Attendance allowance** – to ensure employees turn up. **Guaranteed day rate** – to give employees a minimum payment. **Differential piecework** – to pay efficient workers more for output beyond a given level of output, ie an extra amount per unit.	**Group bonus schemes** – used where employees work as a group. This can include all workers, eg cleaners. This may create problems as the most efficient workers may be held back by the less efficient workers.

Case Study

WESTMID MANUFACTURING: LABOUR PAYMENT

situation

Westmid Manufacturing Company has three factories in the West Midlands making parts for the car industry. Each factory was bought from the previous owners and, as a result, each has a different method for paying its direct labour workforce. The details of the labour payment methods in each factory, together with data on two employees from each factory, are as follows:

WALSALL FACTORY

In this factory, which is involved in heavy engineering, employees are paid on the basis of a time rate. Employees are required to 'clock in' and 'clock out' each day.

John Brown is a machine operator and his clock card for last week shows that he worked 39 hours; his basic pay is £10 per hour.

Stefan Wozniak is a skilled lathe operator and his clock card shows that he worked 42 hours; his basic pay is £12 per hour, with overtime for hours worked beyond 37 hours at 'time-and-a-half'.

DUDLEY FACTORY

This factory operates a number of light engineering production lines making car components such as windscreen wiper blades, headlamp surrounds, interior mirrors etc. The production line employees are all paid on a piecework basis; however, each employee receives a guaranteed time rate which is paid if the piecework earnings are less than the time rate. This may happen if, for example, there are machine breakdowns and the production line has to be halted.

Tracey Johnson works on the line making headlamp surrounds. For each one that passes through her part of the process, she is paid 40p; her guaranteed time rate is 35 hours each week at £10 per hour. Last week's production records show that she processed 910 units.

Pete Bronyah is on the line which makes interior mirrors. For his part of the process he receives £1.00 for each one, with a guaranteed time rate of 35 hours at £10 per hour. Last week there was a machine failure and he was only able to process 250 units.

WOLVERHAMPTON FACTORY

In this factory a number of engineering production lines are operated. The direct labour force is paid on a time rate basis, but a bonus is paid if work can be completed faster than the time allowed. The bonus is for the savings achieved to be shared equally between employer and employee. Wages are, therefore, paid on the following basis: time rate + 50% of (time saved x time rate). If no bonus is due, then the time rate applies.

Martin Lee worked a 38 hour work last week; his time rate is £10 per hour. He is allowed a time of 30 minutes to carry out his work on each unit of production; last week he completed 71 units.

Sara King has a time rate of £11 per hour; last week she worked 40 hours. She is allowed a time of 15 minutes to carry out her work on each unit of production; last week she completed 184 units.

What were the gross earnings of each employee?

solution

WALSALL FACTORY

John Brown	39 hours x £10.00 per hour	=	£390.00
Stefan Wozniak	37 hours x £12.00 per hour = £444		
	5 hours x £18.00 per hour = £90	=	£534.00

DUDLEY FACTORY

Tracey Johnson	Piecework rate, 910 units x 40p per unit	=	£364.00
	Guaranteed time rate, 35 hours x £10.00 per hour	=	£350.00
	Therefore piecework rate of £364.00 is paid.		
Pete Bronyah	Piecework rate, 250 units x £1.00 per unit	=	£250.00
	Guaranteed time rate, 35 hours x £10.00 per hour	=	£350.00
	Therefore guaranteed time rate of £350.00 is paid.		

WOLVERHAMPTON FACTORY

Martin Lee	Time rate, 38 hours x £10.00 per hour	=	£380.00
	Bonus, time allowed 71 units x 30 minutes each = 35 hours 30 minutes		
	Therefore no time saved, so no bonus payable.		
	Time rate of £380 paid.		
Sara King	Time rate, 40 hours x £11.00 per hour	=	£440.00
	Bonus, time allowed 184 x 15 minutes each = 46 hours		
	Therefore time saved is 6 hours		
	Bonus is 50% of (6 hours x £11.00)	=	£33.00
	Therefore wages are £440.00 + £33.00	=	£473.00

The Case Study illustrates some of the direct labour payment methods in use, however it should be appreciated that there are many variations on these to be found.

OVERTIME, IDLE TIME AND EQUIVALENT UNITS

In Chapter 1 we divided labour costs between:

- **direct costs,** labour costs of production-line employees
- **indirect costs,** labour costs of other employees, such as supervisors, office staff, etc

Whilst this distinction appears clear enough, there are times when a proportion of the labour costs of production-line employees is classed as an indirect cost (rather than a direct cost) and is included amongst the overheads of the business. This is done if part of the cost of wages of the direct workers cannot be linked to specific work.

overtime payments and overtime premium

When production-line employees work overtime they are usually paid at a rate above the time rate. For example, overtime might be paid at 'time-and-a-half'; thus an employee with a time rate of £12 an hour will receive **overtime payments** of £18 an hour. The additional £6 per hour is called **overtime premium**. For normal cost accounting purposes, any overtime worked is charged at £12 an hour to direct labour, and £6 an hour to indirect labour.

Example:

A group of employees on a production line have a working week consisting of 35 hours each. Anything over that time is paid at time-and-a-half. One employee has worked 40 hours during the week at a normal rate of £10.

- direct wages cost is 40 hours at £10 = £400
- overtime premium is 5 hours at £5 (half of £10) = £25, which is charged to indirect labour
- total wages cost £425 (35 hours at £10, plus 5 hours at £15)

The overtime premium is spread across all output and is not charged solely to the output being worked on during the overtime period. As another issue, management will wish to know why there was the need to work overtime, and will seek to control such an increase in labour costs.

However, where a customer requests overtime to be worked to get a rush job completed, then the full overtime rate (£15 an hour in the above example) is charged as direct labour, and passed on as a cost to the customer.

Other additional payments made to employees – such as a bonus – will be treated in a similar way to overtime premium and will normally be treated as an indirect labour cost.

idle time

Idle time occurs when production is stopped through no fault of the production-line employees – for example, a machine breakdown, or a shortage of materials. Employees paid under a piecework or a bonus system will receive time rate for the period of the stoppage. Such wages costs are normally charged to overheads as indirect labour.

Similarly, time spent by direct workers on non-productive work – eg attendance on a training course – would also usually be treated as an overhead.

equivalent units

When production employees are paid on the basis of output, a calculation of equivalent units may need to be made. This happens when part of the production at the end of the accounting period is work-in-progress for the labour content.

Example:

10,000 units have been completed during the month and, at the month-end, 2,000 units are work-in-progress and are 50 per cent complete for the labour content. The equivalent units completed for the month will be:

10,000 units + (2,000 units x 50%) = 11,000 equivalent units

USING A TIME SHEET

In order to calculate gross wages, as noted earlier (page 66), a business or organisation must obtain information about hours worked and/or work done.

A time sheet is used for each employee to record:

- hours worked each day, split between production and indirect work
- amount of basic pay each day (using the hourly rate paid to the employee)
- amount of overtime premium each day (using the hourly rate)
- total pay each day
- total hours worked for the week
- total basic pay, overtime premium and pay for the week

A time sheet, which includes overtime premium is shown in the Case Study which follows:

Case Study

CALCULATING THE PAY

situation

You are an Accounts Assistant at Onslow Limited and have been asked to help with calculating labour costs.

The cost accountant has given you the following time sheet for one of Onslow Limited's employees, P Cusack, who is paid as follows:

- For a basic seven-hour shift every day from Monday to Friday – basic pay at £12.00 per hour
- For any overtime in excess of the basic seven hours on any day from Monday to Friday – the extra hours are paid at time-and-a-half (basic pay plus an overtime premium equal to half of basic pay)
- For any hours worked on a Saturday or Sunday – double-time (basic pay plus an overtime premium equal to basic pay)

You are to complete the time sheet columns headed basic pay, overtime premium and total pay (enter a zero figure, '0', in the columns where nothing is to be paid).

Note: overtime premium is just the premium paid for the extra hours worked.

The employee's weekly time sheet for week ending 14 June 20-2 is shown below.

Employee:	P Cusack		Profit Centre: Metal cutting			
Employee number:	260		Basic pay per hour: £12.00			
	Hours spent on production	Hours worked on indirect work	Notes	Basic pay £	Overtime premium £	Total pay £
Monday	7	0				
Tuesday	5	2	2pm-4 pm first aid course			
Wednesday	7	0				
Thursday	6	1	8 am-9 am cleaning			
Friday	8	0				
Saturday	3	0				
Sunday	0	0				
Total	36	3				

solution

P Cusack's time sheet is completed as follows:

Employee: P Cusack			Profit Centre: Metal cutting			
Employee number: 260			Basic pay per hour: £12.00			
	Hours spent on production	Hours worked on indirect work	Notes	Basic pay £	Overtime premium £	Total pay £
Monday	7	0		84	0	84
Tuesday	5	2	2pm-4 pm first aid course	84	0	84
Wednesday	7	0		84	0	84
Thursday	6	1	8 am-9 am cleaning	84	0	84
Friday	8	0		96	6	102
Saturday	3	0		36	36	72
Sunday	0	0		0	0	0
Total	36	3		468	42	510

BOOKKEEPING FOR LABOUR COSTS

In this section we look at the cost bookkeeping entries to record labour costs – the transfer of labour costs to production and to overheads. These entries form part of the bookkeeping system for costing.

A **wages control account** – which may also include salaries – links to the payroll accounting system. It is used to charge labour costs to the various cost, profit, or investment centres of a business or organisation. In this way:

- direct labour costs are charged to production
- indirect labour (eg factory supervisor) costs are charged to production overheads
- administration labour (eg office staff) costs are charged to non-production overheads

Note:

- production overheads are also referred to as operating overheads
- non-production overheads are also referred to as non-operating overheads

With labour costs the general ledger entries are:

- **transfer of direct labour costs to production**
  - debit production
  - credit wages control
- **transfer of indirect labour costs to production overheads**
  - debit production overheads
  - credit wages control
- **transfer of administration labour costs to non-production overheads**
  - debit non-production overheads, eg administration
  - credit wages control

The cost bookkeeping entries for labour costs are shown diagrammatically below:

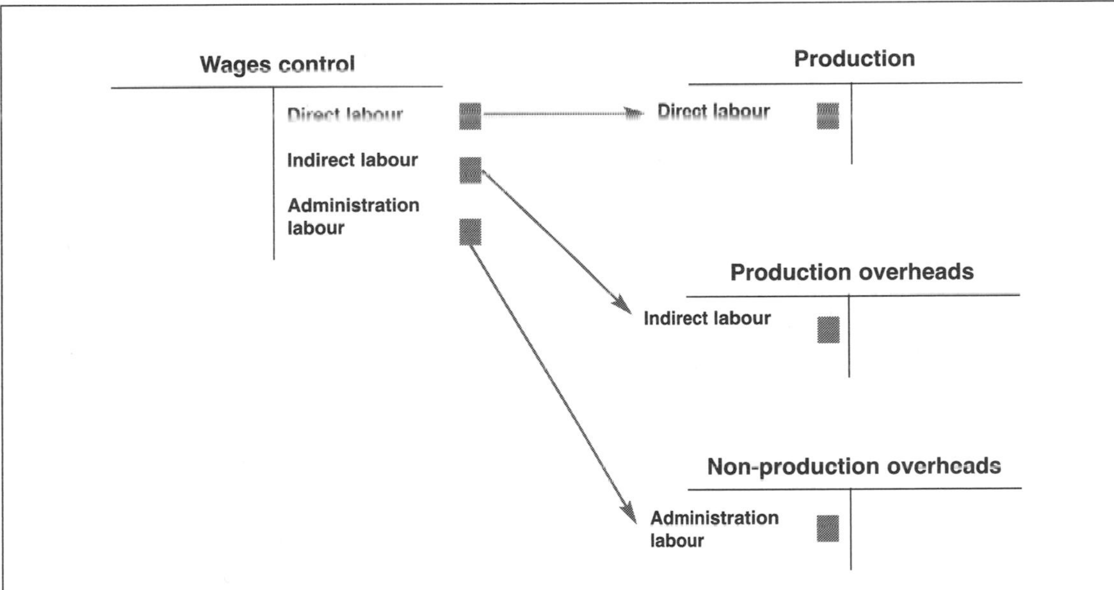

Note: Here all of the labour costs have been transferred to production and overheads. From time-to-time, however, some part of labour costs may relate to capital expenditure – for example, own workforce used to build an extension to the premises; here the bookkeeping entries for the relevant labour costs are:

- debit premises account (or relevant capital expenditure account)
- credit wages control account

Case Study

BLUE JEANS LIMITED: BOOKKEEPING FOR LABOUR COSTS

situation

Blue Jeans Limited manufactures and sells denim jeans and jackets. The payroll for the week ended 21 May 20-4 has been completed with the following amounts to pay:

• net wages to be paid to employees	£5,000
• Income Tax and National Insurance Contributions (NIC) to HMRC	£1,000
• pension contributions to be paid to the pension fund	£500
Total	£6,500

The payroll for the week has been analysed as:

• direct labour costs	£3,500
• indirect labour costs	£2,000
• administration labour costs	£1,000
Total	£6,500

All of the direct labour costs are for the manufacture of blue jeans. The following cost accounting codes are in use to record labour costs:

Code number	Description
2200	production – blue jeans
2400	production overheads
2600	non-production overheads – administration
4200	wages control

As an Accounts Assistant at Blue Jeans Limited, you are asked to prepare the wages control account and to fill in the table below to record the journal entries which show how the total cost of the payroll is split between the various cost centres of the business.

20-4	Code number	Debit £	Credit £
21 May	2200		
21 May	4200		
21 May	2400		
21 May	4200		
21 May	2600		
21 May	4200		

solution

Wages control account is prepared as follows:

Dr	Wages Control Account (4200)		Cr
	£		£
Cash/bank (net wages)	5,000	Production (direct labour)	3,500
HM Revenue & Customs		Production overheads	
(income tax and NIC)	1,000	(indirect labour)	2,000
Pension contributions	500	Non-production overheads	
		(administration)	1,000
	6,500		6,500

The cost bookkeeping entries are:

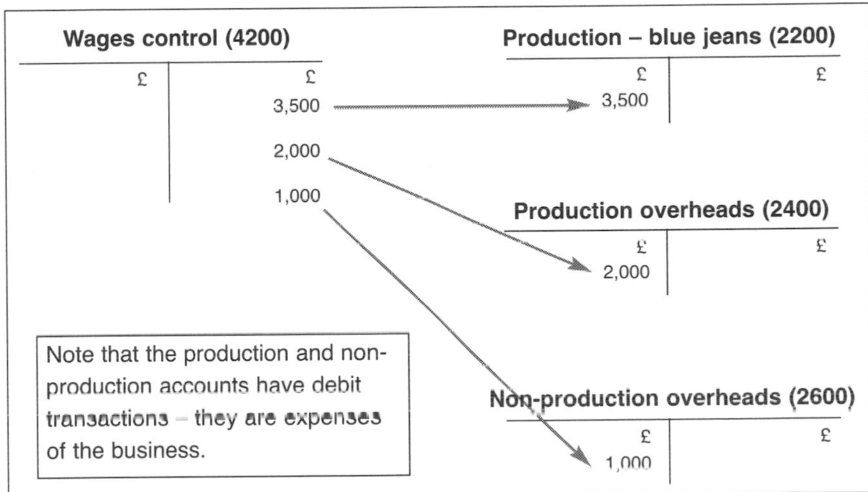

The cost bookkeeping transactions are recorded as journal entries in the following way:

20-4	Code number	Debit £	Credit £
21 May	2200	£3,500	
21 May	4200		£3,500
21 May	2400	£2,000	
21 May	4200		£2,000
21 May	2600	£1,000	
21 May	4200		£1,000

In this way, the total cost of the payroll is split between the various cost centres of the business.

Chapter Summary

- Labour costs – the costs of wages and salaries – are incurred in every kind of business.
- Levels of wage rates paid to employees are influenced by a number of factors including the rates paid by similar local businesses, national living wage rate and national averages.
- The main labour payment methods are based either on time or amounts of work done or on a combination of both.
- Certain wages costs of the direct workers may be classed as indirect labour costs: these include overtime premium and payment for idle or non-productive time.
- Cost bookkeeping entries are made to charge labour costs to the various cost centres of a business or organisation.

Key Terms

time rate labour payment method based on the time worked by an employee, giving the formula:

hours worked x rate per hour

piecework rate labour payment method based on the work done by an employee, giving the formula:

number of items produced x rate per unit

bonus system labour payment method in which an employee is paid a time rate and then receives a bonus if output is better than expected when comparing the time allowed with the time taken – the bonus is calculated as an agreed percentage of the time saved multiplied by the time rate

time sheet method by which employees record the hours they have worked

clock card where employees 'clock in' at the start of work, and 'clock out' at the end

piecework ticket documentation completed by employees who work on a batch of output

job card documentation completed by employees which records the amount of time spent on each job

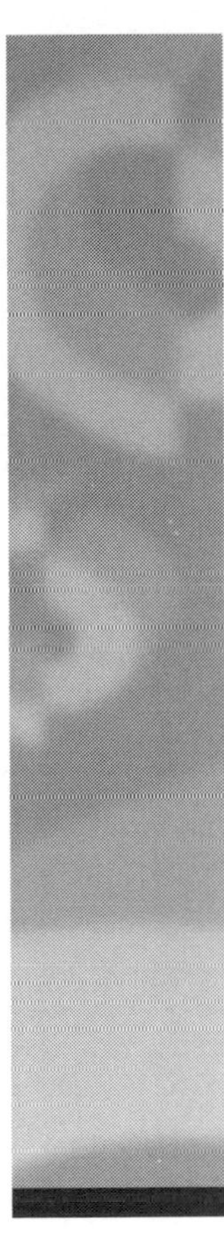

route card — documentation which follows a product through the production process – employees record the amount of time they spend working on the product

overtime payment — an overtime pay rate paid at more than time rate, for example, 'time-and-a-half'

overtime premium — the additional pay above normal rates which is paid to employees working overtime, for example, the premium part of 'time-and-a-half' is the extra 'half' of the hourly rate

idle time — time during which work is stopped, due to reasons such as machine breakdown or shortage of materials; employees usually receive time rate for idle time, and the cost is normally classified as an indirect cost

equivalent units — completed units plus work-in-progress at the percentage complete for labour

wages control account — used to charge labour costs to the various cost, profit or investment centres:

- direct labour to production
- indirect labour to production overheads
- administration labour to non-production overheads

Activities

3.1 A manufacturing business pays its production workers on a time rate basis. A bonus is paid where production is completed faster than the time allowed for a standard hour's production; the bonus is paid at half of the time rate for production time saved. How much will each of the following employees earn for the week?

Employee	Time rate	Hours worked	Time allowed (output per hour)	Actual production
N Ball	£11.00 per hour	35	30 units	1,010 units
T Smith	£9.00 per hour	37	40 units	1,560 units
L Lewis	£10.00 per hour	38	20 units	820 units
M Wilson	£12.00 per hour	36	25 units	950 units

3.2 A company pays its production-line employees on a piecework basis, but with a guaranteed time rate. How much will each of the following employees earn during the week?

Employee	Time rate	Hours worked	Production	Piecework rate
L Fry	£10.00 per hour	40	1,200 units	30p per unit
R Williams	£12.00 per hour	37	500 units	90p per unit
P Grant	£9.50 per hour	36	725 units	50p per unit

3.3 Print 'n Go is a print shop that specialises in printing headed notepaper for businesses. It employs two printers, Steve Kurtin and Pete Singh. Both are paid a basic rate per hour for a 35-hour week with two overtime rates: time-and-a-third for weekdays (rate 1), and time-and-a-half for week-ends (rate 2). In addition, a production bonus is paid of 50p per 1,000 copies printed.

Details for last week are as follows:

	Steve Kurtin	Pete Singh
Basic rate per hour	£10.50	£12.00
Total hours worked	39	42
Overtime hours: rate 1	4	3
rate 2	–	4
Number of copies printed	45,000	57,000

You are to

- calculate the gross wages earned by each employee for last week
- calculate the piecework rate per 1,000 copies printed that would be equal to the gross wages earned by Steve Kurtin for the week, assuming the same output level of 45,000 copies.

3.4 Wyvern Fabrication Company has two departments – moulding and finishing. Data relating to labour for a four-week period is given on the labour cost sheet below.

The company uses a bonus scheme whereby employees receive 50 per cent of the time saved in each department, paid at the actual labour rate per hour. This is not included in the actual wages cost, which shows actual hours multiplied by the actual wage rate.

LABOUR COST SHEET for the four weeks ended 26 February 20-7		
	MOULDING	FINISHING
Actual wages cost (£)	£41,160	£45,450
Time allowed	4,000 hours	5,000 hours
Time taken	4,100 hours	4,500 hours
Time saved		
Bonus (£)		
Total labour cost (£)		

You are to calculate the total labour cost for each department.

3.5 The direct workers of Haven Limited are paid a basic wage of £10.20 per hour. For time worked above 40 hours per week, they receive overtime pay at time-and-a-half. For two particular weeks, we have the following information for a team of 10 direct workers:

Week 1: Total hours worked = 450 hours, including 50 hours of overtime.

Week 2: Total hours worked = 400 hours, including 20 hours of non-production work, clearing up and re-organising a section of the factory during a machine breakdown.

For each of the two given weeks you are to:

- Calculate the gross earnings in total for the team of 10 employees.
- State how much of the gross earnings would normally be treated as an indirect labour cost.

3.6 You are an Accounts Assistant at Durning Limited and have been asked to help with calculating labour costs.

The cost accountant has given you the following time sheet for one of Durning Limited's employees, T Mantle, who is paid as follows:

- For a basic six-hour shift every day from Monday to Friday – basic pay.
- For any overtime in excess of the basic six hours on any day from Monday to Friday – the extra hours are paid at time-and-a-half (basic pay plus an overtime premium equal to half of basic pay).
- For three contracted hours each Saturday morning – basic pay.
- For any hours worked in excess of three hours on a Saturday or any hours worked on a Sunday – double-time (basic pay plus an overtime premium equal to basic pay).

You are to complete the time sheet columns headed basic pay, overtime premium and total pay (enter a zero figure, '0', in the columns where nothing is to be paid).

Note: overtime premium is just the premium paid for the extra hours worked

Employee's weekly time sheet for week ending 15 April 20-6

Employee: T Mantle			Profit Centre: Finishing			
Employee number: 170			Basic pay per hour: £14.00			
	Hours spent on production	Hours worked on indirect work	Notes	Basic pay £	Overtime premium £	Total pay £
Monday	6	0				
Tuesday	5	2	8am-10am maintenance			
Wednesday	7	0				
Thursday	6	3	9am-12 noon training			
Friday	8	0				
Saturday	5	0				
Sunday	0	0				
Total	37	5				

3.7 Breeden Bakery Limited makes 'homestyle' cakes which are sold to supermarket chains. The payroll for the week ended 26 March 20-4 has been completed with the following amounts to pay:

	£
• net wages to be paid to employees	£7,500
• Income Tax and National Insurance Contributions (NIC) to HMRC	£1,450
• pension contributions to be paid to the pension fund	£750
Total	£9,700

• direct labour costs	6,500
• indirect labour costs	2,700
• administration labour costs	500
Total	9,700

As an Accounts Assistant at Breedon Bakery you have been given the following tasks:

Task 1

Prepare wages control account for the week ended 26 March 20-4:

Dr		**Wages Control Account**	Cr
	£		£

Task 2

All of the direct labour costs are for the manufacture of fruit cakes. The following cost accounting codes are in use to record labour costs:

Code number	**Description**
3300	production – fruit cakes
3500	production overheads
3700	non-production overheads – administration
5200	wages control

Complete the table on the next page to record the journal entries which show how the total cost of the payroll is split between the various cost centres of the business.

20-4	Code number	Debit £	Credit £
26 March			
26 March			
26 March			
26 March			
26 March			
26 March			

3.8 Icod Limited manufactures golf clubs. The following data relates to the production of its 'Mulligan' brand of clubs for October 20-4:

Total direct labour hours worked	16,000 hours
Normal time hours	14,400 hours
Overtime hours	1,600 hours
Normal time rate per hour	£10 per hour
Overtime premium per hour	£5 per hour

In the company's cost bookkeeping system all direct labour overtime payments are included in direct costs.

The following cost accounting codes are in use to record labour costs:

Code number	**Description**
1500	production – 'Mulligan' clubs
5000	wages control

You are to:

- Calculate the total cost of direct labour for October.
- Show the cost bookkeeping entries, together with account codes, in order to transfer the direct labour costs to production.

3.9 Wyvern Manufacturing Limited pays some of its production employees on a piecework system, based on an agreed output per hour – standard hours produced – that they are allowed to manufacture components.

The following information relates to one of these employees last week:

Day	**Actual hours worked**	**Standard hours produced**
Monday	8	7
Tuesday	7	7
Wednesday	9	10
Thursday	10	11
Friday	10	8

The employee is paid £15 per standard hour produced.

You are to complete the sentences below by entering the correct figures:

(a) The employee's total pay for the week was £ [ ]

Now assume that the company offers a guaranteed minimum daily payment of £120.

(b) The employee's total pay for the week would now be £ [ ]

Now assume that, instead of a guaranteed minimum daily payment, the company offers a guaranteed minimum weekly payment of £650.

(c) The employee's total pay for the week would now be £ [ ]

Now assume that, instead of a guaranteed minimum weekly payment, the company pays for actual hours worked at the standard hour rate, together with a flat-rate bonus of £75 for the week.

(d) The employee's total pay for the week would now be £ [ ]

3.10 Excalibur Limited, a manufacturing business, has a Production Department where the employees work in teams. Their basic rate is £10.00 per hour and there are two rates of overtime as follows:

Overtime rate 1: basic pay + 25%

Overtime rate 2: basic pay + 50%

Excalibur sets a target for production of every component each month. A team bonus equal to 5% of basic hourly rate is payable for every equivalent unit of production in the month in excess of the target.
The target for March was 10,000 units.

In March the production was 12,000 equivalent units.

All overtime and bonuses are included as part of the direct labour cost.

(a) Complete the gaps in the table below to calculate the total labour cost.

Labour cost	**Hours**	£
Basic pay	416	
Overtime rate 1	30	
Overtime rate 2	15	
Total cost before team bonus	461	
Bonus payment		
Total cost including team bonus		

(b) Calculate the total labour cost per equivalent unit of the finished production for March. Give your answer in £s to **two** decimal places.

The direct labour cost per equivalent unit for March is £ [ ]

(c) Excalibur has forecast the following information for the Production Department for April:

The basic hourly rate will be increased to £10.60 per hour. The target for production is still 10,000 units and the bonus, equal to 5% of basic hourly rate, is still payable for equivalent units of production in excess of this.

9,800 units will be completed in April and the closing work in progress is expected to be 1,500 units which will be 80% complete with regard to labour. No opening work in progress was expected at the start of April.

Complete the following sentence by filling in the blanks.

The equivalent units of production with regard to labour for April will be [ ] and the bonus payable will be £ [ ] .

4 Overheads and expenses

this chapter covers...

In this chapter we turn our attention to the way in which the overheads and expenses of a business are incorporated into the cost of the output. In particular we look at:

- *the nature of overheads as period costs*
- *the need to recover the cost of overheads through units of output*
- *the process of allocating and apportioning the cost of overheads into the units of output*
- *the different bases of apportionment of overheads*
- *apportionment of service department costs, using the direct and step-down methods*
- *the commonly-used overhead absorption (recovery) rates and their relative merits in given circumstances*
- *the bookkeeping entries for overheads*

OVERHEADS

In Chapter 1 'An Introduction to Cost Accounting' we saw that costs could be classified as follows:

	Direct materials		Indirect materials
+	Direct labour	+	Indirect labour
+	Direct expenses	+	Indirect expenses
=	Total direct costs or Prime cost	=	Total indirect costs or Overheads

Direct costs are product costs which can be identified directly with each unit of output, whilst indirect costs (overheads) are period costs which cannot be identified directly with each unit of output.

The indirect costs – indirect materials, indirect labour, and indirect expenses – form the overheads of a business. Overheads do not relate to particular units of output but must, instead, be shared amongst all the cost units (units of output to which costs can be charged) to which they relate. For example, the cost of the factory rent must be included in the cost of the output.

The important point to remember is that all the overheads of a business, together with the direct costs must be covered by revenue from the output – the sales of products or services.

In practice, businesses usually plan – or budget – their overheads in advance, often on an annual basis. By doing this they can work out how to 'recover' the overheads through their output – using an overhead absorption rate.

In larger businesses and organisations, overheads are usually classified by function under headings such as:

- factory or production, eg factory rent and rates, indirect factory labour, indirect factory materials, heating and lighting of factory
- selling and distribution, eg salaries of sales staff, vehicle costs, delivery costs
- administration, eg office rent and rates, office salaries, heating and lighting of office, indirect office materials
- finance, eg bank interest

Each of these functions or sections of the business is likely to be what is known as a cost centre, a term which was defined in Chapter 1 as follows:

Cost centres are segments of a business or organisation to which costs can be charged.

As well as cost centres, businesses may also have profit centres, investment centres and revenue centres – all four types of centres are collectively called responsibility centres.

In order to deal with the overheads we need to know the responsibility centres of the organisation. This will depend on the size of the business and the way in which the work is organised.

COLLECTING OVERHEADS IN RESPONSIBILITY CENTRES

Depending on the type of cost, overheads are either **allocated** to responsibility centres – cost centres, profit centres or investment centres – or they are **apportioned** to centres.

allocation of overheads

Some overheads belong entirely to one particular centre, for example:

- the wages of a supervisor who works in only one centre
- the rent of a separate building in which there is only one centre
- the cost of indirect materials that have been issued to one particular centre

Overheads like these can therefore be allocated to the centre to which they belong.

Allocation of overheads is the charging to a particular responsibility centre of overheads that are incurred entirely by that centre.

apportionment of overheads

Overheads that cannot be allocated to a particular centre have to be shared or **apportioned** between those responsibility centres that have shared the benefits of the relevant cost.

Apportionment of overheads is the sharing of overheads over a number of responsibility centres to which they relate. Each centre is charged with a proportion of the overhead cost.

For example, a department which is a cost centre within a factory will be charged a proportion of the factory rent and rates. Another example is where a supervisor works within two departments, both of which are separate cost centres: the indirect labour cost of employing the supervisor is shared between the two cost centres.

With apportionment, a suitable **basis** – or method – must be found to apportion overheads between centres; the basis selected should be related to the type of cost. Different methods might be used for each overhead.

Look at the example below.

Overhead	Basis of apportionment
rent, rates	floor space (or volume of space) of centres
heating, lighting	floor space (or volume of space) of centres
buildings insurance	floor space (or volume of space) of centres
buildings depreciation	floor space (or volume of space) of centres
machinery insurance	cost or value of machinery and equipment
machinery depreciation	value of machinery; or machine usage (hours)
canteen	number of employees in each centre
supervisory costs	number of employees in each centre, or labour hours worked by supervisors in each centre

It must be stressed that apportionment is used only for those overheads that cannot be allocated to a particular centre. For example, if a college's Business Studies Department occupies a building in another part of town from the main college building, the local authority business rates for the building can clearly be allocated to the Business Studies cost centre. By contrast, the business rates for the main college building must be apportioned amongst the cost centres on the main campus.

review of allocation and apportionment

It is important that the allocation and apportionment of overheads are reviewed at regular intervals to ensure that the methods being used are still valid. For example:

- **allocation**

  The role of a supervisor may have changed – whereas previously the supervisor worked in one department only, he or she might now be working in two departments.

- **apportionment**

  Building work may have expanded the floor space of a department, so that the apportionment basis needs to be reworked.

Any proposed changes to allocation and apportionment must be discussed with senior staff and their agreement obtained before any changes to methods are implemented. Accounting personnel will often have to consult with personnel (such as managers and supervisors) working in operational departments, to discuss how overheads are charged to their departments, and to resolve any queries.

apportionment and ratios

It is important to understand the method of apportionment of overheads using ratios. For example, overheads relating to buildings are often shared in the ratio of the floor space used by the cost centres.

Now read through the Worked Example and the Case Study which follow.

worked example: apportionment using ratios

A business has four cost centres: two production departments, A and B, and two non-production cost centres, stores and maintenance. The total rent per year for the business premises is £12,000. This is to be apportioned on the basis of floor space, given as:

	Production dept A	**Production dept B**	**Stores**	**Maintenance**
Floor space (square metres)	400	550	350	200

Step 1

Calculate the total floor space: 400 + 550 + 350 + 200 = 1,500 square metres

Step 2

Divide the total rent by the total floor space: £12,000 ÷ 1,500 = £8

This gives a rate of £8 per square metre.

Step 3

Multiply the floor space in each cost centre by the rate per square metre. This gives the share of rent for each cost centre. For example, in Production Department A, the share of rent is 400 x £8 = £3,200. The results are shown in the table:

	Production dept A	**Production dept B**	**Stores**	**Maintenance**
Floor space (square metres)	400	550	350	200
Rent apportioned	£3,200	£4,400	£2,800	£1,600

Step 4

Check that the apportioned amounts agree with the total rent:

£3,200 + £4,400 + £ 2,800 + £1,600 = £12,000.

Case Study

PILOT ENGINEERING LIMITED: OVERHEAD ALLOCATION AND APPORTIONMENT

situation

Pilot Engineering Limited, which makes car engine components, uses some of the latest laser equipment in one department, while another section of the business continues to use traditional machinery. Details of the factory are as follows:

Department X is a 'hi-tech' machine shop equipped with laser-controlled machinery which cost £80,000. This department has 400 square metres of floor space. There are three machine operators: the supervisor spends one-third of the time in this department.

Department Y is a 'low-tech' part of the factory equipped with machinery which cost £20,000. The floor space is 600 square metres. There are two workers who spend all their time in this department: the supervisor spends two-thirds of the time in this department.

The budgeted overheads for the next financial year to be allocated or apportioned are:

1	Factory rates	£12,000
2	Wages of the supervisor	£21,000
3	Factory heating and lighting	£2,500
4	Depreciation of machinery	£20,000
5	Buildings insurance	£2,000
6	Insurance of machinery	£1,500
7	Specialist materials for the laser equipment	£2,500

How should each of these be allocated or apportioned to each department?

solution

The recommendations are:

1 Factory rates – apportioned on the basis of floor space.

2 Supervisor's wages – apportioned on the basis of time spent, ie one-third to Department X, and two-thirds to Department Y. If the time spent was not known, an alternative basis could be established, based on the number of employees.

3 Factory heating and lighting – apportioned on the basis of floor space.

4 Depreciation of machinery – apportioned on the basis of the cost of machinery.

5 Buildings insurance – apportioned on the basis of floor space.

6 Insurance of machinery – apportioned on the basis of the cost of machinery.

7 Specialist materials for the laser equipment – allocated to Department X because this cost belongs entirely to Department X.

It is important to note that there are no fixed rules for the apportionment of overheads – the only proviso is that a fair proportion of the overhead is charged to each department which has shared the benefits of the relevant cost. Methods of apportionment will need to be reviewed at regular intervals to ensure that they are still valid; changes can only be implemented with the agreement of senior staff.

The apportionment of budgeted overheads for Pilot Engineering Limited is as follows (sample workings are shown below the table):

Budgeted overheads	Basis Of Apportionment	Total	Dept X	Dept Y
		£	£	£
Factory rates	Floor space	12,000	4,800	7,200
Wages of supervisor	Time spent	21,000	7,000	14,000
Heating and lighting	Floor space	2,500	1,000	1,500
Dep'n of machinery	Cost of machinery	20,000	16,000	4,000
Buildings insurance	Floor space	2,000	800	1,200
Machinery insurance	Cost of machinery	1,500	1,200	300
Specialist materials	Allocation	2,500	2,500	–
		61,500	33,300	28,200

workings:

For example, the floor space of the two departments are:

Dept X	400	square metres
Dept Y	600	square metres
Total	1,000	square metres

Factory rates are apportioned as follows:

$$\frac{£12{,}000}{1{,}000} = £12 \text{ per square metre}$$

Dept X rates:	£12 x 400 =	£4,800
Dept Y rates	£12 x 600 =	£7,200
Total (check)		£12,000

SERVICE DEPARTMENTS

Many businesses have departments which provide services within the business; for example, maintenance, transport, stores or stationery. Each service department is likely to be a cost centre, to which a proportion of overheads is charged. As service departments do not themselves have any cost units to which their overheads may be charged, the costs of each service department must be re-apportioned to the production departments (which do have cost units to which overheads can be charged). A suitable basis of re-apportionment must be used, for example:

- the overheads of a maintenance department might be re-apportioned to production departments on the basis of value of machinery or equipment, or on the basis of time spent in each production department
- the overheads of a stores or stationery department could be re-apportioned on the basis of value of goods issued to production departments
- the overheads of a subsidised canteen could be re-apportioned on the basis of the number of employees

Re-apportionment of service department overheads is considered in the next section.

RE-APPORTIONMENT OF SERVICE DEPARTMENT OVERHEADS

The overheads of service departments are charged to production cost centres using:

- either **direct apportionment** is used where service departments provide services to production departments only
- or the **step-down method** is used where service departments provide services to production departments *and* to other service departments

To illustrate re-apportionment, we will apply these techniques to a business with two production departments, A and B, and two service departments, stores and maintenance. After allocation and apportionment of production overheads, the totals are:

	Total £	Production dept A £	Production dept B £	Stores £	Maintenance £
Overheads	20,400	10,000	5,000	2,400	3,000

direct apportionment

Initially, we will assume that the service departments do not provide services to one another. Their costs are directly apportioned to production departments using a suitable basis. In the example on the previous page:

- stores overheads are re-apportioned on the basis of the number of stores requisitions – department A has made 150 requisitions; department B has made 50
- maintenance overheads are re-apportioned on the value of machinery – department A has machinery with a net book value of £20,000, department B's machinery has a value of £10,000

Using direct apportionment, the overheads of the service departments are re-apportioned as shown in the table below. The method of calculation using ratios is the same as we used for apportionment.

Notice that the total is taken out of the service cost centre column when it is shared between the production cost centres.

	Total £	Production dept A £	Production dept B £	Stores £	Maintenance £
Overheads	20,400	10,000	5,000	2,400	3,000
Stores	–	1,800	600	(2,400)	–
Maintenance	–	2,000	1,000	–	(3,000)
	20,400	13,800	6,600	–	–

Thus all the overheads have now been charged to the production departments where they can be 'absorbed' into the cost units which form the output of each department. We will see how the absorption is carried out later in this chapter.

step-down method

This is used where, as well as to production departments, one service department provides services to another. We will now assume this is the case and, using the example, the stores department deals with requisitions from the maintenance department, but no maintenance work is carried out in the stores department. Under the step-down method we re-apportion firstly the overheads of the stores department (because it does not receive any services from the maintenance department), and secondly the overheads of the maintenance department:

- stores requisitions
  - department A 150
  - department B 50
  - maintenance 50
- value of machinery
  - department A £20,000
  - department B £10,000

The re-apportionment of the production overheads of the service departments, using the step-down method, is as follows:

	Total	Production dept A	Production dept B	Stores	Maintenance
	£	£	£	£	£
Overheads	20,400	10,000	5,000	2,400	3,000
Stores	–	1,440	480	(2,400)	480
				–	*3,480
Maintenance	–	2,320	1,160	–	(3,480)
	20,400	13,760	6,640	–	–

* Note that a new total is calculated for the maintenance department before it is re-apportioned. £480 from stores is added to the original £3,000 overheads in the maintenance department.

All the overheads have now been charged to the production departments.

ALLOCATION AND APPORTIONMENT – A SUMMARY

The diagram on the next page summarises the allocation and apportionment of overheads that we have seen in this chapter. It shows:

- allocation of overheads directly to cost centres
- apportionment of overheads on an equitable basis to cost centres
- re-apportionment of service department costs to production cost centres

The Case Study which follows on page 99 is a comprehensive example of allocation and apportionment – it is based on AAT sample Assessment tasks.

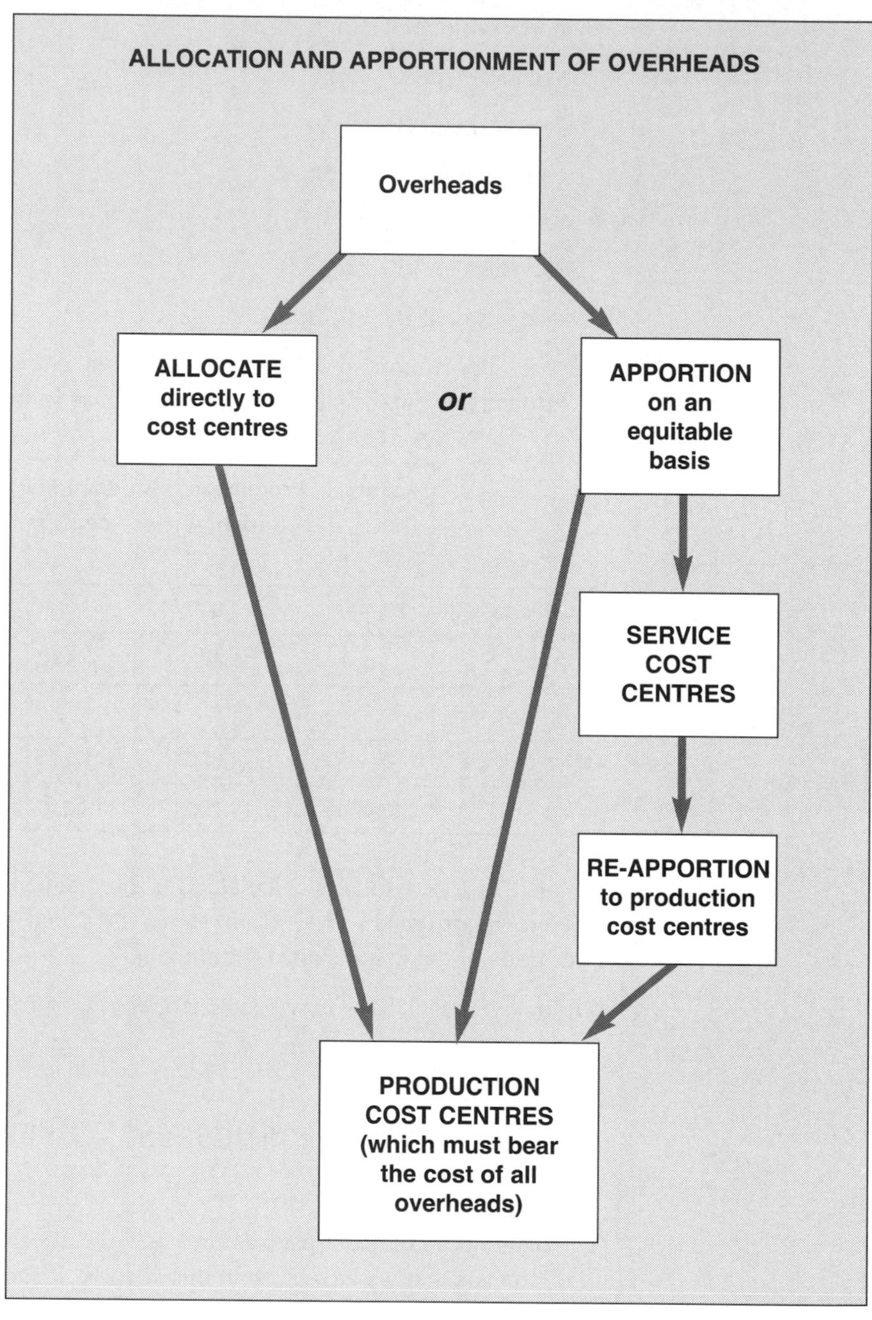
ALLOCATION AND APPORTIONMENT OF OVERHEADS
Overheads
ALLOCATE directly to cost centres
or
APPORTION on an equitable basis
SERVICE COST CENTRES
RE-APPORTION to production cost centres
PRODUCTION COST CENTRES (which must bear the cost of all overheads)

PREPARING FOR ASSESSMENT: ALLOCATION AND APPORTIONMENT OF OVERHEADS

Tutorial note:
This Case Study gives the floor space for support cost centres and not for production centres – this means that any costs apportioned by floor space must be charged to the support cost centres. When re-apportionment takes place the costs will be charged to production centres in the proportion that they have used the support centres.

situation

You work as an Accounts Assistant for Korecki Limited, a manufacturing business. The company has two production centres: cutting and assembly – and three support cost centres: maintenance, stores and administration.

Korecki Limited's budgeted overheads for the next financial year are:

	£	£
Depreciation charge for machinery		3,900
Power for production machinery		4,680
Rent and rates of premises		21,450
Light and heat for premises		8,250
Indirect labour costs:		
Maintenance	45,400	
Stores	27,250	
Administration	62,100	
Totals	134,750	38,280

The following information is also available:

See table on the next page.

Overheads are allocated or apportioned on the most appropriate basis. The total overheads of the support cost centres are then re-apportioned to the two production centres, using the direct method.

- 75% of the maintenance cost centre's time is spent maintaining production machinery in the cutting production centre and the remainder in the assembly production centre.
- The stores cost centre makes 60% of its issues to the cutting production centre, and 40% to the assembly production centre.
- Administration supports the two production centres equally.
- There is no reciprocal servicing between the three support cost centres.

Department	Carrying amount of machinery	Production machinery power usage (KwH)	Floor space (square metres)	Number of employees
Production centres:				
Cutting	175,000	25,500	600	6
Assembly	85,000	13,500	400	8
Support cost centres:				
Maintenance			300	3
Stores			200	2
Administration			150	4
Total	260,000	39,000	1,650	23

You are to use the information to allocate and apportion the budgeted overheads for the next financial year.

solution

Before completing an apportionment table you identify that:

- indirect labour is to be allocated to the support cost centres
- all other overheads are to be apportioned to the production centres and support cost centres, using a suitable basis

The basis of apportionment you decide to use is:

- depreciation charge for machinery – carrying amount of machinery
- power for production machinery – power usage
- rent and rates of premises – floor space
- light and heat for premises – floor space

As noted earlier, the indirect labour of the support centres will be allocated.

The apportionment table, including the re-apportionment of the service cost centres, is completed as follows:

Budgeted overheads	Basis of apportionment	Cutting £	Assembly £	Maintenance £	Stores £	Admin £	Totals £
Depreciation charge for machinery	Carrying amount of machinery	2,625	1,275				3,900
Power for production machinery	Power usage	3,060	1,620				4,680
Rent and rates of premises	Floor space	7,800	5,200	3,900	2,600	1,950	21,450
Light and heat for premises	Floor space	3,000	2,000	1,500	1,000	750	8,250
Indirect labour	Allocated			45,400	27,250	62,100	134,750
Totals		16,485	10,095	50,800	30,850	64,800	173,030
Re-apportion Maintenance		38,100	12,700	(50,800)			
Re-apportion Stores		18,510	12,340		(30,850)		
Re-apportion Administration		32,400	32,400			(64,800)	
Total overheads to production centres		105,495	67,535				173,030

OVERHEAD ABSORPTION (RECOVERY)

Once overheads have been allocated or apportioned to profit centres or production cost centres, the final step is to ensure that the overheads are charged to cost units. In the language of cost accounting this is known as 'absorption' or 'recovery', ie the cost of overheads is charged to the cost units which pass through that particular production department.

For example, if you take a car to be repaired at a garage, the bill may be presented as follows:

	£
Parts	70.00
Labour: 3 hours at £40 per hour	120.00
Total	190.00

Within this bill are the three main elements of cost: materials (parts), labour and overheads. The last two are combined as labour – the garage mechanic is not paid £40 per hour; instead the labour rate might be £15 per hour, with the rest, ie £25 per hour, being a contribution towards the overheads and profit of the garage. Other examples are accountants and solicitors, who charge a 'rate per hour', part of which is used to contribute to the cost of overheads and profit.

To be profitable, a business must ensure that its selling prices more than cover all its costs:

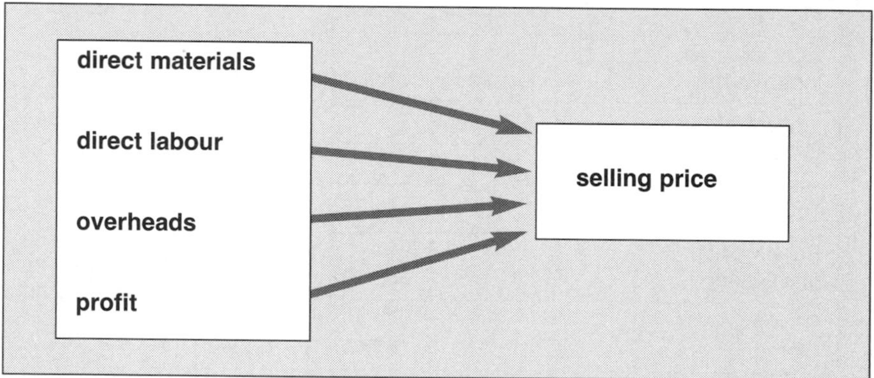

calculating overhead absorption (recovery) rates

In order to recover the overheads of a department, there are two steps to be followed:

1 calculation of the overhead absorption rate (OAR)

2 application of this rate to actual work done

The overhead absorption rate is calculated using estimated or budgeted figures as follows, for a given time period:

$$OAR = \frac{\textit{total budgeted cost centre overheads}}{\textit{total planned work in the cost centre}}$$

The amount of work must be measured in a suitable way – for a manufacturing business this is usually:

- direct labour hours, or
- machine hours

For manufacturing businesses, an alternative to direct labour hours is to use a percentage add-on to the direct labour cost. Other businesses and organisations – especially those which provide a service – will use other ways, eg an accountancy firm may use an hourly rate, or a bus company may use miles travelled.

Methods of overhead absorption are illustrated on the next page.

direct labour hour method

With this method, production overhead is absorbed on the basis of the number of direct labour hours worked. It is most commonly used where production is labour intensive.

1 Calculation of the overhead absorption rate, using budgeted figures:

$$\frac{\textit{total cost centre overheads}}{\textit{total direct labour hours (in cost centre)}} = \textit{cost per direct labour hour}$$

2 Application of the rate:

direct labour hours worked x overhead absorption rate

= overhead absorbed

worked example

Department A	total budgeted cost centre overheads for year	£40,000
	expected direct labour hours for year	5,000
	actual direct labour hours in March	450

1 Overhead absorption rate:

$$\frac{£40{,}000}{5{,}000 \text{ hours}} = £8 \text{ per direct labour hour}$$

2 Application of the rate:

450 hours x £8 = £3,600 of overhead absorbed in March

machine hour method

Here the production overhead is absorbed on the basis of machine hours. It is most commonly used where production is machine intensive.

1 Calculation of the overhead absorption rate, using budgeted figures:

$$\frac{\textit{total cost centre overheads}}{\textit{total machine hours (in cost centre)}} = \textit{cost per machine hour}$$

2 Application of the rate:

machine hours worked x overhead absorption rate

= overhead absorbed

worked example

Department B	total budgeted cost centre overheads for year	£216,000
	expected machine hours for year	36,000
	actual machine hours in March	3,500

1 Overhead absorption rate:

$$\frac{£216{,}000}{36{,}000 \text{ hours}} = £6 \text{ per machine hour}$$

2 Application of the rate:

3,500 hours x £6 = £21,000 of overhead absorbed in March

other methods – direct labour percentage add-on

With this method, which is a variant of the direct labour hours basis, a percentage is added on to the cost of direct labour.

1 Calculation of the overhead absorption rate, using budgeted figures:

$$\frac{\textit{total cost centre overheads x 100}}{\textit{total direct labour cost (in cost centre)}} = \textit{direct labour percentage add-on}$$

2 Application of the rate:

direct labour cost x direct labour percentage add-on

= overhead absorbed

worked example

Department C	total budgeted cost centre overheads for year	£32,000
	expected direct labour cost for year	£80,000
	actual direct labour cost in March	£6,000

1 Overhead absorption rate:

$$\frac{£32{,}000 \times 100}{£80{,}000} = 40\% \text{ direct labour percentage add-on}$$

2 Application of the rate:

£6,000 x 40% = £2,400 of overhead absorbed in March

service sector – hourly rate (or sales price/unit method)

This method is often used by businesses such as accountants, solicitors, dentists, garages, where the overhead is absorbed on the basis of chargeable time or sales price or units sold.

1 Calculation of the overhead absorption rate, using budgeted figures:

$$\frac{\textit{total cost centre* overheads}}{\textit{total chargeable hours** (in cost centre)}} = \textit{cost per hour of chargeable time}$$

* for a firm of accountants, an example of a cost centre would be a department (eg tax department), or the whole of a small office

** can be adapted to use sales price/units sold

2 Application of the rate:

chargeable hours (or sales price/units sold) x overhead absorption rate

= overhead absorbed

worked example

Tax department of accounting firm

total budgeted cost centre overheads for year	£120,000
expected chargeable hours for year	6,000
actual chargeable hours in May	450

1 Overhead absorption rate:

$$\frac{£120{,}000}{6{,}000 \text{ hours}} = £20 \text{ per chargeable hour}$$

2 Application of the rate:

450 chargeable hours x £20 = £9,000 of overhead absorbed in May

service sector – miles travelled

Here the overhead is absorbed on the basis of miles travelled.

1 Calculation of the overhead absorption rate, using budgeted figures:

$$\frac{\textit{total cost centre* overheads}}{\textit{total miles travelled (in cost centre)}} = \textit{cost per mile travelled}$$

* for a bus company, an example of a cost centre would be a route number, a bus or a garage

2 Application of the rate:

miles travelled x overhead absorption rate = overhead absorbed

worked example

Buses on route 73	total budgeted cost centre overheads for year	£100,000
	expected miles travelled for year	200,000
	actual miles travelled in March	18,000

1 Overhead absorption rate:

$$\frac{\pounds 100{,}000}{200{,}000 \text{ miles}} = \pounds 0.50 \text{ per mile travelled}$$

2 Application of the rate:

18,000 miles travelled x £0.50 = £9,000 of overhead absorbed in March

which method to use?

Only one overhead absorption rate will be used in a particular department, and the method selected must relate to the reason why the costs are incurred. For example, a cost centre which is machine based, where most of the overheads incurred relate to machinery, will use a machine hour basis.

The direct labour hour method is a very popular method (eg the garage mentioned earlier) because overheads are absorbed on a time basis. Thus the cost unit that requires twice the direct labour of another cost unit will be charged twice the overhead. However this method will be inappropriate where some units are worked on by hand while others quickly pass through a machinery process and require little direct labour time.

A machine hour rate is particularly appropriate where expensive machinery is used in the department. However, it would be unsuitable where not all products pass through the machine but some are worked on by hand: in the latter case, no overheads would be charged to the cost units.

It is important to select the best method of overhead absorption for the particular business, otherwise wrong decisions will be made on the basis of the costing information. The particular absorption method selected for a department will need to be reviewed at regular intervals to ensure that it is still valid. For example, the direct labour hour method is unlikely to continue to be appropriate where a machine has been brought in to automate processes that were previously carried out by hand. Any proposed changes must be discussed with senior personnel and their agreement obtained before any changes to methods are implemented. The changes will need to be discussed with personnel (such as managers and supervisors) working in operational departments to explain how overheads will be charged to their departments in the future, and any queries will need to be resolved.

using a pre-determined rate

Most businesses and organisations calculate a pre-determined overhead absorption rate for each department. This is then applied to all production passing through that department.

The OAR is calculated in advance using estimates – this avoids having to calculate the rate regularly, which may result in changes over quite short time periods. Instead the rate is smoothed out over fluctuations in cost and activity over a longer accounting period.

Appropriate consultation will need to be made with personnel from the operating departments before a pre-determined rate is established for a particular department.

OVER- OR UNDER-ABSORPTION OF OVERHEADS

Most businesses will find that the amount of overheads absorbed into the cost of their actual work during the year is not the same as the amount that has been spent. If the amount absorbed is the greater, the difference is called 'over-absorption' or 'over-recovery' of overheads. If the amount absorbed is less than the amount spent, the difference is called 'under-absorption' or 'under-recovery'.

Over-absorption or under-absorption (recovery) is the difference between the total amount of overheads absorbed (recovered) in a given period and the total amount spent on overheads.

over-absorption of overheads

The following example shows a calculation for over-absorption – with the overhead absorption rate based on direct labour hours.

worked example

Department C

overhead absorption rate (based on direct labour hours)	£6.00 per labour hour
actual labour hours in year	6,300 hours
actual overheads for year	£36,000

- actual overheads for the department are £36,000
- actual overhead absorbed: 6,300 hours x £6.00 per hour = £37,800
- over-absorption of overhead: £37,800 – £36,000 = £1,800

At the end of the financial year the statement of profit or loss is credited with the amount of over-absorbed overhead.

On first impressions, over-absorption of overheads seems to be a 'bonus' for a business – profits will be higher; however, it should be remembered that the overhead rate may have been set too high. As a consequence, sales might have been lost because the selling price has been too high. The overhead absorption rate (OAR) will need to be reviewed with the manager and supervisors of the operational department if over-absorption continues on a regular basis – they may be able to explain the reason for the difference.

under-absorption of overheads

With under-absorption, the actual overhead absorbed is less than the actual overheads for the department. For example, if in Department C (above) actual labour hours in the year were 5,500, the calculations would be:

- actual overheads for the department are £36,000
- actual overhead absorbed: 5,500 hours x £6.00 per hour = £33,000
- under-absorption of overhead: £36,000 – £33,000 = £3,000

At the end of the financial year the statement of profit or loss is debited with the amount of under-absorbed overhead.

Under absorption of overheads is a cost to a business, so reducing profitability. It may be that the selling price of output has been set too low, or output is less than expected, or actual overhead is more than expected. The OAR will need to be revised if under-absorption continues on a regular basis.

BOOKKEEPING ENTRIES FOR OVERHEADS

In this section we look at the cost bookkeeping entries to record the transfer of the cost of overheads to production, together with the entries for over- or under-absorption of overheads (which are transferred to the statement of profit or loss – sometimes referred to as the income statement). These entries form part of the bookkeeping system for costing.

A production overheads account is used to:

- transfer production overheads to production
- credit the amount of over-absorbed overheads to the statement of profit or loss
- debit the amount of under-absorbed overheads to the statement of profit or loss

The cost bookkeeping entries are:

- **transfer production overheads (amount absorbed) to production**
  - debit production
  - credit production overheads
- **credit over-absorbed overheads to the statement of profit or loss**
  - debit production overheads
  - credit statement of profit or loss

  Here, the amount of over-absorbed overheads reduces the total cost of production, and so increases profits.
- **charge under-absorbed overheads to the statement of profit or loss**
  - debit statement of profit or loss
  - credit production overheads

  Here the amount of under-absorbed overheads adds to the total cost of production, and so reduces profits.

These cost bookkeeping entries are shown diagrammatically as shown below.

Bookkeeping entries for overheads

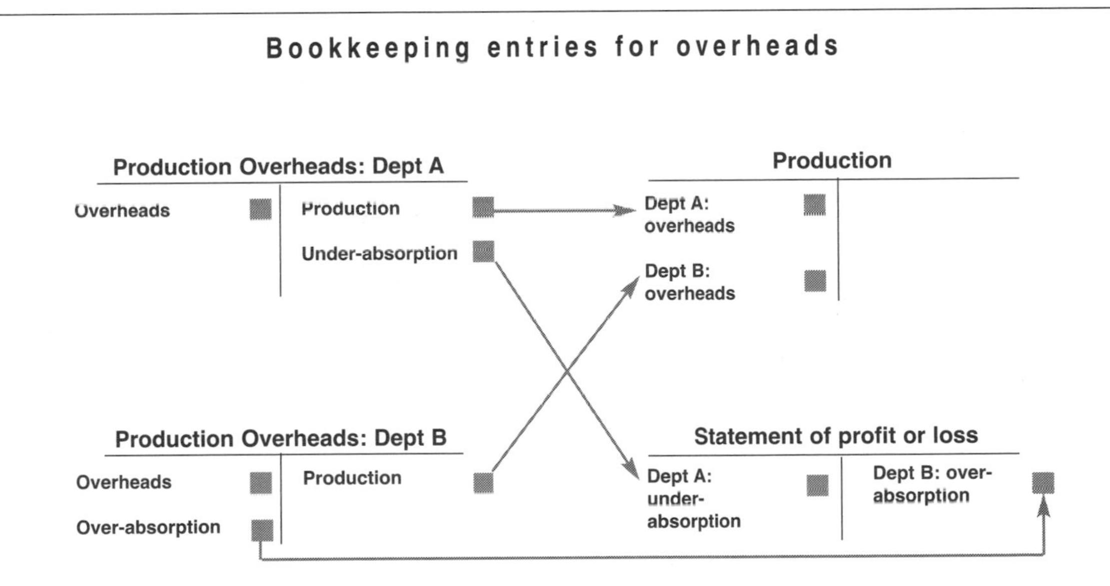

Note: instead of transferring the over- or under-absorption of overheads direct to the statement of profit or loss, an alternative is to use a holding account for the amounts. At the end of the financial year, the balance of this account is then transferred to the statement of profit or loss – as either a debit or a credit entry, depending on the balance.

Case Study

BOXIT LIMITED: BOOKKEEPING FOR OVERHEADS

situation

Boxit Limited manufactures and sells cardboard boxes which are used for packaging and storage. The boxes pass through two departments – cutting and assembly. Details of overheads for the departments for the four weeks ended 24 March 20-8 are as follows:

Cutting Department

- overhead absorption rate is £10.00 per machine hour
- machine hours worked were 1,000
- actual cost of production overhead was £11,000

Assembly Department

- overhead absorption rate is £4.00 per direct labour hour
- direct labour hours worked were 2,000
- actual cost of production overhead was £7,500

The following cost accounting codes are in use to record overheads:

Code number	Description
2200	production
2500	production overheads: cutting department
2600	production overheads: assembly department
5500	statement of profit or loss

As an Accounts Assistant at Boxit Limited, you are asked to prepare the two production overheads accounts and to fill in the table below to record the journal entries for the overheads and for the over- and under-absorption of overheads.

20-8	Code number	Debit £	Credit £
24 March	2200		
24 March	2500		
24 March	2200		
24 March	2600		
24 March	5500		
24 March	2500		
24 March	2600		
24 March	5500		

solution

The production overheads accounts are prepared as follows:

Dr	Production Overheads Account: Cutting Department (2500)		Cr
	£		£
Bank (overheads incurred)	11,000	Production	10,000
		Statement of profit or loss (under-absorption)	1,000
	11,000		11,000

Dr	Production Overheads Account: Assembly Department (2600)		Cr
	£		£
Bank (overheads incurred)	7,500	Production	8,000
Statement of profit or loss (over-absorption)	500		
	8,000		8,000

The cost bookkeeping entries are:

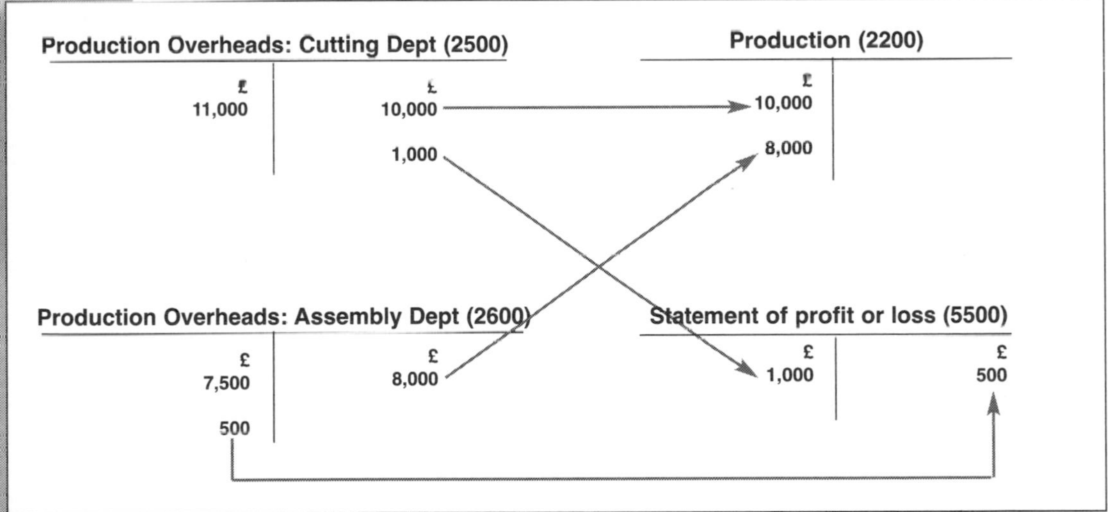

The cost bookkeeping entries to record the journal entries are as follows:

20-8	Code number	Debit £	Credit £
24 March	2200	10,000	
24 March	2500		10,000
24 March	2200	8,000	
24 March	2600		8,000
24 March	5500	1,000	
24 March	2500		1,000
24 March	2600	500	
24 March	5500		500

In this way, the cost of the pre-determined overhead rates is charged to production, while the amount of over- or under-absorption of overheads is transferred to the statement of profit or loss.

Chapter Summary

- Overheads are the indirect costs – indirect materials, indirect labour and indirect expenses.
- Overheads are:
  - allocated to a specific responsibility centre, if they belong entirely to that centre
  - apportioned between centres, if they are shared
- Apportionment is done on a suitable basis, using ratios of floor space, numbers of employees and so on.
- Methods of allocation and apportionment should be reviewed regularly.
- The total overheads allocated and apportioned to the service cost centres are then re-apportioned to profit centres or production cost centres using either direct apportionment or the step-down method.
- After re-apportionment of the service cost centre overheads, the total overheads in each profit centre or production cost centre can be calculated.
- All the above steps can be carried out using expected or budgeted overhead amounts.
- Overhead absorption rates are calculated using the total expected or budgeted overheads in each cost centre.

- An overhead absorption rate is calculated as follows:

$$\textit{overhead absorption rate} = \frac{\textit{total budgeted cost centre overheads}}{\textit{total planned work in cost centre}}$$

  where the planned amount of work may be measured, often in terms of direct labour hours or machine hours for a manufacturing company, although service sector organisations will use other methods, eg miles travelled for a bus company.

- Overhead absorption rates are applied to the actual work carried out. A direct labour hour absorption rate is applied as follows, for example:

  Direct labour hours worked x overhead absorption rate

  = overhead absorbed

- At the end of a given period, the amount of overhead absorbed may differ from the amount actually spent on the overheads. The difference is:
  - either, an over absorption (when the amount absorbed is more than the amount spent)
  - or, an under-absorption (when the amount absorbed is less than the amount spent)

- Cost bookkeeping entries are made to record:
  - overheads debited to production
  - over-absorption of overheads credited to the statement of profit or loss
  - under-absorption of overheads debited to the statement of profit or loss

Key Terms

overheads	indirect costs, made up of: indirect materials + indirect labour + indirect expenses
cost centres	segments of a business to which costs can be charged
allocation of overheads	the charging to a particular responsibility centre of overheads that are incurred entirely by that centre
apportionment of overheads	the sharing of overheads over a number of responsibility centres to which they relate – each centre is charged with a proportion of the overhead cost
service department	a non-production cost centre that provides services to other cost centres in the business

re-apportionment of service department overheads	the sharing of the total overheads from a service department, a proportion being charged to each cost centre it serves; after all re-apportionment has been carried out, the overheads will be charged to profit centres or production cost centres
direct apportionment	method of re-apportionment used where service departments provide services to production departments only
step-down	method of re-apportionment used where service departments provide services to production departments *and* to other service departments
absorption (recovery)	the charging of overheads to cost units (units of output)
overhead absorption rate (OAR) of overheads	the rate used to charge overheads to cost units – calculated in advance, as: budgeted total overhead ÷ planned amount of work
basis of absorption	the measurement of work used to calculate the overhead absorption rate, for example: – direct labour hours – machine hours – direct labour percentage add-on – miles travelled
over- or under-absorption (recovery)	the difference between the total amount of overheads absorbed (recovered) in a given period and the total amount spent on overheads
over-absorption of overheads	overheads absorbed are more than the amount spent on overheads
under-absorption of overheads	overheads absorbed are less than the amount spent on overheads

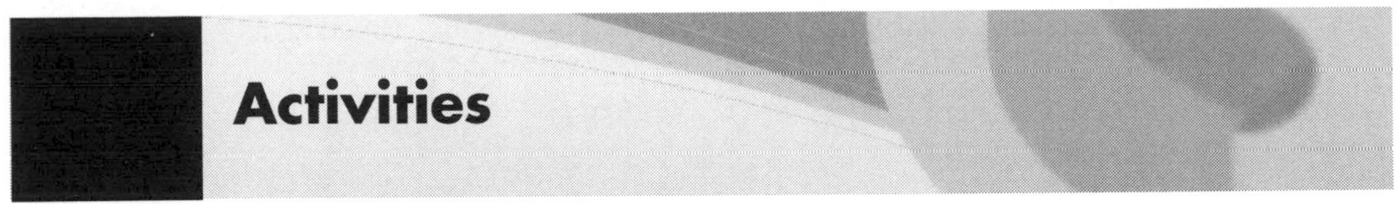

Activities

4.1 Wyvern Fabrication Company has two production departments – moulding and finishing.

The company charges overheads on the basis of machine hours and the following overhead analysis information is available to you (note that service department overheads have already been apportioned to production departments):

OVERHEAD ANALYSIS SHEET		
	MOULDING	FINISHING
Budgeted total overheads (£)	9,338	3,298
Budgeted machine hours	1,450	680
Budgeted overhead absorption rate (£)		

Details of a particular job of work are as follows:

JOB OVERHEAD ANALYSIS SHEET		
	MOULDING	FINISHING
Job machine hours	412	154
Budgeted overhead absorption rate (£)		
Overhead absorbed by job (£)		

You are to:

(a) Calculate the overhead absorption rate (to two decimal places) for each of the two departments and complete the overhead analysis sheet.

(b) Calculate the production overhead absorbed by the job (to two decimal places) and complete the job overhead analysis sheet.

(c) Suggest another overhead absorption rates that the company might use and comment on the circumstances that would make it appropriate.

4.2 ABC Limited is a manufacturing business with three cost centres: Departments A, B and C. The following are the budgeted factory overheads for the forthcoming year:

Rent and rates	£7,210
Depreciation of machinery	£10,800
Supervisor's salary	£12,750
Insurance of machinery	£750

Departmental information is:

	Dept A	Dept B	Dept C
Floor space (sq m)	300	150	250
Value of machinery	£25,000	£15,000	£10,000
Number of production-line employees	8	4	3

You are to:

(a) Using the following table, apportion the overheads to the cost centres, stating the basis of apportionment.

Budgeted overheads	Basis of apportionment	Total	Dept A	Dept B	Dept C
		£	£	£	£

(b) Calculate the overhead absorption rate (to two decimal places) of each department, based on direct labour hours. Note that the factory works a 37 hour week for 48 weeks in a year.

4.3 Wye Engineering Limited offers specialist engineering services to the car industry. It has two production departments – machining and finishing – and a service department which maintains the machinery of both departments. Expected production overheads for the forthcoming year are:

	£
Rent and rates	5,520
Buildings insurance	1,320
Insurance of machinery	1,650
Lighting and heating	3,720
Depreciation of machinery	11,000
Supervisory salaries	30,000
Maintenance department salary	16,000
Factory cleaning	4,800

The following information is available:

	Machining	**Finishing**	**Maintenance**
Floor space (square metres)	300	200	100
Number of employees	6	3	1
Value of machinery	£40,000	£15,000	–

The factory works a 35 hour week for 47 weeks each year.

You are to:

Using the following table:

(a)
- Prepare an analysis of production overheads showing the basis of allocation and apportionment to the three departments of the business
- Re-apportion the service department overheads to production departments on the basis of value of machinery.

Budgeted overheads	**Basis of apportionment**	**Total**	**Machining**	**Finishing**	**Maintenance**
		£	£	£	£

continued

(b) Calculate an overhead absorption rate (to two decimal places) based on direct labour hours for each of the two production departments.

(c) Discuss alternative overhead absorption rates that the company could use.

4.4 Mercia Tutorial College has two teaching departments – business studies and general studies – and two service departments – administration and technical support. The overheads of each department are as follows:

	£
• Business studies	40,000
• General studies	20,000
• Administration	9,600
• Technical support	12,000

The basis for re-apportioning the overheads of the service departments is:

- technical support, on the value of equipment in each department – business studies, £50,000; general studies, £25,000; administration, £25,000
- administration, on the number of students in the teaching departments – business studies, 500; general studies, 250

You are to use the table below and the step-down method to re-apportion the two service department overheads to the two teaching departments.

Budgeted overheads	Total	Business studies	General studies	Admin	Technical support
	£	£	£	£	£

4.5 Rossiter and Rossiter is a firm of chartered accountants, with two partners. Overhead costs for next year are estimated to be:

	£
Office rent	10,000
Office salaries	30,000
Rates	4,800
Heating and lighting	2,400
Stationery	2,000
Postage and telephone	5,100
Car expenses	5,600

The two partners plan to work for 47 weeks next year. They will each be in the office for 40 hours per week, but will be working on behalf of their clients for 35 hours per week.

(a) What is the overhead absorption rate per partner hour (to two decimal places)?

(b) If each partner wishes to earn a salary of £30,000 per year, what is the combined hourly rate per partner they should charge to clients, which includes overheads and their salaries (to two decimal places)?

(c) If both partners actually work on their clients' behalf for 37 hours per week, what will be the total over-absorption of overheads for the year (to two decimal places)?

4.6 A friend of yours is about to start in business making garden seats. She plans to make two different qualities – 'Standard' and 'De Luxe'. Costs per unit for direct materials and labour are expected to be:

	Standard	**De Luxe**
	£	£
Direct materials	12.50	20.00
Direct labour:		
3 hours at £8.00 per hour	24.00	–
3.5 hours at £10.00 per hour	–	35.00
	36.50	55.00
Machine hours	1	2.5

Production overheads are expected to be £1,000 per month.

Production is expected to be 80 'Standard' seats and 40 'De Luxe' seats per month.

(a) Suggest and calculate two different methods by which overheads can be absorbed.

(b) Calculate the production cost (to two decimal places) of each of the two qualities of garden seats using the two different methods of overhead absorption.

(c) Compare the results of your calculations and suggest to your friend the most appropriate method of overhead absorption for this business.

4.7 Durning Limited manufactures and sells household furniture. The company's operations are organised by departments, as follows:

- Warehouse
- Manufacturing
- Sales
- Administration

The budgeted fixed overheads of the company for November 20-1 were as follows:

	£
Depreciation of non-current assets	9,150
Rent	11,000
Other property overheads	6,200
Administration overheads	13,450
Staff costs:	
– warehouse	3,600
– indirect manufacturing	9,180
– sales	8,650
– administration	5,940
Total budgeted fixed overheads	67,170

The following information is also relevant:

Department	**% of floor space occupied**	**Net book value/ carrying amount of non-current assets** *£000*
Warehouse	15%	120
Manufacturing	60%	400
Sales	10%	20
Administration	15%	60
	100%	600

Overheads are allocated and apportioned between departments using the most appropriate basis.

Task 1

Please see next page.

Task 2

Manufacturing fixed overheads are absorbed on the basis of budgeted machine hours. The budgeted number of machine hours for November 20-1 was 10,000 hours.

You are to calculate the budgeted fixed overhead absorption rate (to two decimal places) for the manufacturing department for November 20-1.

Task 1

Complete the following table showing the allocation and apportionment of budgeted fixed overheads between the four departments.

Budgeted fixed overheads for November 20-1	**Basis**	**Total** £	**Warehouse** £	**Manufacturing** £	**Sales** £	**Administration** £
Depreciation		9,150				
Rent		11,000				
Other property overheads		6,200				
Administration overheads		13,450				
Staff costs		27,370				
		67,170				

4.8 You work as an Accounts Assistant at the Trevaunance Hotel which is part of a group of hotels. Each month it is one of your tasks to record and report cost information to head office.

The Trevaunance Hotel has fifty bedrooms and its operations are organised into five departments, as follows:

- Accommodation
- Restaurant
- Bar
- Kitchen
- Administration

The budgeted fixed overheads for the Trevaunance Hotel for August 20-3 were as follows:

	£
Bedroom repairs	3,200
Electricity	1,700
Rent	9,000
Kitchen repairs	1,025
Staff costs:	
– accommodation	4,550
– restaurant	6,740
– bar	3,045
– kitchen	2,310
– administration	6,950
Other property overheads	4,000
Total budgeted fixed overheads	42,520

The following information is also relevant:

Department	**% of floor space occupied**	**Metered electricity costs** £
Accommodation	65%	550
Restaurant	15%	250
Bar	10%	150
Kitchen	5%	700
Administration	5%	50
	100%	1,700

Overheads are allocated and apportioned to the five departments using the most appropriate basis. The total administration overheads are then re-apportioned to the other four departments using the following percentages:

- Accommodation 60%
- Restaurant 20%
- Bar 10%
- Kitchen 10%

Task 1

Complete the following table showing the allocation and apportionment of budgeted fixed overheads between the five departments.

Budgeted fixed overheads for August 20-3	Basis	Total £	Accommodation £	Restaurant £	Bar £	Kitchen £	Administration £
Bedroom repairs		3,200					
Electricity		1,700					
Rent		9,000					
Kitchen repairs		1,025					
Staff costs		23,595					
Other property overheads		4,000					
		42,520					
Administration							( )
		42,520					

Task 2

Kitchen fixed overheads are absorbed on the basis of budgeted labour hours. The budgeted number of labour hours for the kitchen during August 20-3 was 1,000 hours.

You are to calculate the budgeted fixed overhead absorption rate per labour hour (to two decimal places) for the kitchen for August 20-3.

4.9 You work as an Accounts Assistant for Sekula Limited, a manufacturing business. The company has two production centres: moulding and finishing – and three support cost centres: maintenance, stores and administration.

Sekula Limited's budgeted overheads for the next financial year are:

	£	£
Depreciation charge for machinery		1,950
Power for production machinery		2,604
Rent and rates of premises		4,275
Light and heat for premises		2,925
Indirect labour costs:		
Maintenance	32,200	
Stores	17,150	
Administration	28,450	
Totals	77,800	11,754

The following information is also available:

Department	**Carrying amount of machinery**	**Production machinery power usage (KwH)**	**Floor space (square metres)**	**Number of employees**
Production centres:				
Moulding	80,000	16,000	300	4
Finishing	50,000	8,000	160	5
Support cost centres:				
Maintenance			120	2
Stores			140	1
Administration			180	2
Total	130,000	24,000	900	14

Overheads are allocated or apportioned on the most appropriate basis. The total overheads of the support cost centres are then re-apportioned to the two production centres, using the direct method.

- 75% of the maintenance cost centre's time is spent maintaining production machinery in the moulding production centre and the remainder in the finishing production centre.
- The stores cost centre makes 60% of its issues to the moulding production centre, and 40% to the finishing profit centre.
- Administration supports the two production centres equally.
- There is no reciprocal servicing between the three support cost centres.

You are to complete the apportionment table below using the data above.

Budgeted overheads	**Basis of apportionment**	**Moulding** £	**Finishing** £	**Maintenance** £	**Stores** £	**Admin** £	**Totals** £
Depreciation charge for machinery							
Power for production machinery							
Rent and rates of premises							
Light and heat for premises							
Indirect labour							
Totals							
Re-apportion Maintenance							
Re-apportion Stores							
Re-apportion Administration							
Total overheads to production centres							

4.10 Wentworth Limited's budgeted overheads and activity levels for the next quarter are:

	Cutting	**Assembly**
Budgeted overheads (£)	165,600	318,750
Budgeted direct labour hours	18,400	12,750
Budgeted machine hours	8,280	4,250

(a) What would be the budgeted overhead absorption rate for each department if this were set based on their both being heavily automated?

(a)	cutting £9 per hour; assembly £25 per hour	
(b)	cutting £9 per hour; assembly £75 per hour	
(c)	cutting £20 per hour; assembly £25 per hour	
(d)	cutting £20 per hour; assembly £75 per hour	

(b) What would be the budgeted overhead absorption rate for each department if this were set based on their both being labour intensive?

(a)	cutting £9 per hour; assembly £25 per hour	
(b)	cutting £9 per hour; assembly £75 per hour	
(c)	cutting £20 per hour; assembly £25 per hour	
(d)	cutting £20 per hour; assembly £75 per hour	

Additional data

At the end of the quarter actual overheads incurred were found to be:

	Cutting	**Assembly**
Actual overheads (£)	158,200	322,250

(c) Assuming that exactly the same amount of overheads was absorbed as budgeted, what were the budgeted under or over absorptions in the quarter?

(a)	cutting over-absorbed £7,400; assembly over-absorbed £3,500	
(b)	cutting over-absorbed £7,400; assembly under-absorbed £3,500	
(c)	cutting under-absorbed £7,400; assembly under-absorbed £3,500	
(d)	cutting under-absorbed £7,400; assembly over-absorbed £3,500	

4.11 AggieSurf Limited manufactures and sells surfboards. The boards pass through two departments – moulding and finishing. Details of production overheads for the departments for the four weeks ended 26 May 20-6 are as follows:

Moulding Department

- overhead absorption rate is £8.00 per machine hour
- machine hours worked were 600
- actual cost of production overhead was £5,000

Finishing Department

- overhead absorption rate is £5.00 per direct labour hour
- direct labour hours worked were 1,500
- actual cost of production overhead was £7,000

The following cost accounting codes are in use to record production overheads:

Code number	Description
3000	production
3400	production overheads: moulding department
3500	production overheads: finishing department
6000	statement of profit or loss

As an Accounts Assistant at AggieSurf Limited, you are asked to prepare the two production overheads accounts and to fill in the table as at 26 May 20-6 to record the journal entries for the overheads and the over- and under-absorption of overheads.

Dr **Production Overheads Account: Moulding Department (3400)** Cr

	£		£

Dr **Production Overheads Account: Finishing Department (3500)** Cr

	£		£

20-6	Code number	Debit £	Credit £
26 May	3000		
26 May	3400		
26 May	3000		
26 May	3500		
26 May	6000		
26 May	3400		
26 May	3500		
26 May	6000		

4.12 Fancy Cakes Limited manufactures and sells iced cakes and chocolate cakes. The cakes pass through two departments – baking and finishing. Details of production overheads for the departments for the four weeks ended 11 March 20-4 are as follows:

Baking Department

- overhead absorption rate is £10.00 per machine hour
- machine hours worked were 1,200
- actual cost of production overhead was £11,500

Finishing Department

- overhead absorption rate is £6.00 per direct labour hour
- direct labour hours worked were 800
- actual cost of production overhead was £5,000

The following cost accounting codes are in use to record production overheads:

Code number	**Description**
2000	production
2600	production overheads: baking department
2800	production overheads: finishing department
5000	statement of profit or loss

As an Accounts Assistant at Fancy Cakes Limited, you are asked to prepare the two production overheads accounts and to fill in the table as at 11 March 20-6 to record the journal entries for the overheads and the over- and under-absorption of overheads.

Dr	Production Overheads Account: Baking Department (2600)	Cr
£		£

Dr	Production Overheads Account: Finishing Department (2800)	Cr
£		£

20-6	Code number	Debit £	Credit £
11 March	2000		
11 March	2600		
11 March	2000		
11 March	2800		
11 March	2600		
11 March	5000		
11 March	5000		
11 March	2800		

5 Methods of costing

this chapter covers...

In this chapter we examine appropriate methods of costing for different types of businesses and organisations. We look at:

- *the principles of unit costing*
- *the methods of costing used for separate jobs: job costing and batch costing*
- *the methods of costing used when the work is continuous: service costing and process costing*
- *the method of costing that would be used in various types of businesses and organisations*
- *the calculation of job or batch costs and selling prices from given data*
- *the calculation of average costs per cost unit in service costing and in process costing*
- *the bookkeeping entries for process costing*

UNIT COSTING

Unit costing is the cost incurred to produce one cost object.

A **cost object** is a unit of product, service or activity for which costs can be ascertained. Examples of cost objects in unit costing are:

- for a manufacturing business, per item manufactured
- for a chemical business, per kilogram (kg) or litre of output
- for a transport company, per passenger mile/kilometre (km)
- for a hospital, per day per patient

Note that, in the service sector, the units of output are often composite cost units (see page 5) which comprise two variables.

The principles of unit costing are the same whatever method of costing is used by the business or organisation. The unit cost of production or output is always calculated as:

$$\frac{\textit{cost of production or output}}{\textit{number of cost units}} = \textit{unit cost}$$

There are four unit costs that can be calculated:

- prime cost
- marginal cost
- absorption cost
- total cost

Each of these includes different costs of production, as follows:

Direct costs

- direct materials
- direct labour
- variable production overheads

Direct materials and direct labour together give the **prime cost** of production.

Prime cost plus variable production overheads gives the **marginal cost** of production.

Indirect costs

- fixed production overheads

Marginal cost plus fixed production overheads gives the **absorption cost** of production.

Fixed non-production overheads

- such as administration, selling and distribution

Absorption cost plus fixed non-production overheads gives the **total cost** of production.

Study the worked example below, where the unit cost is calculated.

worked example – unit costing

A toy manufacturer makes a popular type of doll. During the four-week period which has just ended 10,000 dolls were produced, with the following costs:

Product: doll	
Direct costs	£
Direct materials	16,500
Direct labour	17,500
Prime cost	**34,000**
Variable production overheads	5,000
Marginal cost of production	**39,000**
Indirect costs	
Fixed production overheads	15,000
Absorption cost of production	**54,000**
Fixed non-production overheads	15,000
Total cost of production	**69,000**

The unit costs are calculated as follows:

- prime cost of one unit $\dfrac{\text{£34,000}}{\text{10,000 dolls}}$ = £3.40
- *marginal cost of one unit $\dfrac{\text{£39,000}}{\text{10,000 dolls}}$ = £3.90
- *absorption cost of one unit $\dfrac{\text{£54,000}}{\text{10,000 dolls}}$ = £5.40
- total cost of one unit $\dfrac{\text{£69,000}}{\text{10,000 dolls}}$ = £6.90

*We will look at marginal and absorption costing in more detail in Chapter 6.

In this chapter we will be looking at a number of different costing methods and will see that most calculate a unit cost of production.

We look firstly at costing methods for specific orders, and secondly at costing methods for continuous work (page 138).

COSTING METHODS FOR SPECIFIC ORDERS

Specific order costing is where customers order what they want, before it is made. Thus, the customer places the specific order, and agrees to buy the product before the work is done.

Many service businesses also carry out work to customers' requirements, for example, accountants and solicitors. Each piece of work is different and is kept separate from the others.

Costing methods which are used by business to collect costs and to calculate the total cost of their output include:

- job costing
- batch costing

These are used in conjunction with absorption costing to recover the cost of overheads. Remember that businesses must recover their overheads in the total price charged to their customers – this applies both to manufacturing businesses and to service industries, such as hairdressers, banks, shops and transport companies.

Case Study

RACERS LIMITED: MANUFACTURING RACING BIKES

situation

Otto Kranz, a former cycling champion, is setting up a company to manufacture racing bikes. The business is to be called Racers Limited.

Otto is aware that he has two very distinct markets into which to sell his bikes:

- Some of his bikes will be produced to the specific requirements of individual customers for international level competition racing – this is the area which really interests Otto. He can charge a premium price for these custom-built designs.
- He also has to sell to the mass-market for quality racing bikes which will be made in batches of 20 to standard designs. These will be sold in specialist shops and are cheaper, both to manufacture and in terms of selling price.

But Otto is confused about how he is going to cost out these two different methods of production – the 'one-off' and the standard design. He says:

'I can record the costs of the direct materials and labour hours used to make the 'one-off' bike and the batches of 20. But what about the overheads? Will I need more than one costing system here?'

solution

Racers Limited is likely to use two different methods of costing, depending on the kind of work being done:

- job costing – for the one-off designs
- batch costing – for the mass-market bikes

JOB COSTING

Job costing is used where each job can be separately identified from other jobs and costs are charged to the job.

The job becomes the cost unit to which costs are charged.

Examples of job costing include engineering firms that produce 'one-offs' to the customer's specifications, printing businesses, vehicle repairs, jobbing builders, painters and decorators.

The diagram below shows the main steps involved in job costing.

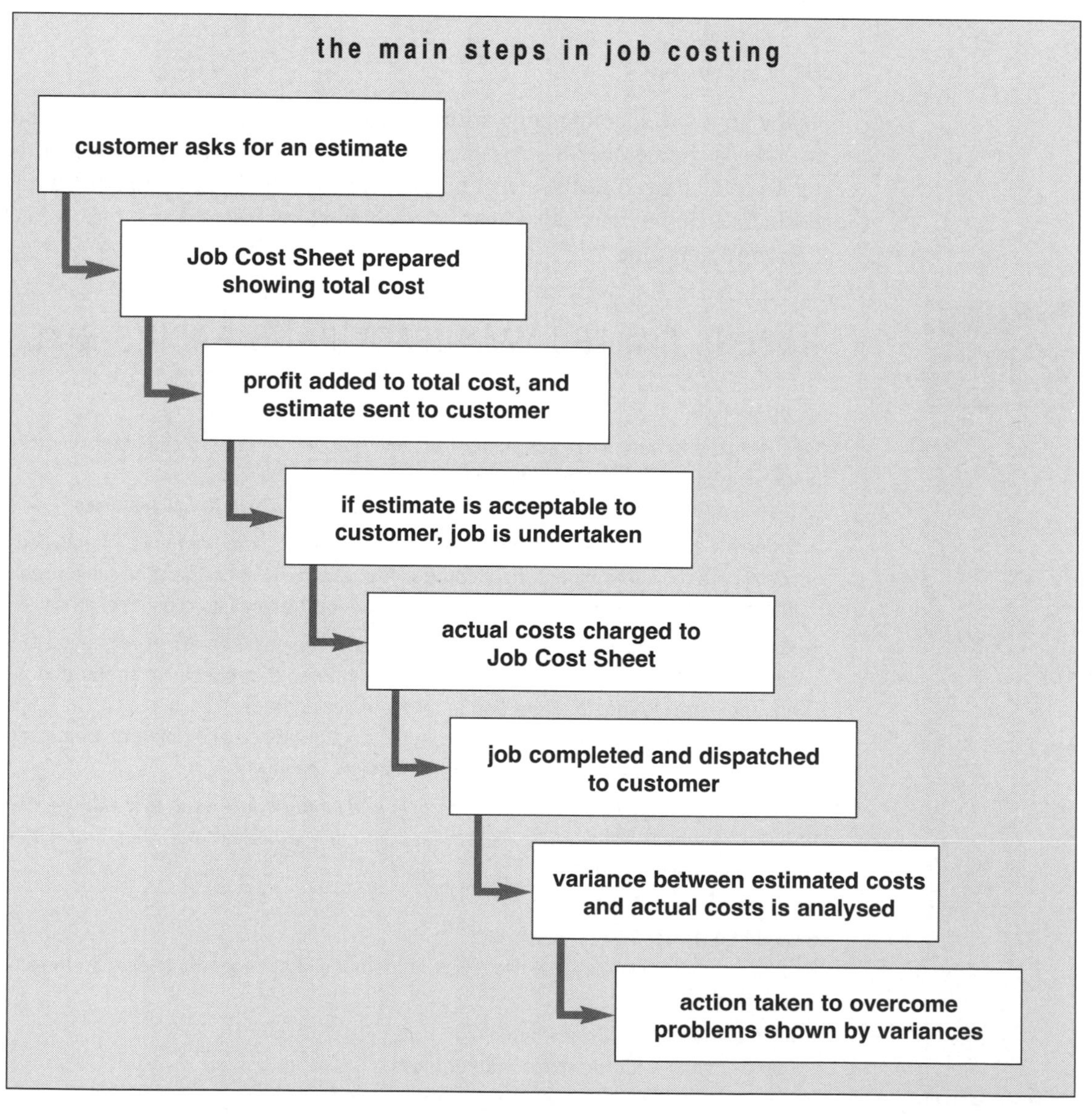

The important points to note from the diagram are:

- each job is given a number, in order to identify it
- a separate job cost sheet is prepared for each job, listing the estimates of direct materials, direct labour, direct expenses and overheads (most businesses nowadays use a computer spreadsheet program to help with their costing and, in practice, the job cost sheet is held as a computer file)
- the actual costs incurred are compared with the estimated costs, and the differences (called 'variances') between the two are analysed; action can then be taken to correct the variances, which will help when preparing future estimates

FASHION AID: JOB COSTING A CHARITY PROGRAMME

situation

The youth group at a local church has decided to organise an evening fashion show, to be called 'FashionAid'. The objective of the show is to raise money to send to a children's charity working in Central Africa. One of the organisers has asked for your help in arranging the printing of a programme for the evening's events. You approach Pearshore Printers for an estimate of the cost of printing 500 copies of a sixteen page programme.

solution

Pearshore Printers allocate a reference number to the job. They prepare a Job Cost Sheet on their computer database as follows:

JOB NO. 6789
'FashionAid' Programme: 500 copies

	£
Direct Materials	
Paper for text: white glossart paper code 135	82.00
Paper for cover: coated board code 235	55.00
Printing plates	25.00
Direct Labour	
Printing: 5 hours at £12.00 per hour	60.00
Finishing: 2 hours at £9.00 per hour	18.00
Overheads (based on direct labour hours)	
7 hours at £20.00 per hour	140.00
TOTAL COST	380.00
Profit (40% of total cost)	152.00
SELLING PRICE	532.00

These estimated costs will be obtained as follows:

- **direct materials**, from the inventory records for materials already held, and from the firm's Purchasing Department for items that need to be bought in especially for this job
- **direct labour**, from the payroll records of the different grades of labour to be employed on this job
- **overheads**, from the pre-determined overhead absorption rate based, for this job, on direct labour hours

Assuming that the price is acceptable to the customer, the job will go ahead and Pearshore Printers will record the actual costs of the job. These can then be compared with the estimated costs, and any differences or 'variances' between the two can be investigated. For example, it might be that actual labour costs are much higher than was estimated – this could mean that the employees took longer to do the job than was expected, or that pay rates had increased, or that more skilled staff – earning higher rates of pay – were used to do the job. This type of analysis, called 'variance analysis', will be covered in Chapter 7.

BATCH COSTING

Batch costing is used where the output consists of a number of identical items which are produced together as a batch.

Examples of batch costing include a bakery producing a batch of standard white loaves, and then a batch of croissants; or a clothing factory producing a batch of jackets, and then a batch of trousers, or a batch of blue scarves, and then a batch of red scarves. Each batch is the cost unit to which the costs are charged. Once the batch has been produced, the total cost per unit is calculated as follows:

$$\frac{\textit{total batch cost}}{\textit{number of units of output}} = \textit{total cost per unit}$$

In essence, batch costing is very similar to job costing, but in a batch a number of identical units are produced. The batch is costed as a job during manufacture and the costs are collected together. Upon completion of the batch, the cost per unit can be calculated.

Batch numbers are frequently used to identify the output of a particular time – examples include paint colours, wallpaper production. The reason for identifying batches in this way is that there might be slight production variations – for example, in the quantities of raw materials used.

Case Study

AMBER LIMITED: BATCH COSTING FOR CHILDREN'S CLOTHES

situation

Amber Limited is a company that designs and manufactures children's clothes. The company's products are noted for their design flair, and the use of fabrics that appeal to children and also wear well. The clothes sell through specialist shops and department stores.

This week, Amber Limited is making a batch of 1,000 sequin dresses for a department store. The costs of the batch are expected to be:

- direct materials, £3,500
- direct labour: cutting, 100 hours at £11 per hour
  sewing, 200 hours at £10 per hour
  finishing, 100 hours at £12 per hour
- the overhead absorption rate is £6 per direct labour hour
- a profit mark-up of 40% is added to the total cost

The Accounts Supervisor asks you, an Accounts Assistant, to calculate the total cost of producing the batch of sequin dresses, and to add the profit mark-up. She also asks you to calculate the company's cost per dress and the selling price per dress.

solution

Batch cost: 1,000 sequin dresses

		£	£
Direct materials			3,500
Direct labour:			
	cutting, 100 hours at £11 per hour	1,100	
	sewing, 200 hours at £10 per hour	2,000	
	finishing, 100 hours at £12 per hour	1,200	
			4,300
Variable overheads:	400 direct labour hours at £6 per hour		2,400
TOTAL COST			10,200
Profit (40% x £10,200)			4,080
SELLING PRICE			14,280

- total cost per unit = $\frac{\text{total batch cost}}{\text{number of units of output}}$ = $\frac{£10,200}{1,000}$ = £10.20

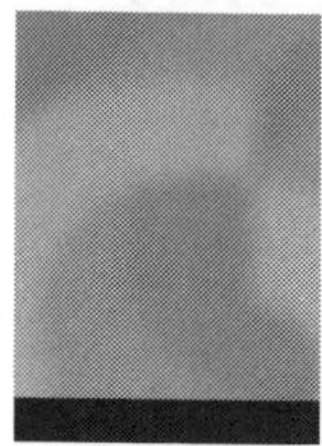

- selling price $= \dfrac{\text{total batch cost + profit}}{\text{number of units of output}} = \dfrac{£14,280}{1,000} = £14.28$

As with most types of costing, the estimated costs above will need to be compared with the actual costs of making the batch. Any significant differences or 'variances' will need to be investigated.

SUMMARY – SPECIFIC ORDER COSTING

The diagram which follows summarises the costing methods for specific orders. Note that each of these separate pieces of work is a **cost object**, ie an item for which costs can be ascertained.

SPECIFIC ORDERS (separate pieces of work)

job costing	**batch costing**
for example: • making one racing bike • preparing one client's accounts • putting a central heating system into one house	for example: • making a batch of bikes to a standard design • producing a batch of wallpaper • baking a batch of loaves

COSTING METHODS FOR CONTINUOUS WORK

In both manufacturing and service industries, work may be done continuously rather than in separate jobs. This requires specific costing methods appropriate to those types of business. For example:

- a bus company runs a continuous service of buses, available for customers to use and customers pay for their use of the service – the business will be costed using the **service costing** method
- in the manufacture of chocolate bars, production is a continuous process and the chocolate bars are available for customers to buy at all times – the business will be costed using the **process costing** method

These two methods are summarised as follows:

CONTINUOUS WORK

service costing	**process costing**
for example: • running a nursing home • providing a bus service • providing banking services	for example: • making chocolate bars • brewing beer or cider • manufacturing paint or chemicals

We will now look at these two methods in turn.

SERVICE COSTING

This method of costing applies to service industries. By using service costing, the cost per passenger mile of a bus or train service, the cost of cleaning an office, and the cost per student hour at a school or college, can be calculated. (However, a bus company quoting for a trip to the seaside for a pensioners' group, or a college tendering for an in-house course, would use job costing.)

worked example – service costs

A nursing home has capacity for twenty residents at any one time. The home achieves an occupancy rate of 90%, ie an average of eighteen beds are occupied at any one time. Costs for last year were:

	£
direct costs	
food and other supplies	54,580
nursing and medical staff	232,680
other support services	45,300
indirect costs	
overheads	58,820
	391,380

The cost per day of each resident is calculated as follows:

- The occupancy in days is (20 residents x 365 days) x 90% = 6,570 days
- Cost per day per resident is: $\frac{\text{total cost}}{\text{number of days}} = \frac{£391{,}380}{6{,}570} = £59.57$ per resident
- This is the unit cost for this organisation

PROCESS COSTING

This method of costing is used for continuous manufacturing processes, such as the manufacture of chocolate bars, cider, chemicals and so on. The process continually produces identical units of output.

The total costs of the process for a given time period are collected together. To obtain an average cost per unit of output, the total cost is divided by the number of units of output in the period.

$$\textit{cost per cost unit} = \frac{\textit{total costs of continuous work for the period}}{\textit{total cost units for the period}}$$

worked example – process costing

Chox Limited manufactures chocolate bars in a continuous process. In a given time period 400,000 bars are made and the costs of the process are as follows:

	£
Direct materials (ingredients)	40,000
Direct labour (machine operators)	24,000
Production overheads	32,000
Total costs of production for period	96,000

Unit cost of production $= \frac{£96{,}000}{400{,}000} = £0.24$ per bar

Many products pass through more than one separate process before they are completed. For example, the unleaded petrol with which you fill the tank of your car started the production process as crude oil – this is passed through a number of refining processes before it is suitable to use in cars. Similarly, the production of chemicals starts with raw materials which pass through various processes – often with further chemicals being added – before the finished product is completed.

In process costing we need to know the costs of each process in order to find out the total cost of the finished goods, and also the cost per unit.

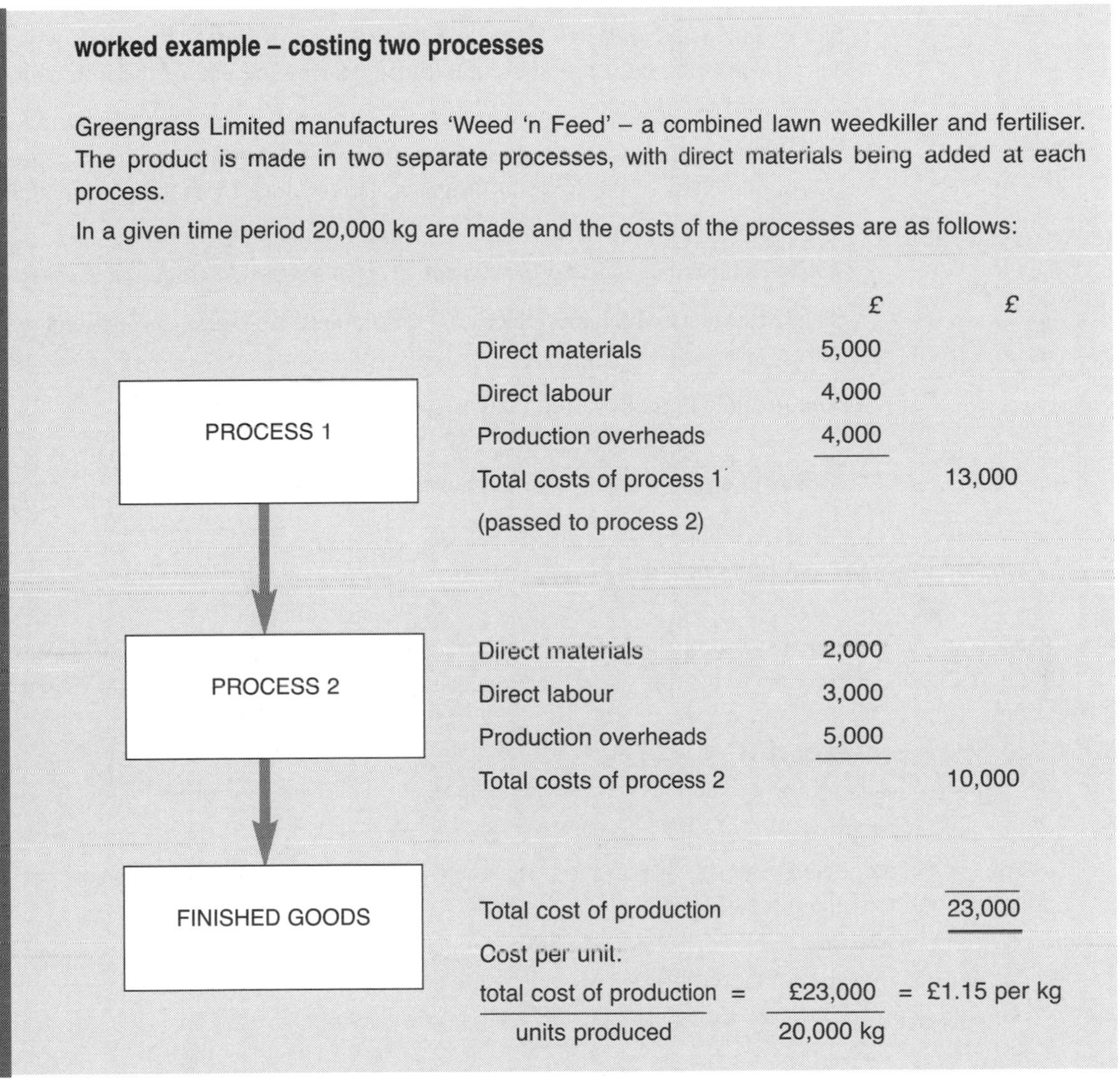

worked example – costing two processes

Greengrass Limited manufactures 'Weed 'n Feed' – a combined lawn weedkiller and fertiliser. The product is made in two separate processes, with direct materials being added at each process.

In a given time period 20,000 kg are made and the costs of the processes are as follows:

	£	£
Direct materials	5,000	
Direct labour	4,000	
Production overheads	4,000	
Total costs of process 1		13,000
(passed to process 2)		
Direct materials	2,000	
Direct labour	3,000	
Production overheads	5,000	
Total costs of process 2		10,000
Total cost of production		23,000

Cost per unit:

$$\frac{\text{total cost of production}}{\text{units produced}} = \frac{£23{,}000}{20{,}000 \text{ kg}} = £1.15 \text{ per kg}$$

The bookkeeping entries for process costing are explained on pages 144-155.

PROCESS COSTING AND WORK-IN-PROGRESS

Process costing is straightforward if all the items on the production line are completed at the end of the accounting period. In a more complex environment there will be items that have been started but not completed. This is known as **part-finished goods** or **work-in-progress** – see also Chapter 2 (page 50) – which can be calculated using either FIFO or AVCO.

For example, the production line at a car factory will always have cars which vary from being only just started, to those nearing the end of the line which are almost complete.

In calculating the cost per unit, it is necessary to take into account the degree of completeness of the work-in-progress. This is done by making equivalent unit calculations:

number of units in progress x percentage of completeness = equivalent units

Thus, 100 units which are exactly 40% complete are equal to 40 completed units.

The formula for calculating the cost per unit now becomes:

$$\frac{\text{total cost of production}}{\text{number of units of output + equivalent units-in-progress}} = \text{cost per unit}$$

worked example – work-in-progress

Cradley Cider Company brews a popular local cider at its cider house in rural Herefordshire. The figures for the first month of the new season's production of its award-winning 'Triple X' variety are:

total cost of production	£8,500
units completed	800 barrels
units in progress	100 barrels

The units in progress are exactly half-finished. The equivalent units in progress, and the cost per barrel, for the month are as follows:

completed units		= 800 barrels
equivalent units	100 x 50%	= 50 barrels
cost per unit	$\frac{\text{£8,500}}{800 + 50}$	= £10 per barrel

Although, in the example above, it was assumed that the work-in-progress was exactly half-finished, this may well not be the case for all the elements of cost. For example, while direct materials might be 100% complete, direct labour, and variable production overheads might be 50% complete.

Allowance has to be made for these differences in the calculation of the valuation of work-in-progress, and the layout used in the example below is one way in which the calculations can be made.

worked example – work-in-progress

The Toy Manufacturing Company makes a plastic toy called a 'Humber-Wumber'. The figures for the first month's production are:

direct materials	£6,600
direct labour	£3,500
variable production overheads	£4,000
units completed	900
units in progress	200

The units in progress are complete as regards materials, but are 50% complete for direct labour and variable production overheads.

Cost element	Costs	Completed units	Work-in-progress			Total equivalent units	Cost per unit	WIP value
			Units	% complete	Equivalent units			
	A	B	C	D	E	F	G	H
					C x D	B + E	A ÷ F	E x G
	£			%			£	£
Direct materials	6,600	900	200	100	200	1,100	6.00	1,200
Direct labour	3,500	900	200	50	100	1,000	*3.50	350
Production overheads	4,000	900	200	50	100	1,000	4.00	400
Total	14,100						13.50	1,950

Note: columns are lettered to show how calculations are made.

Using an average cost basis (AVCO), the cost per unit of the first month's production, and the month-end valuation figure for work-in-progress (WIP) is as follows:

900 completed units at £13.50 each	=	£12,150
work-in-progress valuation	=	£1,950
costs for month	=	£14,100

*Note how the direct labour cost has been calculated for equivalent units: £3,500 ÷ 1,000 units = £3.50 per equivalent unit

BOOKKEEPING ENTRIES FOR PROCESS COSTING

In this section we look at the cost bookkeeping entries to record process costing transactions. The account to be used is a **process account**, which carries out a similar function to the production account that we have used previously for the bookkeeping entries.

The basic layout of a process account, which has inputs on the debit side and outputs on the credit side, is shown below.

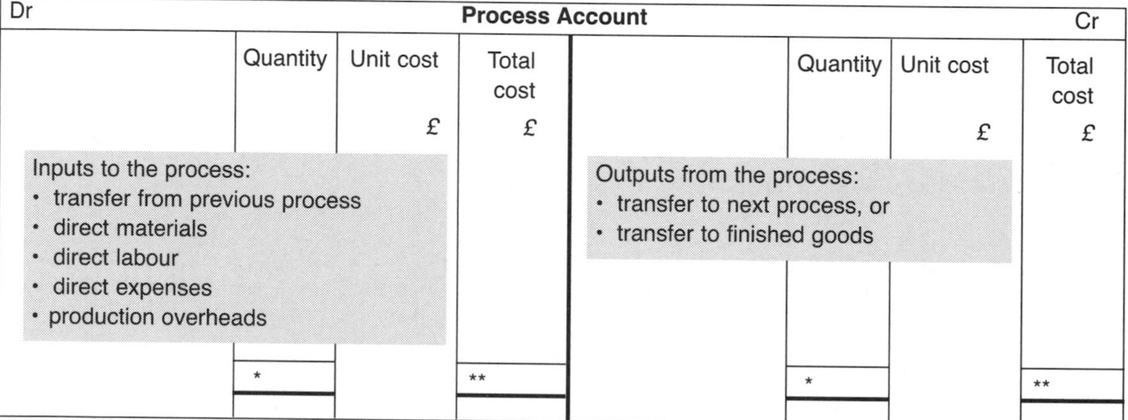

* must total to the same quantity

** must total to the same total cost

Note:

- there are columns for the quantity of goods (eg kg, litres) input to, and output from, the process
- there are money columns for the unit cost (eg cost per kg, cost per litre), and for the total
- inputs to the process can include a transfer from a previous process (if any), and any direct costs and production overheads that are added to this stage of the process
- outputs from the process are either a transfer to the next process or, if this is the last or only process, to finished goods
- where there is more than one process involved in production, each will have a separate account, eg 'Process 1 Account', 'Process 2 Account' (the Case Study on page 156 illustrates the use of two processes)
- in the process account the columns for quantity and total cost must total to the same quantity and total cost for the debit and credit columns

losses and gains in process costing

An important feature of process costing is that you don't always get out what you put in to the process. This is illustrated by the example of ordering a steak in a restaurant; the menu will say '250g fillet steak' (explaining that this is the uncooked weight); what comes on the plate will weigh rather less because, when the steak is grilled, fat and liquids are cooked away. Thus, in the 'process' of cooking a steak, the output is less than the input. This is unlike other costing, where the input always equals the output, for example, input the components for 100 computers, and the output will be 100 computers.

The aspect of process costing where you don't get out what you put in is mainly described as a **normal loss**. This is an unavoidable loss arising from the production process. For example, the normal loss on a 250g steak might be 50g. Normal losses, which occur as a result of factors such as evaporation, breakage, sampling and testing, are included as part of the cost of the output.

Once a standard of normal loss has been established for a process, this then forms the expectation for future processing. Any variation from this normal loss is treated separately in the bookkeeping and will be either:

- **abnormal loss**, where the loss is greater than normal, or
- **abnormal gain**, where the loss is less than normal

If any of the normal losses can be sold as **scrap sales**, the amount of money so received is treated as a reduction in the total costs of the process. Examples include: wood chippings and shavings sold off from wood processing, scrap metal from an engineering company.

With normal loss, abnormal loss, abnormal gain, and scrap sales to consider, there are seven possible outcomes from process costing. These are shown in the following diagram:

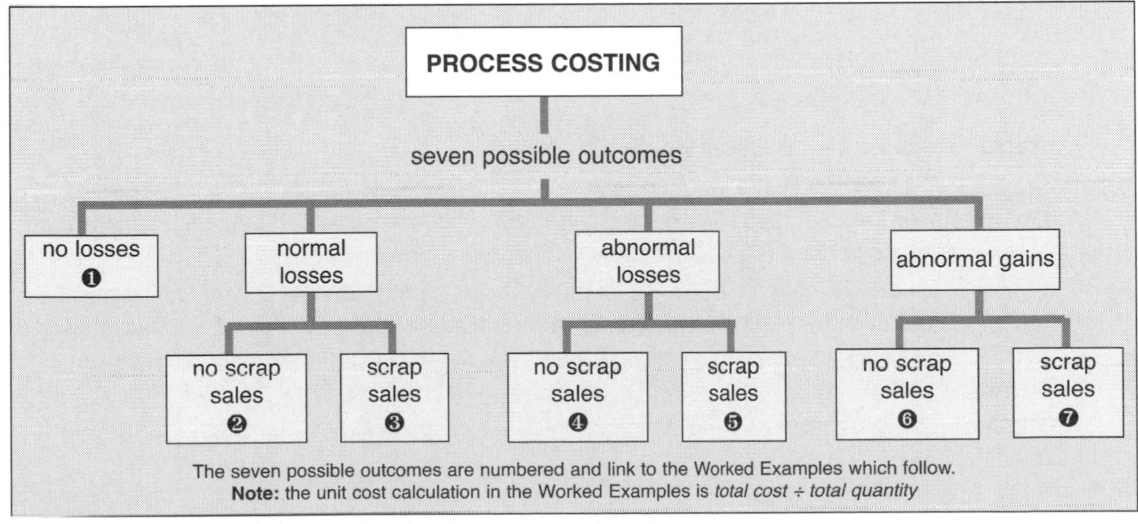

The seven possible outcomes are numbered and link to the Worked Examples which follow.
Note: the unit cost calculation in the Worked Examples is *total cost ÷ total quantity*

no losses within the process

Here the process account is debited with inputs and credited with the output, which is transferred either to the next process or to finished goods.

The cost bookkeeping entries are:

- **transfer inputs to the process account**
  - debit process account
  - credit materials, labour, production overhead accounts
- **transfer outputs to the next process or to finished goods stock**
  - debit next process account, or finished goods account
  - credit process account

The cost bookkeeping entries are shown diagrammatically as follows:

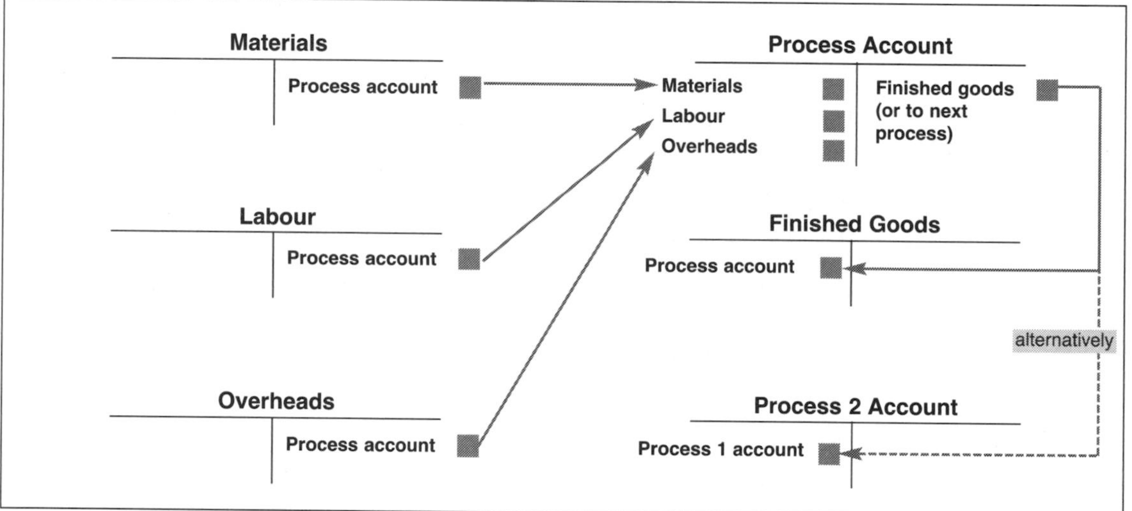

worked example 1 – no losses within the process

Garden Eezee Limited manufactures granular fertiliser for use on flowers and vegetables. The fertiliser is made in one production process.

For the four weeks ended 30 January 20-4 the company input 11,000 kg of direct materials and had an output of 11,000 kg. The input costs were; materials £6,600, labour £3,300, overheads £1,100. There was no opening or closing inventory at the beginning and end of the process; all output was complete.

The process cost account for the period is prepared as follows (note: unit cost = total cost ÷ quantity):

Dr			Process Account				Cr
	Quantity	Unit cost	Total cost		Quantity	Unit cost	Total cost
	(kg)	£	£		*(kg)*	£	£
Materials	11,000	0.60	6,600	Finished goods	11,000	1.00	11,000
Labour		0.30	3,300	(or to next process)			
Overheads		0.10	1,100				
	11,000		11,000		11,000		11,000

Notes:

- here the unit costs for inputs of materials, labour and overheads total £1.00 (60p + 30p + 10p) – this figure will be used in the subsequent Worked Examples
- inputs could also include the costs of a previous process
- the columns for quantity and total cost total to the same quantity and total cost for the debit and credit columns – check this in the subsequent Worked Examples

normal losses, with no scrap sales

Here the process account is credited with the expected amount of the normal loss. The amount is recorded in the quantity column only, with no amounts in the money columns. In this way, the cost of the normal loss is included as part of the costs of the output.

worked example 2 – normal losses, with no scrap sales

Garden Eezee Limited has had to change the chemical composition of its granular fertiliser in order to comply with new regulations. As a result of this, not all of the output can be sold to gardeners. The company's scientists have established that, with an input of 11,000 kg of raw materials there will be an output of 10,000 kg and a normal loss of 1,000 kg.

For the four weeks ended 27 February 20-4, the process account is prepared as follows (with the same input costs from Worked Example 1 and shading showing the change):

Dr			Process Account				Cr
	Quantity	Unit cost	Total cost		Quantity	Unit cost	Total cost
	(kg)	£	£		*(kg)*	£	£
Inputs (see Worked Example 1)	11,000	1.00	11,000	Normal loss	1,000	–	–
				Finished goods (or to next process)	10,000	1.10	11,000
	11,000		11,000		11,000		11,000

The cost of the normal losses is included as part of the costs of the output, so the cost per unit is:

$$\frac{\text{input cost}}{\text{expected output (input – normal loss)}} = \frac{£11{,}000}{10{,}000 \text{ kg}} = £1.10 \text{ per kg}$$

The cost of the output is transferred to finished goods (or to the next process).

normal losses, with scrap sales

If any of the normal losses from a process can be sold – called 'scrap sales' – the process account is credited with the revenue. The amount of such revenue is recorded in the money column against the normal loss. In this way, the revenues from scrap sales reduce the cost of the output.

worked example 3 – normal losses, with scrap sales

Garden Eezee Limited is now able to sell its normal losses to a specialist reprocessing company. The price it receives for the scrap sales is 50p per kg.

For the four weeks ended 26 March 20-4 the process account is prepared as follows (with the same input costs and normal loss as Worked Example 2 and shading showing the change):

Process Account

Dr	Quantity	Unit cost	Total cost		Quantity	Unit cost	Total cost Cr
	(kg)	£	£		*(kg)*	£	£
Inputs (see Worked Example 1)	11,000	1.00	11,000	Normal loss (scrap sales)	1,000	0.50	500
				Finished goods (or to next process)	10,000	1.05	10,500
	11,000		11,000		11,000		11,000

The value of the scrap sales reduces the cost per unit of the expected output to:

$$\frac{\text{input cost – scrap value of normal loss}}{\text{expected output (input – normal loss)}} = \frac{£11{,}000 – £500}{10{,}000 \text{ kg}}$$

= £1.05 per kg

Normal loss account is debited with £500 by transfer from the process account. The revenues from scrap sales are then credited to this account and debited to either bank account (cash received), or trade receivables account (sold on credit terms). Normal loss account then appears as:

Dr	Normal Loss Account		Cr
	£		£
Process account	500	Bank/trade receivables	500

abnormal losses, with no scrap sales

An abnormal loss is, as we have seen, where output is lower than after a normal loss. For example:

	kg
input	11,000
less normal loss	1,000
expected output	10,000
actual output	9,400
abnormal loss	600

Clearly, if there are recurring abnormal losses, the managers will wish to investigate the causes and to take corrective action. Causes of abnormal losses can include poor quality raw materials, wastage and spillages caused by poor handling, faults in the process.

For cost bookkeeping, the value of the abnormal loss is credited to the process account at the same cost per unit as the expected output; the value is debited to a separate **abnormal loss account**. These cost bookkeeping entries are shown diagrammatically as follows:

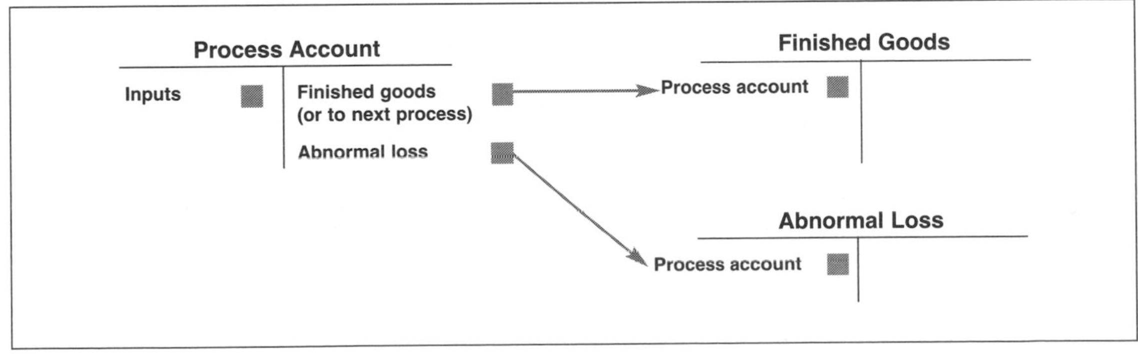

worked example 4 – abnormal losses, with no scrap sales

For the four weeks ended 23 April 20-4, Garden Eezee Limited inputs 11,000 kg of direct materials. Output transferred to finished goods is 9,400 kg – the difference of 1,600 kg being made up of a normal loss of 1,000 kg and an abnormal loss of 600 kg. For technical reasons, none of the losses was able to be sold as scrap.

The process account is prepared as follows (with the same input costs as Worked Example 1 and shading showing the change):

Dr		Process Account					Cr
	Quantity	Unit cost	Total cost		Quantity	Unit cost	Total cost
	(kg)	£	£		*(kg)*	£	£
Inputs (see Worked Example 1)	11,000	1.00	11,000	Normal loss	1,000	–	–
				Finished goods (or to next process)	9,400	1.10	10,340
				Abnormal loss	600	1.10	660
	11,000		11,000		11,000		11,000

Both the transfer to finished goods (or to the next process) and the abnormal loss are valued at the cost per unit of the expected output, ie

$$\frac{\text{input cost}}{\text{expected output}} = \frac{£11{,}000}{10{,}000 \text{ kg}} = £1.10 \text{ per kg}$$

The amount of abnormal loss is debited to abnormal loss account:

Dr	Abnormal Loss Account		Cr
	£		£
Process account	660		

At the end of the financial year, the balance of abnormal loss account is debited to the statement of profit or loss:

– debit statement of profit or loss

– credit abnormal loss account

In this way, abnormal losses are treated as a period cost instead of being included with the closing inventory valuation.

abnormal losses, with scrap sales

Where there are revenues from scrap sales for both normal losses and abnormal losses, we must be careful to distinguish between the two amounts:

- revenues for scrap sales from normal losses are credited to the process account (where they reduce the cost of the output – including the abnormal loss)
- revenues for scrap sales from abnormal losses are credited to abnormal loss account (where they reduce the amount of the abnormal loss and, at the end of the financial year, the amount debited to the statement of profit or loss)

worked example 5 – abnormal losses, with scrap sales

Here the details are the same as Worked Example 4, except that all losses – both normal and abnormal – are sold to a specialist reprocessing company at a price of 50p per kg.

For the four weeks ended 21 May 20-4, the process account and abnormal loss account are prepared as follows (with the same input costs and normal and abnormal loss as Worked Example 4 and shading showing the changes):

Dr		Process Account					Cr
	Quantity	Unit cost	Total cost		Quantity	Unit cost	Total cost
	(kg)	£	£		*(kg)*	£	£
Inputs (see Worked Example 1)	11,000	1.00	11,000	Normal loss	1,000	0.50	500
				Finished goods (or to next process)	9,400	1.05	9,870
				Abnormal loss	600	1.05	630
	11,000		11,000		11,000		11,000

Both the transfer to finished goods (or to the next process) and the abnormal loss are valued at the cost per unit of the expected output, ie

$$\frac{\text{input cost} - \text{scrap value of normal loss}}{\text{expected output}} = \frac{£11{,}000 - £500}{10{,}000 \text{ kg}} = £1.05 \text{ per kg}$$

The amount of abnormal loss (600 kg x £1.05 per kg = £630) is debited to the abnormal loss account; the revenues from scrap sales from either bank or trade receivables are then credited to the abnormal loss account.

Dr	Abnormal Loss Account		Cr
	£		£
Process account	630	Bank/trade receivables (600 kg x 50p)	300

If there are no more abnormal losses, the balance of this account (£630 – £300 = £330) will be debited as an expense to the statement of profit or loss at the end of the company's financial year:

– debit statement of profit or loss

– credit abnormal loss account

Normal loss account is debited with £500 by transfer from the process account; revenues from scrap sales are credited to the account (as in Worked Example 3):

Dr	Normal Loss Account		Cr
	£		£
Process account	500	Bank/trade receivables	500

abnormal gains, with no scrap sales

An abnormal gain is, as we have seen, where output is higher than after a normal loss. For example:

	kg
input	11,000
less normal loss	1,000
expected output	10,000
actual output	10,200
abnormal gain	200

If there are recurring abnormal gains, the managers will wish to investigate the causes with a view to reducing the amount of the normal loss. Causes of abnormal gains can include good quality raw materials, less wastage and spillage caused by improved handling techniques, improved processing caused by the introduction of better machinery.

For cost bookkeeping, the value of the abnormal gain is debited to the process account at the same cost per unit as the expected output; the value is credited to a separate **abnormal gain account**. The cost bookkeeping entries are shown diagrammatically as follows:

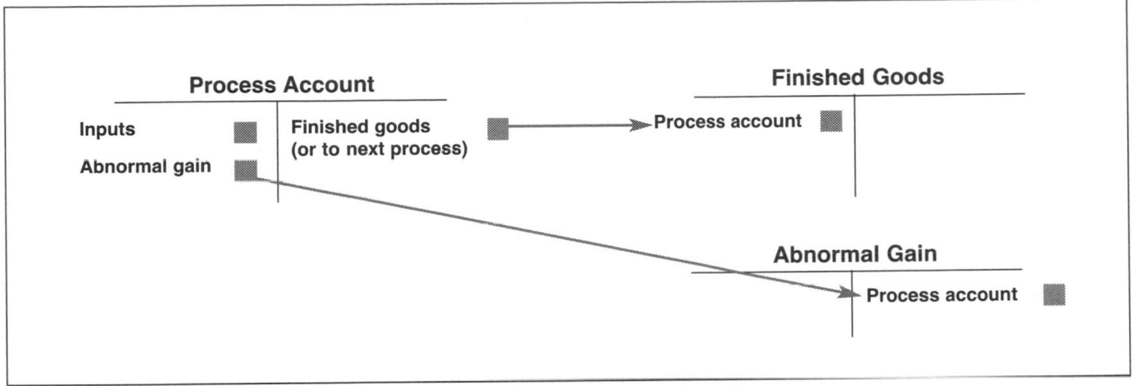

worked example 6 – abnormal gains, with no scrap sales

For the four weeks ended 18 June 20-4, Garden Eezee Limited inputs 11,000 kg of direct materials. Output transferred to finished goods is 10,200 kg – the difference of 800 kg being made up of a normal loss of 1,000 kg and an abnormal gain of 200 kg. For technical reasons, none of the losses was able to be sold as scrap.

The process account is prepared as follows (with the same input costs as Worked Example 1 and shading showing the change):

Dr			Process Account				Cr
	Quantity	Unit cost	Total cost		Quantity	Unit cost	Total cost
	(kg)	£	£		*(kg)*	£	£
Inputs (see Worked Example 1)	11,000	1.00	11,000	Normal loss	1,000	–	–
Abnormal gain	200	1.10	220	Finished goods (or to next process)	10,200	1.10	11,220
	11,200		11,220		11,200		11,220

Both the transfer to finished goods (or to next process) and the abnormal gain are valued at the cost per unit of the expected output, ie

$$\frac{\text{input cost}}{\text{expected output}} = \frac{£11,000}{10,000 \text{ kg}} = £1.10 \text{ per kg}$$

The amount of the abnormal gain is credited to the abnormal gain account:

Dr	Abnormal Gain Account		Cr
	£		£
		Process account	220

At the end of the financial year, the balance of abnormal gain account is credited to the statement of profit or loss:

– debit abnormal gain account

– credit statement of profit or loss

In this way, abnormal gains are treated as a period gain instead of being included with the closing inventory valuation.

abnormal gains, with scrap sales

Where there are normal losses (with a scrap sales value) and abnormal gains, we must be careful to distinguish between the two amounts:

- the value of the full amount of normal losses is credited to the process account (notwithstanding the fact that normal losses are reduced because of the abnormal gains)
- the value of abnormal gains is debited to the process account and credited to abnormal gains account (at the cost per unit of the expected output)

worked example 7 – abnormal gains, with scrap sales

Here the details are the same as Worked Example 6, except that normal losses have a scrap value of 50p per kg.

For the four weeks ended 16 July 20-4, the process account and abnormal gain account are prepared as follows (with the same input costs and abnormal gain as Worked Example 6 and shading showing the changes):

Dr		Process Account					Cr
	Quantity	Unit cost	Total cost		Quantity	Unit cost	Total cost
	(kg)	£	£		*(kg)*	£	£
Inputs (see Worked Example 1)	11,000	1.00	11,000	Normal loss	1,000	0.50	500
Abnormal gain	200	1.05	210	Finished goods (or to next process)	10,200	1.05	10,710
	11,200		11,210		11,200		11,210

Both the transfer to finished goods (or to next process) and the abnormal gain are valued at the cost per unit of the expected output, ie

$$\frac{\text{input cost} - \text{scrap value of normal loss}}{\text{expected output}} = \frac{£11{,}000 - £500}{10{,}000 \text{ kg}} = £1.05 \text{ per kg}$$

Dr	Abnormal Gain Account		Cr
	£		£
Normal loss account	100	Process account	210

If there are no more abnormal gains, the balance of this account (£210 – £100 = £110) will be credited to the statement of profit or loss at the end of the company's financial year:

– debit abnormal gain account

– credit statement of profit or loss

The transactions on abnormal gain account are:

	Quantity	Unit cost	Total cost
	(kg)	£	£
■ credit (transfer from process account)	200	1.05	210
■ debit (transfer to normal loss account)	200	0.50	100
■ balance		0.55	110

The reason for the transfer of £100 to normal loss account is to leave only the amount of the abnormal gain, £110. This is 55p per kg, which is left after deducting the value of normal losses of 50p from the cost per unit of expected output of £1.05. By doing this, we highlight the value of abnormal gains above the normal efficiency of the process.

At the end of the financial year, the balance of abnormal gain account is credited to the statement of profit or loss.

Dr	Normal Loss Account		Cr
	£		£
Process account	500	Bank/trade receivables	400
		Abnormal gain account	100
	500		500

Here, normal loss account is debited with £500 by transfer from the process account. Credits to the account come from two sources:

- revenue of £400 (ie 800 kg sold at 50p per kg) from bank or trade receivables
- transfer of £100 (ie 200 kg at 50p per kg) from abnormal gain account

Case Study

PERRAN CHEMICALS LIMITED: TWO PROCESSES

Tutorial note: This Case Study illustrates normal losses, abnormal losses and abnormal gains using the example of a two-process company.

situation

Perran Chemicals Limited manufactures a product, Xenova, within two separate processes. For the week ended 14 May 20-4 the details were:

- *Process 1*
  - materials input, 2,000 kg at £4 per kg
  - labour, £720
  - overheads, £1,440
- *Process 2*
  - materials input, 3,100 kg at £6 per kg
  - labour, £960
  - overheads, £480

Normal outputs are:

- Process 1, 80% of input
- Process 2, 90% of input

All losses are sold at a scrap value of £1 per kg to a specialist reprocessing company.

There was no work-in-progress at either the beginning or end of the week.
Output during the week was 1,400 kg from Process 1 and 4,200 kg from Process 2.
As an Accounts Assistant at Perran Chemicals Limited you are asked to prepare the process 1 account, process 2 account, normal loss account, abnormal loss account, and abnormal gain account for the week ended 14 May 20-4. Note: show the cost per unit of expected output to the nearest penny.

solution

Process 1 Account

Dr	Quantity	Unit cost	Total cost		Quantity	Unit cost	Total cost Cr
	(kg)	£	£		*(kg)*	£	£
Materials	2,000	4.00	8,000	Normal loss (20%)	400	1.00	400
Labour			720	Transfer to process 2	1,400	6.10	8,540
Overheads			1,440	Abnormal loss*	200	6.10	1,220
	2,000		10,160	* 600 kg loss, minus normal loss 400 kg = 200 kg abnormal loss	2,000		10,160

Dr			Process 2 Account				Cr
	Quantity	Unit cost	Total cost		Quantity	Unit cost	Total cost
	(kg)	£	£		*(kg)*	£	£
Transfer from process 1	1,400	6.10	8,540	Normal loss (10%)	450	1.00	450
Materials	3,100	6.00	18,600	Finished goods	4,200	6.95	29,172
Labour			960				
Overheads			480				
	4,500		28,580				
Abnormal gain*	150	6.95	**1,042				
	4,650		29,622		4,650		29,622

* 300 kg loss, minus normal loss 450 kg = 150 kg abnormal gain

**This figure is rounded down in order to balance the account

Dr	Normal Loss Account		Cr
	£		£
Process 1 account	400	Bank/trade receivables	400
Process 2 account	450	Abnormal gain account	*150
		Bank/trade receivables	300
	850		850

*see abnormal gain account

Dr	Abnormal Loss Account		Cr
	£		£
Process 1 account	1,220	Bank/trade receivables (200 kg x £1.00)	200

Dr	Abnormal Gain Account		Cr
	£		£
Normal loss account	*150	Process 2 account	1,042
* 150 kg x £1.00 per kg			

Tutorial notes *(amounts calculated to the nearest penny):*

- In process 1, the cost per unit of expected output is:

$$\frac{£10,160 - £400}{1,600 \text{ kg*}} = £6.10 \text{ per kg}$$

* ie 2,000 kg x 80%

- In process 2, the cost per unit of expected output is:

$$\frac{£28{,}580 - £450}{4{,}050 \text{ kg}^{**}} = £6.95 \text{ per kg}$$

** ie 4,500 kg x 90%

For calculating the finished goods, leave the cost per kilo unrounded in your calculator.

- At the end of the financial year:
  - the balance of abnormal loss account, here £1,020 (ie £1,220 - £200), is debited to the statement of profit or loss
  - the balance of abnormal gain account, here £892 (ie £1,042 - £150), is credited to the statement of profit or loss

Note re AAT Assessments

In the example of process costing we have seen how the process account is written up, together with the accounts for normal loss, abnormal loss and abnormal gain. In AAT Assessments the main focus will be on the process account rather than the associated loss and gain accounts. Nevertheless, you should be prepared to state amounts entered in these accounts and whether they are debit or credit entries.

Chapter Summary

- The method chosen for cost accounting within a business depends on the kind of work being done.
- In manufacturing and in service industries, work may consist of separately identifiable jobs or it may be continuous.
- Separately identifiable jobs are usually done to a customer's specific order.
- Costs are calculated for each separately identifiable job.
- The costing method to be used for specific orders (separate jobs) is:
  - job costing for a single unit of work
  - batch costing for a batch of identical units
- The costing method to be used for continuous work is:
  - process costing for continuous manufacturing processes
  - service costing for continuous services
- To obtain a cost per cost unit for continuous work, the total costs for a time period are first collected together, then divided by the number of cost units produced or provided in the time period, ie

$$\textit{total cost per cost unit} = \frac{\textit{total costs of continuous work for the period}}{\textit{total cost units for the period}}$$

- If there is work-in-progress at the end of the period, the number of equivalent complete units is calculated, for example 500 units that are 50% complete are equivalent to 500 x 50% = 250 completed units.

- Bookkeeping for process costing uses a process account to calculate the cost per unit of expected output. Possible outcomes of process costing to be recorded in the accounts are:
  - no losses within the process
  - normal losses, with or without scrap sales
  - abnormal losses, with or without scrap sales
  - abnormal gains, with or without scrap sales

  At the end of a financial year, the balance of abnormal loss account is debited to the statement of profit or loss, while the balance of abnormal gain account is credited.

Key Terms

costing method — a technique used to collect costs and to calculate the total cost of output

unit costing — the cost incurred to produce one cost object (product/service/activity)

job/batch costing — a form of specific order costing which applies costs to jobs/batches

service costing — a form of costing for service industries; costs are averaged to find the cost per unit

job cost sheet — sheet (or record on a computer database) which shows the estimated and actual direct and indirect costs for a particular job

variance — the difference between an estimated cost and an actual cost

process costing — method of costing applied to continuous manufacturing processes

work-in-progress (WIP) — part-finished goods at a particular time

equivalent units — number of units in progress x percentage of completeness

cost per unit — $\frac{\textit{total costs}}{\textit{number of units (including equivalent units)}}$

process account — bookkeeping account used in process costing to calculate the cost per unit of expected output

normal loss — an unavoidable loss arising from the production process

abnormal loss — where the loss in a process is greater than the normal loss

abnormal gain — where the loss in a process is less than the normal loss

Activities

5.1 State, with reasons, the method of costing you think would be appropriate for:

- an accountant
- a bus company
- a baker
- a sports centre
- a hotel

5.2 A clothing manufacturer has been asked to give a quotation for the supply of a batch of uniforms for a band. Materials for the uniforms will be:

- 100 metres of cloth at £7.50 per metre
- 75 metres of braiding at £4.00 per metre

It is estimated that the job will take the machinists a total of 35 hours.

They are paid at the rate of £10.00 per hour.

The overhead absorption rate is £8.50 per direct labour hour.

You are to:

(a) Calculate the total cost of the job.

(b) Calculate the selling price if the company is to make a profit of 20% on the total cost price.

5.3 Rowcester Engineering Limited is asked to quote for the supply of a replacement cylinder head for a large stationary engine installed in a local factory.

The item will need to be cast in the foundry and then passed to the finishing shop for machining to specification.

Materials needed will be a 100 kg ingot of high-strength steel, which costs £10 per kg.

Direct labour will be 10 hours in the foundry, and 15 hours in the finishing shop. It will need 12 hours of machine hours in the finishing shop.

Foundry workers are paid £10 per hour, while machine operators in the finishing shop are paid £12 per hour.

Overheads are charged on the basis of 80% of direct labour cost in the foundry, and on the basis of £20 per machine hour in the finishing shop.

Profit is to be 25% of cost price.

You are to complete the following Job Cost Sheet to show the estimated total cost of the job, and the selling price.

JOB COST SHEET Replacement Cylinder Head	£
Direct Materials	
Direct Labour	
Foundry:	
Finishing:	
Overheads	
Foundry:	
Finishing:	
TOTAL COST	
Profit	
SELLING PRICE	

5.4 City Transit plc is a small train operating company which runs passenger rail services on a commuter line in a large city. The line links the docks area, which has been redeveloped with flats and houses, with the city centre, and then runs on through the suburbs. An intensive service is operated from early morning to late at night carrying people to and from work, schoolchildren, shoppers and leisure travellers.

The tracks that City Transit uses are leased from the track owner, Railnet plc.

The modern fleet of six diesel trains is owned and maintained by City Transit.

The following information is available in respect of last year's operations:

	Cost	Estimated life
Diesel trains	£1,300,000 each	20 years

Depreciation is on a straight-line basis, assuming a residual value of £100,000 for each train.

Leasing charges for track	£1,000,000 pa
Maintenance charges for trains	£910,000 pa
Fuel for trains	£210,000 pa
Wages of drivers and conductors	£480,000 pa
Administration	£520,000 pa

There were 2.5 million passenger journeys last year with an average distance travelled of five miles.

You are to calculate the total cost per passenger mile (to two decimal places) of operating the railway for last year.

5.5 A manufacturer of plastic toys has the following information concerning the first month of production:

Direct materials	£11,500
Direct labour	£9,000
Variable production overheads	£18,000
Toys completed	20,000
Toys in progress	5,000

The work-in-progress is complete as regards materials, but is 50% complete as regards direct labour and variable production overheads.

You are to complete the following layout to show the cost per toy (to two decimal places) of the first month's production and the month-end valuation for work-in-progress.

Cost element	Costs	Completed units	Work-in-progress			Total equivalent units	Cost per unit	WIP valuation
			Units	% complete	Equivalent units			
	A	B	C	D	E	F	G	H
	£				C x D	B + E	A ÷ F £	E x G £
Direct materials								
Direct labour								
Variable production overheads								
Total								

5.6 Agro Chemicals Limited produces a chemical, which is made in one production process.

For the four weeks ended 27 February 20-8, the company input 22,000 litres of direct materials, had an output of 20,000 litres and a normal loss of 2,000 litres. The input costs were: materials £5,500, labour £3,300, overheads £2,200. Normal losses were sold to a specialist reprocessing company for 20p per litre.

There was no opening or closing inventory at the beginning and end of the process; all output was complete.

(a) As an Accounts Assistant, you are to complete the following process account for the four weeks ended 27 February 20-8.

Dr			Process Account				Cr
	Quantity *(litres)*	Unit cost £	Total cost £		Quantity *(litres)*	Unit cost £	Total cost £
Materials				Normal loss			
Labour				Finished goods			
Overheads							

(b) Identify the entry to be made in normal loss account.

	Debit £	Credit £
Normal loss account		

5.7 GrowFast Limited produces a granular lawn fertiliser, which is made in one production process.

For the four weeks ended 21 May 20-7, the company input 42,000 kg of direct materials, had an output of 39,500 kg – the difference of 2,500 kg was made up of a normal loss of 2,000 kg and an abnormal loss of 500 kg.

The input costs were: materials £10,500, labour £4,200, overheads £2,100. All losses were sold to a specialist reprocessing company for 20p per kg.

There was no opening or closing inventory at the beginning and end of the process; all output was complete.

As an Accounts Assistant, you are to complete the following process account, the abnormal loss account, and the normal loss account for the four weeks ended 21 May 20-7.

Dr			Process Account				Cr
	Quantity *(kg)*	Unit cost £	Total cost £		Quantity *(kg)*	Unit cost £	Total cost £
Materials				Normal loss			
Labour				Finished goods			
Overheads				Abnormal loss			

Dr	Normal Loss Account		Cr
	£		£

Dr	Abnormal Loss Account		Cr
	£		£

5.8 RP Industries Limited produces a liquid furniture polish called 'EasyShine'. The product is made in two production processes before completion and transfer to finished goods.

For the four weeks ended 26 November 20-6, details of production of 'EasyShine' were as follows:

	Process 1	**Process 2**
Direct materials (10,000 litres)	£5,000	–
Labour	£4,000	£1,800
Overhead	£2,000	£1,350
Normal loss in process	10% of input	5% of input
Output	9,000 litres	8,300 litres
Scrap value of all losses	£0.40 per litre	£0.50 per litre

There was no opening or closing inventory at the beginning and end of either process; all output was complete. All losses were sold to a specialist reprocessing company.

As an Accounts Assistant, you are to complete the following process 1 account and process 2 account for the four weeks ended 26 November 20-6. Note: show the cost per unit of expected output to the nearest penny.

Dr			Process 1 Account				Cr
	Quantity *(litres)*	Unit cost £	Total cost £		Quantity *(litres)*	Unit cost £	Total cost £
Materials				Normal loss			
Labour				Transfer to			
Overheads				process 2			

Dr			Process 2 Account				Cr
	Quantity *(litres)*	Unit cost £	Total cost £		Quantity *(litres)*	Unit cost £	Total cost £
Transfer from process 1				Normal loss			
Labour				Finished goods			
Overheads				Abnormal loss			

5.9 Zelah Chemicals Limited produces an insect repellant called 'BuzzOff', which is made in one production process.

For the four weeks ended 16 July 20-5, the company input 11,000 litres of direct materials, and had an output of 10,200 litres – the difference of 800 litres was made up of a normal loss of 1,000 litres and an abnormal gain of 200 litres.

The input costs were: materials £5,500, labour £3,850, overheads £2,750. All losses were sold to a specialist reprocessing company for 30p per litre.

There was no opening or closing inventory at the beginning and end of the process; all output was complete.

As an Accounts Assistant, you are to complete the following process account, abnormal gain account, and normal loss account for the four weeks ended 16 July 20-5.

Dr			Process Account				Cr
	Quantity *(litres)*	Unit cost £	Total cost £		Quantity *(litres)*	Unit cost £	Total cost £
Materials				Normal loss			
Labour				Finished goods			
Overheads							
Abnormal gain							

Dr	Abnormal Gain Account		Cr
	£		£

Dr	Normal Loss Account		Cr
	£		£

5.10 Astra Chemicals Limited uses process costing for its products.

The process account for April for one particular process has been partly completed but the following information is also relevant:

- Three employees worked on this process during April. Each employee worked 35 hours per week for 4 weeks and was paid £10 per hour.
- Overheads are absorbed on the basis of £20 per labour hour.
- Astra Chemicals Limited expects a normal loss of 10% during this process, which it then sells for scrap at 80p per kg.

(a) Complete the process account below for April.

Description	kg	Unit cost £	Total cost £	Description	kg	Unit cost £	Total cost £
Material AB4	500	1.50		Normal loss		0.80	
Material AC5	200	2.20		Output	900		
Material AD6	300	4.10					
Labour							
Overheads							

(b) Identify the correct entry for each of the following in a process account.

	Debit	Credit
Abnormal loss		
Abnormal gain		

5.11 Excalibur Limited, a manufacturing business, uses both batch and unit costing as appropriate in its Production Department. It is currently costing a new product, EX321 which will start production in batches of 24,000 units.

It has estimated that the following costs will be incurred in producing one batch of 24,000 units of EX321:

Product EX321 cost estimates	£ **per batch**
Direct materials	8,400
Direct labour	6,240
Variable overheads	4,560
Fixed manufacturing overheads	3,600
Fixed administration, selling and distribution costs	2,880
Total costs	25,680

You are to:

(a) Calculate the prime cost of one unit of EX321.

£ [ ]

(b) Calculate the full absorption cost of one unit of EX321.

£ [ ]

(c) Calculate the marginal cost of one unit of EX321.

£ [ ]

(d) Calculate the marginal production cost of one batch of EX321.

£ [ ]

(e) Calculate the full absorption cost of one batch of EX321.

£ [ ]

6 Marginal, absorption and activity based costing

this chapter covers...

This chapter studies the costing methods of marginal and absorption costing and compares the profit made by a business under each method. Also included is activity based costing, which has developed from absorption costing. The chapter concludes with the layout of a manufacturing account and statement of profit or loss (income statement) and where the different types of inventory – raw materials, work-in-progress, finished goods – are shown in the financial statements.

This chapter explains:

- *the different treatment of product costs and period costs in marginal costing and absorption costing*
- *how marginal costing works, including the calculation of contribution, and its role in short-term decision-making*
- *how absorption costing works, including the valuation of closing inventory*
- *a comparison of profits when marginal costing and absorption costing are used*
- *how activity based costing charges overheads to production on the basis of activities*

MARGINAL AND ABSORPTION COSTING SYSTEMS

These two costing systems are often used in cost accounting, but for different purposes:

- marginal costing – helps with short-term decision-making
- absorption costing – is used to calculate inventory valuations and profit or loss in financial statements

The use of each system is dependent on the information needs of the business or organisation:

- 'can we afford to sell 1,000 units of our product each month to Megastores Limited at a discount of 20 per cent?' (use marginal costing)
- 'what profit have we made this year?' (use absorption costing)

These costing systems use the same product and period costs, but they are treated differently according to their behaviour. Remember that:

- product costs are those costs that become part of the manufactured product
- period costs are those costs that cannot be assigned to the manufactured product

MARGINAL COSTING

Marginal cost is the cost of producing one extra unit of output

To help with short-term decision-making, costs are classified by their behaviour as either variable costs or fixed costs (with semi-variable costs being split between their fixed and variable parts). Such a classification of costs is used in marginal costing to work out how much it costs to produce each extra unit of output.

Marginal cost is often – but not always – the total of the variable costs of producing a unit of output. For most purposes, marginal costing is not concerned with **fixed period costs** (such as the rent of a factory); instead it is concerned with **variable product costs** – direct materials, direct labour, direct expenses, and variable production overheads – which increase as output increases. For most decision-making, the marginal cost of a unit of output is, therefore, the variable cost of producing one more unit.

Knowing the marginal cost of a unit of output enables the managers of a business to focus on the contribution provided by each unit. The contribution is the sales revenue after marginal/variable product costs have been paid. The contribution formula is:

selling price less variable cost = contribution

Contribution can be calculated on a per unit basis, or for a batch of output (eg 1,000 units), or for a whole business.

It follows that the difference between the sales revenue and the variable costs of the units sold in a period is the total contribution that the sales of all the units in the period make towards the fixed period costs of the business. Once these are covered, the remainder of the contribution is profit.

Thus a business can work out its profit, using a marginal costing statement, for any given period from the total contribution and fixed costs figures:

total contribution less fixed production costs = profit from operations

A marginal costing statement can be prepared in the following format:

		£
	Sales revenue	x
less	Variable production costs	x
equals	Contribution	x
less	Fixed production overheads	x
equals	PROFIT FROM OPERATIONS	x

Note from the marginal costing statement how the contribution goes firstly towards the fixed production overheads and, when they have been covered, secondly contributes to profit.

The relationship between marginal costing, contribution and profit is shown in the Case Study which follows.

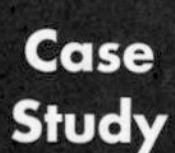

WYVERN BIKE COMPANY: MARGINAL COSTING

situation

The Wyvern Bike Company makes 100 bikes each week and its costs are as follows:

Direct materials	£4,000
Direct labour	£5,000
Production overheads	£5,000

Investigations into the behaviour of costs has revealed the following information:

- direct materials are variable costs
- direct labour is a variable cost
- of the production overheads, £2,000 is a fixed cost, and the remainder is a variable cost

The selling price of each bike is £200.

As an Accounts Assistant at the Wyvern Bike Company, you are asked to:

- calculate the marginal cost of producing each bike
- show the expected contribution per bike
- prepare a marginal costing statement to show clearly the total contribution and the total profit from operations each week

solution

Marginal cost per bike

Variable costs per unit:		£
	Direct materials (£4,000 ÷ 100)	40
	Direct labour (£5,000 ÷ 100)	50
	Production overheads (£3,000* ÷ 100)	30
	Marginal cost per bike	120

* £5,000 – £2,000 fixed costs

Contribution per bike

		£
	Selling price per bike	200
less	Variable cost per bike	120
equals	Contribution per bike	80

Marginal costing statement

		£	£
	Sales £200 x 100 bikes		20,000
less	Variable costs:		
	Direct materials	4,000	
	Direct labour	5,000	
	Production overheads	3,000	
			12,000
equals	Total contribution		8,000
less	Fixed production overheads		2,000
equals	Profit from operations for the week		6,000

ABSORPTION COSTING

Absorption costing absorbs (recovers) the costs of the business amongst the cost units.

Absorption costing answers the question, 'What does it cost to make one unit of output?'

The absorption cost of a unit of output is made up of the following costs:

		£
	Direct materials	x
add	Direct labour	x
add	Direct expenses	x
add	Production overheads (fixed and variable)	x
equals	ABSORPTION COST	x

Note that the production overheads comprise the factory costs of indirect materials, indirect labour, and indirect expenses.

Case Study

WYVERN BIKE COMPANY: ABSORPTION COSTING

situation

The Wyvern Bike Company makes 100 bikes each week and its costs are as follows:

Direct materials	£4,000
Direct labour	£5,000
Production overheads	£5,000

The selling price of each bike is £200.

As an Accounts Assistant at the Wyvern Bike Company, you are asked to:

- calculate the absorption cost of producing each bike
- calculate the total profit from operations each week

solution

Absorption cost per bike

Total costs per week:		£
	Direct materials	4,000
	Direct labour	5,000
	Production overheads	5,000
	Total cost	14,000

The absorption cost of producing one bike is:

$$\frac{\text{Total cost}}{\text{Units of output}} = \frac{£14{,}000}{100 \text{ bikes}} = £140 \text{ per bike}$$

Profit each week

	Selling price (100 bikes x £200)	20,000
less	Total cost	14,000
equals	Profit from operations for the week	6,000

Conclusion

Profit from operations for the week of £6,000 is the same as with the marginal costing method, so we could say 'Does it matter whether we use marginal or absorption costing?' The answer to this is that it does:

- marginal costing, with its focus on variable costs and contribution, is useful for short-term decision-making
- absorption costing is a simple method of calculating the cost of output and is used in financial statements for inventory valuation

As the Case Study shows, each cost unit bears an equal proportion of the costs of the production overheads of the business. Because of its simplicity, absorption costing is a widely used system which tells us how much it costs to make one unit of output. It works well where the cost units are identical, eg 100 identical bikes, but is less appropriate where some of the cost units differ in quality, eg 100 bikes, of which 75 are standard models and 25 are handbuilt to the customers' specifications. It also ignores the effect of changes in the level of output on the cost structure. For example, if the bike manufacturer reduces output to 50 bikes a week:

- will direct materials remain at £40 per bike? (buying materials in smaller quantities might mean higher prices)
- will direct labour still be £50 per bike? (with lower production, the workforce may not be able to specialise in certain jobs, and may be less efficient)
- will the production overheads remain at £5,000? (perhaps smaller premises can be used and the factory rent reduced)

A further costing method – which has developed from absorption costing – is activity based costing (page 177).

MARGINAL AND ABSORPTION COSTING COMPARED

Marginal costing tells the managers of a business or organisation the cost of producing one extra unit of output. Nevertheless, we must always remember that one of the objectives of the costing system is to ensure that all the costs of a business or organisation are recovered by being charged to production. This is achieved by means of overhead absorption (see Chapter 4). We will now make a comparison between marginal and absorption costing:

- **marginal costing**

  Marginal costing recognises that period costs vary with time rather than activity, and identifies the variable production cost of one extra unit. For example, the rent of a factory relates to a certain time period, eg one month, and remains unchanged whether 100 units of output are made or whether 500 units are made (always assuming that the capacity of the factory is at least 500 units); by contrast, the production of one extra unit will incur an increase in variable costs, ie direct materials, direct labour, direct expenses (if any), and variable overheads – this increase is the **marginal cost**.

- **absorption costing**

  This technique absorbs all product costs into each unit of output through the use of an overhead absorption rate (see Chapter 4). Therefore the more units that are produced, the cheaper will be the cost per unit – because the overheads are spread over a greater number of units.

The diagram below demonstrates how the terms in marginal costing relate to the same production costs as those categorised under absorption costing terms. As noted above, when using marginal costing it is the behaviour of the cost – fixed or variable – that is important, not the origin of the cost.

MARGINAL COSTING	ABSORPTION COSTING
variable costs variable direct materials variable direct labour variable direct expenses variable overheads	**direct costs** direct materials direct labour direct expenses
fixed costs fixed direct expenses fixed overheads	**indirect costs** variable overheads fixed overheads

The table on page 180 gives a comparison between marginal costing and absorption costing – together with activity based costing (see page 177) – including a note on the usefulness and the limitations of each.

marginal and absorption costing: profit comparisons

Because of the different ways in which marginal costing and absorption costing treat period costs, the two techniques produce different levels of profit when there is a closing inventory figure. This is because, under marginal costing, the closing inventory is valued at variable production cost; by contrast, absorption cost includes a share of fixed production costs in the closing inventory valuation. This is illustrated in the Case Study which follows, looking at the effect of using marginal costing and absorption costing on the statement of profit or loss of a manufacturing business.

The marginal cost approach is often used to help with short-term decision-making (see Chapter 8). However, for financial statements, absorption costing must be used for inventory valuation purposes in order to comply with IAS 2 (see page 38). Under IAS 2, *Inventories*, the closing inventory valuation is based on the product costs of direct materials, direct labour, direct expenses (if any), and production overheads. Note that non-production overheads are not included, as they are period costs which are charged to the statement of profit or loss in the year to which they relate.

Although these two methods can be used to calculate different levels of profit, they must not be used to manipulate profits. Those working in accounting must apply ethical principles so that the users of profit statements can be assured that such statements have been prepared with objectivity, ie with no manipulation or bias.

Case Study

CHAIRS LIMITED: MARGINAL AND ABSORPTION COSTING

situation

Chairs Limited commenced business on 1 January 20-7. It manufactures a special type of chair designed to alleviate back pain. Information on the first year's trading is as follows:

number of chairs manufactured	5,000
number of chairs sold	4,500
selling price	£110 per chair
direct materials	£30 per chair
direct labour	£40 per chair
fixed production overheads	£100,000
non-production overheads	£50,000

The directors ask for your help in producing profit statements using the marginal costing and absorption costing methods. They say that they will use 'the one that shows the higher profit' to the company's Bank Manager.

solution

CHAIRS LIMITED

Statement of profit or loss for the year ended 31 December 20-7

	MARGINAL COSTING		ABSORPTION COSTING	
	£	£	£	£
Sales revenue at £110 each		495,000		495,000
Variable costs				
Direct materials at £30 each	150,000		150,000	
Direct labour at £40 each	200,000		200,000	
Prime cost	350,000		350,000	
Less Closing inventory (marginal cost)				
500 chairs at £70 each	35,000			
	315,000			
Fixed production overheads	100,000		100,000	
			450,000	
Less Closing inventory (absorption cost)				
500 chairs at £90 each			45,000	
Less Cost of sales		415,000		405,000
GROSS PROFIT		80,000		90,000
Less Non-production overheads		50,000		50,000
NET PROFIT		30,000		40,000

Tutorial notes:

- Closing inventory is always calculated on the basis of this year's costs:

  marginal costing, variable costs only, ie £30 + £40 = £70 per chair

  absorption costing, variable and fixed costs, ie £450,000 ÷ 5,000 chairs = £90 per chair

- The difference in the profit figures is caused only by the closing inventory figures: £35,000 under marginal costing and £45,000 under absorption costing – the same costs have been used, but fixed production overheads have been treated differently.

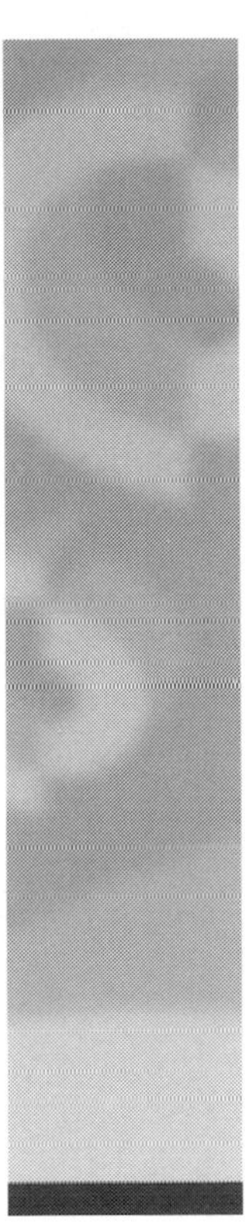

- Only fixed production overheads are dealt with differently using the techniques of marginal and absorption costing.
- Non-production overheads are charged in full to the statement of profit or loss in the year to which they relate.

With marginal costing, the full amount of the fixed production overheads has been charged in this year's statement of profit or loss; by contrast, with absorption costing, part of the fixed production overheads (here, £10,000) has been carried forward in the inventory valuation.

With regard to the directors' statement that they will use 'the one that shows the higher profit', the following points should be borne in mind:

- A higher profit does not mean more money in the bank.
- The two methods simply treat fixed production overheads differently and, in a year when there is no closing inventory, total profits to date are exactly the same – but they occur differently over the years. Over time, profits are identical under both methods.
- For financial statements, Chairs Limited must use the absorption cost inventory valuation of £45,000 in order to comply with IAS 2, *Inventories*.
- Ethical considerations must apply – those working in accounting must prepare profit statements without manipulation or bias.

ACTIVITY BASED COSTING

Activity based costing (ABC) charges overheads to production on the basis of activities.

ABC is a costing method which has developed from absorption costing but with a different approach to charging overheads to production. ABC identifies what causes overheads to be incurred, rather than charging total overheads for a particular period. Instead of using overhead recovery methods based around, for example, labour hours or machine hours, ABC uses cost drivers linked to the way in which a business is conducted.

Cost drivers are activities which cause costs to be incurred.

By identifying relevant cost drivers, as illustrated in the Case Study which follows, the cost per unit of a product can be calculated based on its use of activities.

Case Study

AYEBEE LIMITED: ACTIVITY BASED COSTING

situation

AyeBee Limited manufactures two products: Aye and Bee. Aye is a standard product which is produced in batches of 500 units; Bee is a product which is made for a number of customers who each require different specifications – it is produced in batches of 100 units. Each unit of production – whether Aye or Bee – requires one direct labour hour.

Production of each batch of Aye and Bee incurs the following overheads:

- the machinery to be set up at a cost of £400 per batch (to cover the engineer's time and test running of the machinery)
- quality inspection costs of £200 per batch (to cover inspection time and cost of rejects)

In a typical week the company produces 500 units of Aye and 500 units of Bee, so the set up costs and quality inspection costs are:

1 set-up cost of Aye (1 batch) at £400	=	£400
5 set-up costs of Bee (5 batches) at £400	=	£2,000
1 quality inspection of Aye at £200	=	£200
5 quality inspections of Bee at £200	=	£1,000
WEEKLY TOTAL		£3,600

How should AyeBee Limited charge overheads to production?

solution

As each unit of production requires one direct labour hour, ie product Aye 500 hours, product Bee 500 hours, the overhead costs of set-ups and quality inspections, using a direct labour basis, will be charged to production as follows:

Product Aye	=	£1,800
Product Bee	=	£1,800
TOTAL		£3,600

We can see that this is an incorrect basis on which to charge overheads to production because product Aye required just one set-up and one quality inspection, whereas product Bee required five set-ups and five quality inspections.

By using activity based costing, with set-up and quality inspection as the cost drivers, overheads can be charged to production as follows:

Product Aye:

1 set-up at £400	=	£400
1 quality inspection at £200	=	£200
TOTAL		£600

Product Bee:

5 set-ups at £400	=	£2,000
5 quality inspections at £200	=	£1,000
TOTAL		£3,000

In this way, by using activity based costing, there is a more accurate reflection of the cost of set-ups and quality inspections. The cost of 500 units of product Aye is reduced by £1,200 (ie £1,800 – £600), while the cost of 500 units of product Bee is increased by £1,200 (ie from £1,800 to £3,000). This increased accuracy of costing may have implications for the viability of product Bee, and for the selling price of both products.

other cost drivers

Cost drivers must have a close relationship with an activity, which can then be related to output. Examples of activities and their cost drivers include:

Activity	Cost driver
• set-ups	• number of set-ups
• quality control	• number of quality inspections
• processing orders to suppliers	• number of orders
• processing invoices received	• number of invoices
• processing orders to customers	• number of orders
• processing invoices to customers	• number of invoices
• marketing	• number of advertisements
• telephone sales	• number of telephone calls made

summary

Activity based costing is particularly appropriate for use in capital-intensive industries where overheads are high and complex in nature – requiring analysis into what has caused the overhead to be incurred. The table on the next page compares marginal, absorption and activity based costing.

Comparison of marginal, absorption and activity based costing

	Marginal costing	Absorption costing	Activity based costing
Main use	• to help with short-term decision-making (see Chapter 8) in the forms of – break-even analysis – margin of safety – target profit – contribution sales ratio – limiting factors – 'special order' pricing	• to calculate selling prices using cost plus profit • to calculate inventory valuation for financial statements	• to identify what causes overheads to be incurred for a particular activity
How does it work?	• focuses on product costs • costs are classified as either fixed or variable • contribution to fixed costs is calculated as selling price less variable costs	• focuses on product and period costs • production overheads are charged to production through an overhead absorption rate, often on the basis of direct labour hours or machine hours	• focuses on product costs • cost drivers are identified • production overheads are charged to production on the basis of activities
Main focus	• marginal cost • contribution	• production overheads charged to production • calculating selling prices and profit • calculating inventory values	• identifying cost drivers as a way of charging production overheads to production
Usefulness	• concept of contribution is easy to understand • useful for short-term decision-making, but no consideration of overheads	• acceptable under IAS 2, *Inventories* • appropriate for traditional industries where production overheads are charged to production on the basis of direct labour hours or machine hours	• acceptable under IAS 2 *Inventories* • more accurate calculation of selling prices because production overheads are analysed to the products which use the activities • appropriate for capital-intensive industries where overheads are high and complex in nature
Limitations	• costs have to be identified as either fixed or variable • all overheads have to be recovered, otherwise a loss will be made • not acceptable under IAS 2, *Inventories* • calculation of selling prices may be less accurate than other costing methods	• not as useful in short-term decision-making as marginal costing • may provide less accurate basis for calculation of selling prices where overheads are high and complex in nature	• time-consuming to set up and record costs (because of the detail required) • the selection of cost drivers can be difficult • the cost drivers need to be kept up-to-date • period costs – such as rent and rates – still need to be recovered

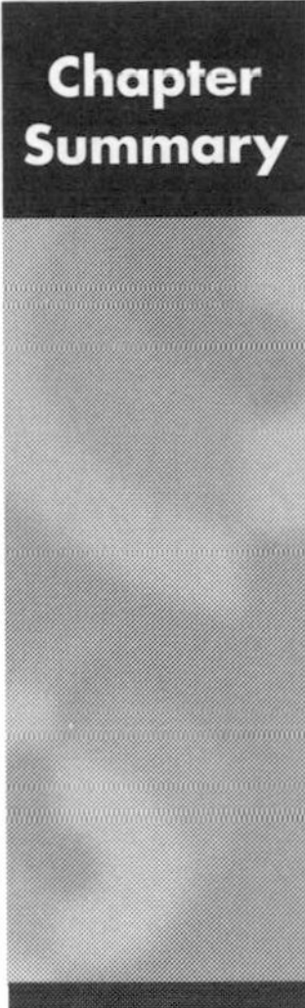

Chapter Summary

- Marginal and absorption costing treat product and period costs differently according to their behaviour.
- Marginal costing classifies costs by their behaviour – variable product costs or fixed period costs. Such a classification is used to cost units of output on the basis of their variable (or marginal) costs.
- Marginal costing helps with short-term decision-making.
- Absorption costing absorbs the period costs of the business amongst the cost units by means of overhead absorption rates. It is used to cost units of output to calculate inventory valuations and profit or loss in financial statements.
- Activity based costing (ABC) charges overheads to production on the basis of activities.
- ABC makes use of cost drivers which are activities which cause costs to be incurred.

Key Terms

product cost — costs that become part of the manufactured product

period cost — costs that cannot be assigned to the manufactured product

marginal cost — the product cost of one extra unit of output

contribution — selling price – variable cost

absorption cost — the period production costs of the business are absorbed amongst the cost units through the use of an overhead absorption rate

objectivity — ethical principle of accounting that does not permit manipulation or bias

activity based costing — technique which charges overheads to production on the basis of activities

cost drivers — activities which cause costs to be incurred

Activities

6.1 Coffeeworks Limited manufactures coffee machines for domestic use. The management of the company is considering next year's production and has asked you to help with certain financial decisions.

The following information is available:

Selling price (per machine)	£80	
Direct materials (per machine)	£25	
Direct labour (per machine)	£20	
Fixed production overheads	£270,000	per year
Non-production overheads	£200,000	per year

The company is planning to manufacture 15,000 coffee machines next year.

(a) Calculate the marginal cost per coffee machine.

(b) Calculate the absorption cost per coffee machine.

(c) Prepare a statement of profit or loss to show the profit or loss if 15,000 coffee machines are sold.

6.2 Cook-It Limited makes garden barbecues. The management of the company is considering the production for next year and has asked for help with certain financial decisions.

The following information is available:

Selling price (per barbecue)	£90	
Direct materials (per barbecue)	£30	
Direct labour (per barbecue)	£25	
Fixed production overheads	£150,000	per year
Non-production overheads	£125,000	per year

The company is planning to manufacture 10,000 barbecues next year.

Required:

You are to calculate:

(a) The marginal cost per barbecue.

(b) The absorption cost per barbecue.

(c) The profit or loss if 10,000 barbecues are sold.

6.3 Maxxa Limited manufactures one product, the Maxx. For the month of January 20-7 the following information is available:

Number of units manufactured	4,000	
Number of units sold	3,000	
Selling price	£8	per unit
Direct materials for month	£5,000	
Direct labour for month	£9,000	
Fixed production overheads for month	£6,000	
Non-production overheads for month	£4,000	

There was no finished goods inventory at the start of the month. Both direct materials and direct labour are variable costs.

Required:

You are to produce statements of profit or loss using marginal costing and absorption costing methods.

6.4 Activtoys Limited commenced business on 1 January 20-1. It manufactures the 'Activ', an outdoor climbing frame. Information on the first year's trading is as follows:

Number of climbing frames manufactured	1,500	
Number of climbing frames sold	1,300	
Selling price	£125	per frame
Direct materials	£25	per frame
Direct labour	£30	per frame
Fixed production overheads	£82,500	
Non-production overheads	£8,000	

Required:

(a) The directors ask for your help in producing statements of profit or loss using the marginal costing and absorption costing methods. They say that they will use 'the one that gives the higher profit' to show to the company's Bank Manager.

(b) Write a note to the directors explaining the reason for the different profit figures and commenting on their statement.

6.5 **(a)** Explain the term 'activity based costing'.

(b) Explain the term 'cost driver'.

6.6 The Financial Director of Elwin Limited is considering changing the method of calculating the selling price of the company's products from absorption cost plus a mark-up to activity based costing plus a mark-up.

Prepare a note for the directors of Elwin Limited which explains the benefits of activity based costing over absorption costing.

6.7 Which **one** of these is an example of ethical behaviour by an accounting technician?

(a)	Agreeing with the business owner to include period costs in the closing inventory	
(b)	Agreeing with the business owner to use marginal costing for the closing inventory	
(c)	Agreeing with the business owner to use absorption costing for the closing inventory	
(d)	Agreeing with the business owner to use either marginal or absorption costing for the closing inventory depending on which gives the higher profit	

7 Aspects of budgeting

this chapter covers...

In this chapter we turn our attention to budgets and how they are used to help with the financial planning of a business or organisation. In particular we see

- *the need for budgets as part of the decision-making, planning and control processes*
- *how budgeted costs and revenues are set*
- *the behaviour of fixed, semi-variable and variable costs*
- *the use of the high/low method to identify the amounts of fixed and variable costs*
- *the preparation of a schedule of forecast revenue and costs*
- *how budgets are a method of cost control through the use of variances*
- *how budgets are used in responsibility accounting to make managers and supervisors responsible for the costs and revenues of their section of the business or organisation, and as a way of motivating employees*
- *the monitoring process for budget reports*
- *the difference between fixed and flexible budgets, together with a practical example of a flexible budget*
- *the causes of variances for costs and revenues*

WHAT IS A BUDGET?

A budget is a financial plan for a business or organisation that is prepared in advance.

Budgets are based on pre-determined costs and revenues set in advance of production. These will be set for materials, labour, overheads, selling prices and profit from operations. Such pre-determined costs and revenues are often referred to as **standard costs** and **standard selling prices**.

All businesses need methods of controlling the costs of materials, labour, and overheads that go to make up the finished product. Imagine a car factory where the cost and amount of materials to make the car is not known; where the hours of work and rates of pay are not known, where the cost of overheads is not known. Under such circumstances, the costs could not be controlled, and it would be impossible to quote a selling price for the product. To overcome this problem many businesses establish budgeted costs and revenues for their output in advance of production. Thus a budgeted cost can be calculated for things as diverse as a product manufactured in a factory, a hospital operation, servicing a car, a meal in a restaurant, a passenger-mile on a bus.

Budgeted/standard costs and revenues are set for:

- **direct materials**

  The quantity and quality of each type of material to be used in producing the output, and the price of such materials is pre-determined. Budgeted materials cost is the expected quantity and quality of materials multiplied by the expected material price.

- **direct labour**

  The labour hours required to manufacture a quantity of goods or provide a service, together with the cost of the labour is pre-determined. Budgeted labour cost is the expected labour hours multiplied by the expected wage rates.

- **production overheads**

  The expected volume of output within a time period, multiplied by the overhead absorption rate, determines the budgeted overhead cost.

- **sales revenue**

  The expected volume of sales within a time period multiplied by the expected selling price determines the budgeted sales revenue.

- **profit from operations**

  The expected profit from operations within a time period (note that profit from operations is sales revenue minus direct materials, direct labour and production and non-production overheads).

Budgets are usually set for each of the responsibility centres – cost, profit or investment centres – of the business or organisation. Once budgets have been set, they can be used as part of the decision-making, planning, and control processes:

- **decision-making**

  The budgeted cost can be used to make pricing decisions, and to consider the effect of using different qualities of materials and grades of labour on the cost of the output.

- **planning**

  Budgets can be prepared to plan the production of goods or services for the next accounting period, and to budget for materials, labour, overheads, sales revenue and profit from operations.

- **control**

  Monitoring can be carried out on a regular basis to identify cost and revenue variances from the budget, together with a reconciliation of budgeted and actual costs, revenues and profit from operations.

FIXED AND VARIABLE COSTS IN BUDGETING AND DECISION-MAKING

In Chapter 1 we saw that:

- fixed costs remain constant over a range of output levels
- variable costs alter directly with changes in output levels
- semi-variable costs combine a fixed and a variable element

Identifying costs as being fixed, semi-variable or variable helps with budgeting and decision-making – the business might be able to alter the balance between fixed and variable costs in order to increase profits. A product could be made:

- either, by using a labour-intensive process, with a large number of employees supported by basic machinery
- or, by using expensive machinery in an automated process with very few employees

In the first case, the cost structure will be high variable costs (direct labour) and low fixed costs (straight-line depreciation of machinery). In the second case, there will be low variable costs and high fixed costs. Management will need to examine the relationship between the costs – together with the likely sales figures, and the availability of finance with which to buy the machinery – before making a decision.

More specifically, a knowledge of the behaviour of costs can be used to help management to:

- identify the amount of fixed costs within a semi-variable cost
- prepare budgets for revenue and costs
- identify the point at which costs are exactly equal to income – known as the break-even point (covered in Chapter 8)

IDENTIFYING THE AMOUNT OF FIXED AND VARIABLE COSTS

With semi-variable costs we have already seen (in Chapter 1) how these combine both a fixed and a variable cost. It is important to be able to identify the amount of each, as this will help with budgeting and decision-making. Where the total costs are known at two levels of output, the amounts of fixed and variable costs can be identified using the 'high/low' method.

example

- at output of 1,000 units, total costs are £7,000
- at output of 2,000 units, total costs are £9,000

What are the fixed costs? What are the variable costs?

Using the 'high/low' method to identify the fixed and variable costs:

- The low output and costs are deducted from the high output and costs, as follows:

	high output	2,000 units	£9,000
less	low output	1,000 units	£7,000
equals	differences	1,000 units	£2,000

- The amount of the variable cost per unit is now calculated as:

$$\frac{\text{difference in cost}}{\text{difference in units}} = \frac{£2,000}{1,000} = £2 \text{ variable cost per unit}$$

- Therefore, at 1,000 units of output the cost structure is:

	total cost	£7,000
less	variable costs (1,000 units x £2 per unit)	£2,000
equals	fixed costs	£5,000

- Check this now at 2,000 units of output when the cost structure is:

	variable costs (2,000 units x £2 per unit)	£4,000
add	fixed costs (as above)	£5,000
equals	total costs	£9,000

The 'high/low' method can only be used when variable costs increase by the same money amount for each extra unit of output (ie there is a constant unit variable cost), and where there are no stepped fixed costs.

BUDGETS FOR REVENUE AND COSTS

Once fixed and variable costs are known for the three elements of costs – materials, labour and expenses – at a particular level of output, it is relatively simple to calculate how the costs will change at different levels of output. For example, if variable materials costs at an output of 1,000 units are £2,000 then, at an output of 1,100 units, they will be £2,200 (ie a 10 per cent increase in both output and cost). By contrast, the fixed expense of factory rent of, say, £5,000 will be unchanged if output increases by 10 per cent. (Note that such calculations assume a constant unit variable cost and that there are no stepped fixed costs.)

Such changes in costs can be incorporated, as part of the planning process, into a **budget for revenue and costs**. This calculates total revenues and costs and shows the cost per unit and profit per unit at changed (either increased or decreased) activity levels, as shown in the Case Study which follows.

BUDGET FOR REVENUE AND COSTS, INCLUDING SEMI-VARIABLE COSTS

situation

Note: In this Case Study batches of output are treated as the units of output.

Cannit Limited makes cans for customers in the food and drink industry. The company has prepared a budget for the next quarter for one of its cans, AB24. This can is produced in batches and the budget is based on producing and selling 800 batches.

One of the customers of Cannit Limited has indicated that it may be significantly increasing its order level for can AB24 for the next quarter and it appears that activity levels of 1,000 batches and 1,500 batches are feasible.

The semi-variable costs should be calculated using the high/low method. If 2,000 batches are sold the total semi-variable cost will be £6,500 and there is a constant unit variable cost up to this volume.

Complete the table below and calculate the budgeted profit per batch of AB24 at the activity levels of 1,000 and 1,500 batches.

Batches produced and sold	**800**	**1,000**	**1,500**
	£	£	£
Sales revenue	24,000		
Variable costs:			
• Direct materials	4,400		
• Direct labour	6,800		
• Overheads	4,800		
Semi-variable costs:	4,100		
• Variable element			
• Fixed element			
Total cost	20,100		
Total profit	3,900		
Profit per batch (to 2 decimal places)	4.88		

solution

- Sales revenue is £30.00 per batch (£24,000 ÷ 800 batches)
- Direct materials are £5.50 per batch (£4,400 ÷ 800)
- Direct labour is £8.50 per batch (£6,800 ÷ 800)
- Overheads are £6.00 per batch (£4,800 ÷ 800)

Each of these can be multiplied by 1,000 and 1,500 to give the revenue and costs at these activity levels as they all vary directly with output.

The semi-variable cost is split between the amounts for fixed and variable costs by using the high/low method:

	high output	2,000	batches	*£6,500
less	low output	800	batches	£4,100
equals	difference	1,200	batches	£2,400

*from text at the start of the Case Study

- The amount of the variable cost per batch is £2.00 (£2,400 ÷ 1,200 batches)
- The amount of the fixed cost is £2,500 (at 800 batches £4,100 – [800 x £2.00])

The schedule of revenue and costs completed for activity levels of 1,000 and 1,500 batches is as follows:

Batches produced and sold	**800**	**1,000**	**1,500**
	£	£	£
Sales revenue	24,000	30,000	45,000
Variable costs:			
• Direct materials	4,400	5,500	8,250
• Direct labour	6,800	8,500	12,750
• Overheads	4,800	6,000	9,000
Semi-variable costs:	4,100		
• Variable element		2,000	3,000
• Fixed element		2,500	2,500
Total cost	20,100	24,500	35,500
Total profit	3,900	5,500	9,500
Profit per batch (to 2 decimal places)	4.88	5.50	6.33

Service businesses

Whilst this Case Study has used the schedule of revenue and costs for a manufacturing business, the same format can be used for a service business. For example, a bus company could budget revenues and costs on the basis of miles travelled, and a hospital could budget revenues and costs on the basis of the number of bed nights.

BUDGETED CONTRIBUTION

Many budgets are set out in such a way as to show the **contribution** to fixed overheads. Contribution, which is **selling price less variable cost**, is an important factor in short-term decision-making and is discussed fully on page 218.

The Case Study which follows shows how a business has gathered its budgeted or standard information and uses this to calculate its costs and contribution per unit, and to calculate a budgeted profit or loss.

MURRAY MANUFACTURING: BUDGETED CONTRIBUTION

situation

Murray Manufacturing Limited makes a single product, the MM6. It has prepared budgeted/standard information for the next financial year, as follows:

	MM6
Sales revenue (£)	137,500
Direct materials (£)	35,000
Direct labour (£)	23,750

The company expects to produce and sell 25,000 units of MM6.
Budgeted fixed overheads are £42,950.

The company directors ask you to prepare information to show the budgeted contribution per unit of MM6 sold, and the company's budgeted profit or loss for the year.

solution

You present your budgeted information in the form of a table, as follows (with working notes shown):

	MM6	
Selling price per unit	£5.50	£137,500 ÷ 25,000 units
Less: variable costs per unit		
Direct materials	£1.40	£35,000 ÷ 25,000 units
Direct labour	£0.95	£23,750 ÷ 25,000 units
Contribution per unit	£3.15	£5.50 - (£1.40 + £0.95)
Sales volume (units)	25,000	
Total contribution	£78,750	£3.15 x 25,000 units
Less: fixed overheads	£42,950	
Budgeted profit	£35,800	£78,750 - £42,950

The table provides useful information for the directors who can see the budgeted information on a per unit basis. From this they can consider the effects of any changes they are able to make regarding sales volume, revenues and costs.

BUDGETS AND VARIANCES

A variance is the budgeted/standard cost or revenue minus the actual cost or revenue.

A particular feature of budgets is their use as a method of cost and revenue control. This is done by comparing the budgeted cost or revenue with the actual cost or revenue of the output in order to establish the variance, ie

budgeted cost or revenue	*minus*	**actual cost or revenue**	*equals*	**variance**

Variances can be either **favourable** (F) or **adverse** (A):

- **favourable variances**
  - a favourable cost variance is where actual costs are lower than budgeted costs
  - a favourable revenue variance is where actual revenues are higher than budgeted revenues
  - a favourable profit from operations is where actual profit is higher than budgeted profit
- **adverse variances**
  - an adverse cost variance is where actual costs are higher than budgeted costs
  - an adverse revenue variance is where actual revenues are lower than budgeted revenues
  - an adverse profit from operations is where actual profit is lower than budgeted profit

management by exception

The control systems of a business will set down procedures for acting on variances, but only for significant variances. This type of system is known as **management by exception**, ie acting on variances that are exceptional. Managers will normally work to **tolerance limits** – a tolerance limit is an acceptable percentage variance on the budgeted amount. If a cost or revenue exceeds the tolerance limit, the variance will be significant and investigative action will need to be taken.

For example, the budgeted labour cost for a production department is £50,000 a month, with a tolerance limit of 5 per cent set. If labour costs in any one month exceed £50,000 x 5%, ie a variance of £2,500, action will have to be taken and the cause investigated.

who needs to know about variances?

Variances against budgeted cost or revenue need to be reported to the **appropriate** level of management within the business. This level will depend on the significance of the variance, as shown in the two extreme examples which follow:

- **the cost of the materials used is going up by 1 per cent**

The Managing Director is unlikely to be interested – it will be up to the purchasing department to see if there is a way around the increase.

- **a major failure in an automated process has cut output by 50 per cent**

This is a matter to bring to the attention of higher management and the directors of the company: production patterns, purchasing and staffing will have to be re-organised so that production can be increased.

motivating employees

As a means of motivating employees, budgets are an example of **responsibility accounting.** Managers and supervisors are made responsible for the costs and revenues of their section but, in order to be effective, managers must participate in the budget-setting process. As a method of motivation, budgets can be seen by employees as either a 'carrot' or a 'stick', ie as a form of encouragement to achieve the amounts set, or as a form of punishment if pre-determined costs are exceeded or sales revenues not achieved.

reporting and investigating variances

The variances for the cost elements and sales revenues are summarised on a **budget report.** Such reports reconcile the budgeted cost and the actual cost for each cost element (materials, labour, expenses and overheads) and the budgeted revenues, and show the variances. An example of a budget report is shown below.

	Budget	Actual	Variance	Favourable (F) or Adverse (A)
Units sold	145,000	145,000		
	£000	*£000*	*£000*	
Sales revenue	870	899	29	F
Less costs:				
Direct materials	200	170	30	F
Direct labour	260	260	0	0
Variable overheads	280	320	40	A
Profit from operations	130	149	19	F

A budget report shows the variances for each cost element and revenue by comparing the budget amount with the actual amount – from the budget report on the previous page:

- cost variance: direct materials £200,000 – £170,000 = £30,000 favourable (F)
- cost variance: direct labour £260,000 – £260,000 = £0, ie no variance, so '0' (zero) is shown in the variance column
- cost variance: variable overheads £280,000 – £320,000 = £40,000 adverse (A)
- revenue variance: sales revenue £870,000 – £899,000 = £29,000 favourable (F), because actual revenue is better than the budget

The effect of variances on profit from operations is that:

- favourable cost variances increase profit
- adverse cost variances reduce profit
- favourable revenue variances increase profit
- adverse revenue variances reduce profit

In the budget report the cost and revenue variances are reconciled to the profit from operations variance, ie the net amount of the variances for costs and revenues is equal to the profit from operations variance – £19,000 favourable in the example on the previous page.

The order for investigating variances shown by the budget report is usually as follows:

- large variances – favourable and adverse
- other adverse variances
- any remaining favourable variances

Note that small variances may not be worth investigating – the cost of the investigation might outweigh the benefits.

The variances need to be investigated by the appropriate level of management:

- less significant variances are dealt with by managers and supervisors
- significant variances need to be referred to a higher level of management who will decide what further investigation is required

Note that constant adverse or favourable variances need to be investigated as the budgeted costs and revenues may have been set incorrectly.

reporting cycle

For budget reports to be used effectively it is essential that employees are trained to record information accurately about actual costs and revenues. The quality of the information must be:

- accurate
- timely
- in the appropriate format, highlighting the major features

The reporting cycle of the budget report will depend on the time periods used. For example, if a business establishes budget reports on the basis of monthly – or four-weekly – periods, then variances are likely to be reported within the first two weeks of the next period – often in the form of a computer report from the finance department. Generally a senior manager will call a meeting at a fixed point in each period – with the staff responsible for the costs and revenues – in order to review variances from the previous period.

revision of budgets

At regular intervals – annually, or more often – the budgeted costs and revenues need to be revised to take note of:

- cost increases caused by inflation, which will affect materials, labour and overheads (although not necessarily to the same extent)
- changes to the specifications and quality of materials, eg an improvement in quality may lead to less wastage and easier, faster, production
- changes to work practices, eg an increase in automation may lead to reduced labour costs, or the employment of different grades of employees
- changes to selling prices, which may be limited by what others are charging for similar products

controllable and non-controllable costs and revenues

When investigating variances, it is important to appreciate that not all of the costs and revenues can be controlled directly by managers and supervisors in the short term.

Period costs, such as the cost of rent paid on the premises is outside the control of the Purchasing Manager – the rent being negotiated by the Administration Manager. Nevertheless, a proportion of rent will be included amongst the budgeted cost of overheads.

By contrast, the Purchasing Manager has control over product costs, such as the cost of materials (unless there is a world price – eg for coffee or crude oil – over which he or she can have no influence).

Thus we can distinguish between:

- **controllable costs** – costs and revenues which can be influenced by the manager/supervisor
- **non-controllable costs** – costs which cannot be influenced by the manager/supervisor in the short term

Note that, in the longer-term, all costs and revenues are controllable. For example, a business may decide to move to premises where the rent is cheaper, or to close its operations at one location, or even – in the extreme – to cease trading altogether.

MONITORING OF BUDGET REPORTS

A business or organisation using budgets will monitor the outcomes by comparing the budgeted amounts set with the results that actually occurred. An outline of the monitoring process is shown in the diagram below.

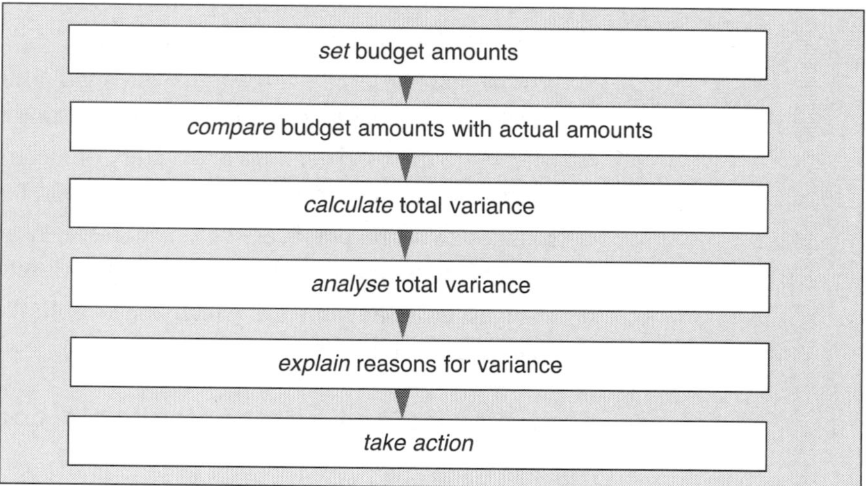

FIXED AND FLEXIBLE BUDGETS

fixed budgets

A fixed budget remains the same whatever the level of activity.

A **fixed budget** is set at the beginning of the time period for planning purposes and then adhered to and monitored, whatever the circumstances – ie the budgeted figures do not change. Fixed budgets are useful in situations where circumstances are stable – for example, a departmental budget for a school or a college, where a set amount of money is allowed for buying stationery each year.

flexible budgets

A flexible budget changes with the level of activity and takes into account different cost behaviour patterns.

In reality, situations do change. For example, the sales revenue can vary quite widely from the figure set in the budget: a new product can be more successful than expected – or it can be a complete disaster. In either case the budgeted figures for sales revenue (and production costs too) will be wide of the mark. The answer is to use a **flexible budget**, which is altered for control purposes to vary in line with the **level of activity** of a business – ie with output of products sold or services provided. By doing this the right costs and revenues are matched and variances can be calculated.

A business may therefore prepare a flexible budget to show different levels of activity. For example, if production is at 80 per cent of the expected amount, then the budget is 'flexed' to 80 per cent and appropriate variances calculated.

flexible budgets – sales revenue, variable and fixed costs

When calculating sales revenue and variable costs for a flexible budget, the revenue or cost per unit is unchanged – it is the total revenue/cost that is 'flexed' to the level of activity. For example, direct materials at £2 per unit: with a budget for 10,000 units, the budgeted cost is £20,000; if the actual performance is 12,000 units, the flexed budget cost is £24,000.

The other costs of making a product or providing a service – the overheads – fall into two categories:

- fixed overheads, eg the rent of a factory
- variable overheads, eg unit costs of telephone calls

The important point to note is that, when preparing a flexible budget, fixed overheads will not change due to changes in the level of output, but they may change due to price (eg the rent is increased). **For an increase in fixed overheads, it is the actual cost that is compared with the budget figure.**

Case Study

PREPARING FOR ASSESSMENT: FLEXIBLE BUDGETS

situation

You work as an Accounts Assistant for Exbury Ltd, a manufacturing business.

Exbury Ltd budgeted to manufacture and sell 10,000 units of product 10EX for the year ended 31 December. However, due to an increase in demand it was able to manufacture and sell 12,000 units.

You are to complete the following table to show a flexed budget and the resulting variances against this budget for the year. Show the actual variance amount, for sales revenue and each cost, in the column headed 'Variance'.

Note:

- Adverse variances must be denoted with a minus sign or brackets
- Enter 0 where any figure is zero

	Original budget	Flexed budget	Actual	Variance
Units sold	10,000	12,000	12,000	
	£000	*£000*	*£000*	*£000*
Sales revenue	250		290	
Less costs:				
Direct materials	80		90	
Direct labour	110		140	
Fixed overheads	30		35	
Profit from operations	30		25	

solution

You complete the table as follows:

	Original budget	Flexed budget	Actual	Variance
Units sold	10,000	12,000	12,000	
	£000	*£000*	*£000*	*£000*
Sales revenue	250	300	290	–10
Less costs:				
Direct materials	80	96	90	6
Direct labour	110	132	140	–8
Fixed overheads	30	30	35	–5
Profit from operations	30	42	25	–17

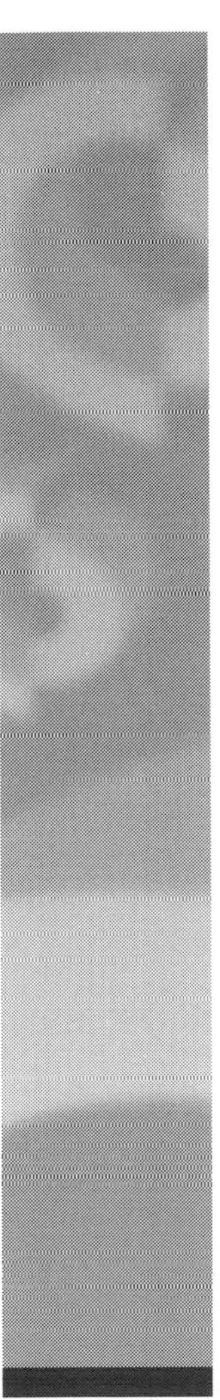

Working notes

- The budget is flexed from 10,000 to 12,000 units. This is 20 per cent increase (2,000/10,000 x 100).

- The budget figures for sales revenue, direct materials and direct labour are all increased by 20 per cent to give the amount for the flexed budget. For example, sales revenue £250,000 x 1.2 = £300,000. Note that variable overheads would be flexed in the same way.

- For fixed overheads, the actual figure of £35,000 is used. The increase from the budget figure of £30,000 shows an adverse variance of £5,000.

- The variance column is completed and the total variance, here £17,000 adverse, is reconciled with the change in profit from operations from that shown by the flexed budget to the actual figure.

What information does the flexed budget tell us?

- Impact on profit

  As the actual profit of £25,000 is £17,000 less than the flexed budget profit of £42,000, the managers of the business will wish to identify which variance has had the greatest impact on decreasing profit from operations. Here, sales revenue is the largest adverse variance and the cause of this will need to be investigated.

- Causes of variances

  There are a number of reasons for variances – as discussed in more detail in the next section. For example, the flexed budget and actual figures show a favourable variance of £6,000 for direct materials. This could be caused by factors such as a decrease in materials prices, less wastage or materials, or a change of specifications to use cheaper materials.

CAUSES OF VARIANCES

Budgeted/standard costs and revenues are set in order to give individual departmental managers, who are responsible for aspects of the business' output, suitable targets to aim for. When actual costs are compared with budgeted costs, an investigation can be carried out to find out the causes of the variances and to see what can be done about them for the future. Note, in particular, the way in which variances are calculated down to a responsibility level of an individual employee, or a small section within the business – **responsibility accounting**.

The main causes of variances are listed on the next page.

Direct materials	Adverse	Favourable
increase in materials prices	✓	
decrease in materials prices		✓
cheaper materials used		✓
more expensive materials used	✓	
more materials wasted	✓	
fewer materials wasted		✓
theft of materials	✓	
change to cheaper specifications		✓
change to more expensive specifications	✓	
Direct labour		
increase in pay	✓	
reduction in pay		✓
more efficient use of labour		✓
less efficient use of labour	✓	
higher paid grade of labour used	✓	
lower paid grade of labour used		✓
Overheads		
increase in price	✓	
reduction in price		✓
stepped fixed cost	✓	
more expensive supplier	✓	
cheaper supplier		✓
Sales revenue		
increase in selling price		✓
decrease in selling price	✓	
increase in number sold		✓
decrease in number sold	✓	

Note the following examples of inter-relationship within variances, referred to as **sub-variances**:

- an adverse direct material variance may be resolved by
  - reducing the amount of materials wasted (material usage variance), or
  - buying the materials at a cheaper price (material price variance), or
  - training staff so that materials are used more efficiently (material usage variance)

- an adverse direct labour variance may be resolved by
  - training staff to work more efficiently (labour efficiency variance), or
  - using labour at a lower grade of pay (labour rate variance), or
  - reorganising the production process so that staff work more efficiently (labour efficiency variance)
- an adverse fixed overhead variance may be resolved by
  - buying from cheaper suppliers (eg telephones, electricity, gas), or
  - more efficient use of overheads (eg sub-letting part of the premises), or
  - making changes to the production process (eg by reviewing the balance between labour work and machine work)

Chapter Summary

- Budgets are based on pre-determined costs and revenues set in advance.
- Budgeted/standard costs and revenues are set for:
  - sales revenue
  - direct materials
  - direct labour
  - overheads
  - profit from operations (sales revenue minus direct materials, direct labour and production overheads)
- Budgets are part of the decision-making, planning and control processes of a business or organisation.
- A knowledge of the behaviour of costs enables:
  - identification of the amounts of fixed and variable costs within a semi-variable cost
  - preparation of budgets for revenue and costs
  - identification of the break-even point
- Variances are used as a method of cost and revenue control. Variances can be either favourable (F) or adverse (A), and are acted upon if they are significant.
- Fixed budgets are set at the beginning of the time period and then adhered to and monitored whatever the circumstances.
- Flexed budgets are altered to vary in line with the level of activity.
- There are a number of reasons why variances occur and, often, there is an inter-relationship (sub-variance) within variances – eg an adverse direct material variance may be resolved by reducing wastage or by buying at a cheaper price.

Key Terms

budget	a financial plan for a business or organisation that is prepared in advance
profit from operations	sales revenue minus direct materials, direct labour and overheads
high/low method	method used to identify the amounts of fixed and variable costs within total costs
budget for revenue and costs	budget which shows the calculation of total cost, total profit, cost per unit, and profit per unit at particular levels of output
variance	budgeted cost or revenue minus actual cost or revenue
favourable variance	where actual costs are lower than budgeted costs, or where actual revenues are higher than budgeted revenues
adverse variance	where actual costs are higher than budgeted costs, or where actual revenues are lower than budgeted revenues
controllable costs	costs which can be influenced by the manager/supervisor
non-controllable costs	costs which cannot be influenced by the manager/supervisor in the short term
fixed budget	budget which remains the same whatever the level of activity
flexible budget	budget which changes with the level of activity and takes into account different cost behaviour patterns

Activities

7.1 The Accounts Supervisor of Nerca Manufacturing Limited has provided you with the following information:

- at 10,000 units of output, total costs are £50,000
- at 15,000 units of output, total costs are £65,000

You are to use the high/low method to identify the amount of fixed costs. The supervisor tells you that there is a constant unit variable cost up to this volume, and that there are no stepped fixed costs.

7.2 Boxster Limited makes boxes for customers in the food and drink industry. The company has prepared a budget for the next quarter for one of its boxes, BB4. This box is produced in batches and the budget is based on selling and producing 1,000 batches.

One of the customers of Boxster Limited has indicated that it may be significantly increasing its order level for box BB4 for the next quarter and it appears that activity levels of 1,200 batches and 2,000 batches are feasible.

The semi-variable costs should be calculated using the high/low method. If 3,000 batches are sold the total semi-variable cost will be £7,500 and there is a constant unit variable cost up to this volume.

Complete the table below and calculate the budgeted profit per batch of BB4 at the different activity levels.

Batches produced and sold	**1,000**	**1,200**	**2,000**
	£	£	£
Sales revenue	35,000		
Variable costs:			
• Direct materials	7,500		
• Direct labour	10,500		
• Overheads	6,000		
Semi-variable costs:	4,500		
• Variable element			
• Fixed element			
Total cost	28,500		
Total profit	6,500		
Profit per batch (to two decimal places)	6.50		

7.3 The budget for direct labour is £10,800; the actual cost is £12,200. The budget for direct materials is £4,600; the actual cost is £4,350.

Which **one** of the following statements is correct?

(a)	direct labour variance £1,400 adverse; direct materials variance £250 adverse	
(b)	direct labour variance £1,400 favourable; direct materials variance £250 favourable	
(c)	direct labour variance £1,400 adverse; direct materials variance £250 favourable	
(d)	direct labour variance £1,400 favourable; direct materials variance £250 adverse	

7.4 The budget for direct labour is £15,900; the actual cost is £14,800. The budget for direct materials is £8,200; the actual cost is £8,650.

Which **one** of the following statements is correct?

(a)	direct labour variance £1,100 adverse; direct materials variance £450 adverse	
(b)	direct labour variance £1,100 favourable; direct materials variance £450 favourable	
(c)	direct labour variance £1,100 adverse; direct materials variance £450 favourable	
(d)	direct labour variance £1,100 favourable; direct materials variance £450 adverse	

7.5 A budget for 8,000 units of output shows a direct materials cost of £17,400 and a direct labour cost of £12,600. Actual output is 9,000 units.

Which **one** of the following gives the correct figures for the flexed budget?

(a)	direct materials £19,575; direct labour £14,175	
(b)	direct materials £19,575; direct labour £12,600	
(c)	direct materials £17,400; direct labour £14,175	
(d)	direct materials £17,400; direct labour £12,600	

7.6 The budget for 10,000 units of output shows a fixed overheads cost of £20,200. Actual output is 12,000 and the actual cost of fixed overheads is £21,000.

For the flexed budget identify whether the following statements are true or false by putting a tick in the relevant column of the table below.

Flexed budget	**True**	**False**
Fixed overheads are shown in the flexed budget at a cost of £24,240		
Fixed overheads are shown in the flexed budget at a cost of £21,000		
Fixed overheads are shown in the flexed budget at a cost of £20,200		
There is a fixed overheads variance of £800 adverse		
There is a fixed overheads variance of £2,040 adverse		
There is no fixed overheads variance		

7.7 Identify the correct variance from the causes of variances given by putting a tick in the relevant column of the table below.

Cause of variance	**Adverse**	**Favourable**
Increase in material prices		
Fewer materials are wasted		
Cheaper materials are used		
Theft of materials		
An increase in direct labour pay		
More efficient usage of direct labour		
Overtime is paid to direct labour		
A cheaper electricity supplier is used for the fixed overhead		
Selling prices are increased		
An increase in the number of units sold		

7.8 You work as an Accounts Assistant for Onslow Limited, a manufacturing business.

You have been given the original budget costs and the actual performance for last month for product O14. Actual output was 90 per cent of budgeted output.

(a) Complete the table below to show a flexed budget and the resulting variances against the budget. Show the actual variance amount, for each cost, in the column headed 'variance'.

Note:

- Adverse variances must be denoted with a minus sign or brackets.
- Enter 0 where any figure is zero.

	Original budget	**Flexed budget**	**Actual**	**Variance**
Output level	100%	90%	90%	
	£	£	£	£
Direct materials	4,700		5,200	
Direct labour	10,800		8,900	
Fixed overheads	4,100		4,500	
Total	19,600		18,600	

(b) Which **one** of the following might have caused the variance for direct materials?

(a) An increase in material prices	
(b) More efficient use of materials	
(c) A decrease in material prices	
(d) Fewer material wasted	

7.9 Wyvern Ltd budgeted to manufacture and sell 30,000 units of product WV10 for the year ending 31 December. However, due to a shortage of raw materials it was only able to manufacture and sell 27,000 units.

(a) Complete the following table to show a flexed budget and the resulting variances against this budget for the year. Show the actual variance amount, for sales revenue and each cost, in the column headed 'Variance'.

Note:

- Adverse variances must be denoted with a minus sign or brackets.
- Enter 0 where any figure is zero.

	Original budget	**Flexed budget**	**Actual**	**Variance**
Units sold	30,000	27,000	27,000	
	£000	*£000*	*£000*	*£000*
Sales revenue	1,800		1,650	
Less costs:				
Direct materials	550		500	
Direct labour	340		297	
Fixed overheads	650		645	
Profit from operations	260		208	

(b) Referring to your answer for part (a), which **one** of the variances has had the greatest impact in increasing the profit from operations?

(a) Sales revenue	
(b) Direct materials	
(c) Direct labour	
(d) Fixed overheads	

7.10 Perran Ltd budgeted to manufacture and sell 22,000 units of product P14 for the year ending 31 December. However, due to an increase in demand it was able to manufacture and sell 27,500 units.

(a) Complete the following table to show a flexed budget and the resulting variances against this budget for the year. Show the actual variance amount, for sales revenue and each cost, in the column headed 'Variance'.

Note:

- Adverse variances must be denoted with a minus sign or brackets.
- Enter 0 where any figure is zero.

	Original budget	**Flexed budget**	**Actual**	**Variance**
Units sold	22,000	27,500	27,500	
	£000	*£000*	*£000*	*£000*
Sales revenue	1,400		1,875	
Less costs:				
Direct materials and direct labour	300		360	
Variable overheads	500		645	
Fixed overheads	420		480	
Profit from operations	180		390	

(b) Which **one** of the following might have caused the variance for direct materials and direct labour?

(a) An increase in material prices	
(b) More efficient use of direct labour	
(c) A increase in employees' pay	
(d) More material wasted	

7.11 Excalibur Limited, a manufacturing business, has prepared budgeted information for three of its products, EX27, EX45 and EX67 for the next financial year.

Product	**EX27**	**EX45**	**EX67**
Sales revenue (£)	57,600	93,600	81,000
Direct materials (£)	20,250	41,400	42,750
Direct labour (£)	17,550	19,800	18,750

The company expects to produce and sell 9,000 units of EX27 and 12,000 units of EX45. The budgeted sales demand for EX67 is 25% greater than that of EX45. Budgeted fixed overheads are £33,845.

Complete the table below (to two decimal places) to show the budgeted contribution per unit of EX27, EX45 and EX67 sold, and the company's budgeted profit or loss for the year from these products.

	EX27 *(£)*	**EX45** *(£)*	**EX67** *(£)*	**Total** *(£)*
Selling price per unit				
Less: variable costs per unit				
Direct materials				
Direct labour				
Contribution per unit				
Sales volume (units)				
Total contribution				
Less: fixed overheads				
Budgeted *profit/loss				

* delete as appropriate

7.12 Excalibur Limited, a manufacturing business, has budgeted to manufacture 10,000 units of product EX94 last month. However, due to an increase in demand, it was able to manufacture 11,200 units.

(a) Complete the table below to show a flexed budget and the resulting variances against this budget for the month. Show the actual variance amount for each cost in the column headed 'Variance'.

Note:

- Adverse variances must be denoted with a minus sign or brackets.
- Enter 0 where any figure is zero.

	Original budget	**Flexed budget**	**Actual**	**Variance**
Units sold	10,000	11,200	11,200	
	£	£	£	£
Raw material A1	3,200		3,925	
Raw material A4	1,250		1,325	
Skilled labour	4,850		5,060	
Unskilled labour	1,225		1,440	
Variable overheads	4,025		4,310	
Fixed overheads	5,740		6,140	
Total costs	20,290		22,200	

(b) Which **one** of the following might have caused the variance for skilled labour?

(a) A increase in employees' pay	
(b) A reduction in employees' pay	
(c) A higher paid grade of labour used	
(d) Less efficient use of skilled labour	

8 Short-term decisions

this chapter covers...

In this chapter we see how cost accounting information is used to help a business or organisation to make short-term decisions. The techniques we will look at include:

- *break-even analysis*
- *margin of safety*
- *target profit*
- *profit-volume (contribution-sales) analysis*
- *limiting factors*
- *'special order' pricing*

These techniques make use of the principles of marginal costing, which have been covered in Chapter 6.

SHORT-TERM DECISIONS

what is meant by short-term decisions?

By short-term decisions we mean those actions which will affect the costs and revenues of a business or organisation over the next few weeks and months, up to a maximum of one year ahead. Long-term decisions – see Chapter 9 – affect the costs and revenues of future years. For example, an ice-cream manufacturer might make the following decisions:

- **short-term** – 'we have to increase production over the summer months in order to meet higher sales'
- **long-term** – 'we need to build a production line so that we can make the new Veneto range of ice creams that we are developing'

types of short-term decisions

The decisions that we will be looking at include:

- Break-even analysis, where the break-even point is the output level (units manufactured or services provided) at which the sales revenue is just enough to cover all the costs. Break-even analysis answers questions such as:
  - what output do we need in order to break-even?
  - at current levels of output we are above break-even, but how safe are we?
  - we have to make a profit of £1,000 per week; what level of output do we need to achieve this?
  - what is the effect on profit if we sell more than we think?
- Limiting factors, where there is a shortage which affects output. Limiting factors include a shortage of materials, skilled labour, machine hours, etc. Once the limiting factor has been identified, the effect of the constraint on output can be minimised in order to achieve the best results for the business or organisation. A knowledge of limiting factors answers questions such as:
  - there is a shortage of materials this week – shall we produce Product Exe or Product Wye?
  - until we complete the training programme we have a shortage of skilled labour; how best can we use the skilled labour that we have available?
  - one of the machines has broken down; both of our products need machine hours – which product takes priority?
- Marginal costing is used in short-term decision-making to identify the

fixed and variable costs that are required to make a product or to provide a service. Once these are known questions about pricing can be answered:

- if we increase prices, sales revenues are expected to fall but how will our profit be affected?
- if we decrease prices, sales revenues are expected to increase but how will our profit be affected?
- a potential customer wants to buy our product but at a lower price than we usually charge; how will our profit be affected?

what information is needed?

Decision-making, both in the short-term and long-term, is concerned with the future and always involves making a choice between alternatives. To help with decision-making it is important to identify **relevant (avoidable) costs** and **irrelevant (unavoidable) costs**.

Relevant costs are those costs that are changed by a decision.

Irrelevant costs are those costs that are not affected by a decision.

In order to make a decision, information is needed about costs and revenues:

- **future costs and revenues**
  - it is the expected future costs and revenues that are relevant
  - past costs and revenues are only useful in so far as they provide a guide to the future
  - costs already spent (called **sunk costs**) are irrelevant to decision-making
- **differential costs and revenues**
  - only those costs which alter as a result of decision-making are relevant and are avoidable costs
  - where costs are the same for each alternative, they are irrelevant and are unavoidable costs
  - thus any cost that changes when a decision is made is a relevant cost

In the short-term, a business or organisation always attempts to make the best use of existing resources. This involves focusing on the relevant costs and revenues that will change as a result of a decision being made, such as:

- selling prices
- variable costs and the variable element of semi-variable costs
- contribution per unit of output, which is selling price minus variable cost
- marginal cost, which is the cost of producing one extra unit of output

Fixed period costs and the fixed element of semi-variable costs are irrelevant in decision-making as they do not alter in short-term decision-making, eg the rent of a car factory is most likely to be the same when 11,000 cars are produced each year instead of 10,000 previously. Although, remember that, in the long-term, all costs are variable. Also, note that, in the long term, all costs are relevant and avoidable – for example, if a business decided to stop production and cease to trade.

reporting decisions

With decision-making – both short- and long-term – it is essential that the costing information of estimated costs and revenues is reported to managers, or other appropriate people, with **professional competence**, in a clear and concise way. **Professional competence** is an **ethical principle** which requires accounting staff to maintain their professional knowledge and skill in order to provide a competent, professional service to employers and clients.

The information reported should include recommendations which are supported by well-presented reasoning. The decisions will not be taken by the person who has prepared the information, but the decision-makers will be influenced by the recommendations of the report. Remember that managers, and other appropriate people, do not always have an accounting background, so any form of presentation must be set out with professional competence and should use as little technical accounting terminology as possible.

Methods of presentation include:

- verbal presentations
- written reports/emails/memorandums

Both of these require a similar amount of preparation; the steps are:

- plan the report
- check that the plan deals with the tasks set
- be aware of the context in which the report is written
- express the report, verbal or written, in clear and concise English

written reports

The written report should include:

- an introduction, which sets out the task or the problem
- the content of the report, which explains the steps towards a solution and may include accounting calculations
- a conclusion, which includes a recommendation of the decision to be taken
- an appendix, which can be used to explain fully the accounting calculations, and to detail any sources of reference consulted

In this chapter we will see two written reports on short-term decisions which make recommendations – see pages 229 and 235. The next chapter includes an example of a report for a long-term decision.

verbal presentations

A verbal presentation requires the same professional competence in preparation and content as a written report and is probably the more difficult to present. Accordingly, verbal presentations often include support material in the form of handouts or computer presentations. Such material can be used to explain accounting data and to make key points and recommendations.

COSTS, CONTRIBUTION AND PROFIT

To help with short-term decision-making, costs are classified by their behaviour as either variable costs or fixed costs (with semi-variable costs being split between their fixed and variable elements). For example, a car manufacturer will need to identify:

- the variable product costs of each car
- the total fixed period costs of running the business over the period

When the manufacturer sells a car it receives the selling price, which covers the variable costs of the car. As the selling price is greater than the variable costs there will also be an amount of money – the contribution – available to pay off the fixed period costs incurred. The contribution formula (which we have seen in Chapter 6) is:

selling price per unit *less* variable cost per unit = contribution per unit

It follows that the difference between the sales income and the variable costs of the units sold in a period is the **total contribution** that the sales of all the units in the period make towards the fixed costs of the business.

A business can work out its profit for any given period from the total contribution and fixed costs figures:

total contribution *less* total fixed costs = profit

A statement of profit or loss (income statement) can be prepared in the following format:

		£
	Sales revenue	x
less	Variable costs	x
equals	Contribution	x
less	Fixed costs	x
equals	PROFIT	x

BREAK-EVEN

Break-even is often referred to as CVP (cost, volume, profit) analysis because we look at the costs of output, the volume of output, and the profit made.

Break-even is the point at which neither a profit nor a loss is made.

The break-even point is the output level (units manufactured or services provided) at which the sales revenue is just enough to cover all the costs. Break-even is the point at which the profit (or loss) is zero. The output level can be measured in a way that is appropriate for the particular business or organisation – either units of output or sales revenue. The break-even formula is:

$$\frac{\textit{fixed costs (£)}}{\textit{contribution per unit (£)}} = \textit{number of units to break-even}$$

The formula for break-even in sales revenue is:

break-even point (units of output) x selling price per unit

This can also be calculated using the profit-volume (PV) ratio – see page 225.

In order to use break-even analysis, we need to know:

- selling price (per unit)
- costs of the product
  - variable costs (such as materials, labour) per unit
  - overhead costs, and whether these are fixed or variable
- limitations, such as maximum production capacity, maximum sales

The Case Study of Fluffy Toys Limited which follows shows how the break-even point can be worked out.

Case Study

FLUFFY TOYS LIMITED: BREAK-EVEN

situation

Fluffy Toys Limited manufactures soft toys and is able to sell all that can be produced. The variable product costs (materials and direct labour) of each toy are £10 and the selling price is £20 each. The fixed period costs of running the business are £5,000 per month. How many toys need to be produced and sold each month for the business to cover its costs, ie to break-even?

solution

This problem can be solved by calculation, by constructing a table, or by means of a graph. Which method is used depends on the purpose for which the information is required:

- the **calculation method** is quick to use and is convenient for seeing the effect of different cost structures on break-even point
- the **table method** shows the amounts of fixed and variable costs, sales revenue, and profit at different levels of production
- the **graph method** is used for making presentations – for example, to the directors of a company – because it shows in a visual form the relationship between costs and sales revenue, and the amount of profit or loss at different levels of production

Often the calculation or table methods are used before drawing a graph. By doing this, the break-even point is known and suitable scales can be selected for the axes of the graph in order to give a good visual presentation.

calculation method

The contribution per unit is:

	selling price per unit	£20
less	variable costs per unit	£10
equals	contribution per unit	£10

Each toy sold gives a contribution (selling price less variable costs) of £10. This contributes towards the fixed costs and, in order to break-even, the business must have sufficient £10 'lots' to meet the fixed costs. Thus, with fixed costs of £5,000 per month, the break-even calculation is:

$$\frac{\textit{fixed costs (£)}}{\textit{contribution per unit (£)}} = \frac{\textit{£5,000}}{\textit{£10}} = \textit{500 toys each month}$$

The break-even point is:

- in units of output, 500 toys each month
- in sales revenue, £10,000 each month (500 toys x £20)

table method

Units of output	Fixed costs A	Variable costs B	Total cost C	Sales revenue D	Profit/(loss)
			A + B		D – C
	£	£	£	£	£
100	5,000	1,000	6,000	2,000	(4,000)
200	5,000	2,000	7,000	4,000	(3,000)
300	5,000	3,000	8,000	6,000	(2 000)
400	5,000	4,000	9,000	8,000	(1,000)
500	5,000	5,000	10,000	10,000	nil
600	5,000	6,000	11,000	12,000	1,000
700	5,000	7,000	12,000	14,000	2,000

graph method

A graphical presentation uses money amounts as the common denominator between fixed costs, variable costs, and sales revenue.

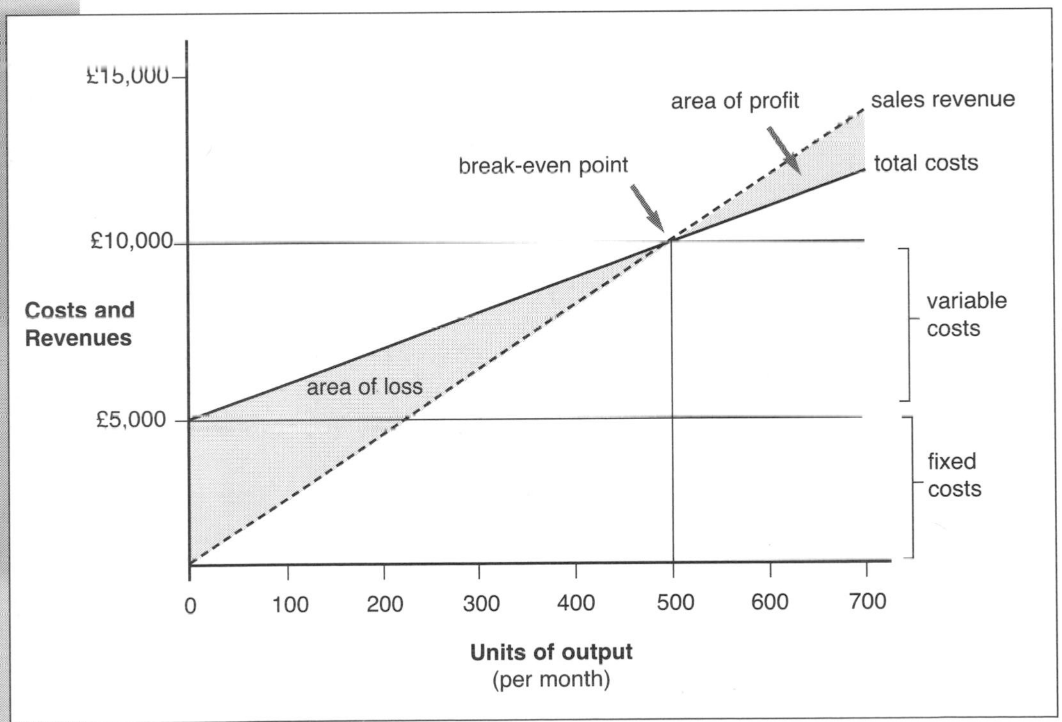

notes to the graph

- With a break-even graph, it is usual for the vertical axis to show money amounts; the horizontal axis shows units of output/sales.
- The sales revenue and total costs lines are straight.
- The fixed costs are unchanged at all levels of output, in this case they are £5,000 (but there might be stepped fixed costs).
- The variable costs commence, on the vertical axis, *from the fixed costs amount*, not from 'zero'. This is because the cost of producing zero units is the fixed costs.
- The fixed costs *plus* the variable costs form the *total costs* line.
- The point at which the total costs and sales revenue lines cross is the break-even point.
- From the graph we can read off the break-even point both in terms of units of output, 500 units on the horizontal axis, and in sales revenue, £10,000 on the vertical axis.
- The 'proof' of the break-even chart is:

		£
	Sales revenue (500 units at £20 each)	10,000
less	Variable costs (500 units at £10 each)	5,000
equals	Contribution	5,000
less	Fixed costs	5,000
equals	PROFIT/LOSS	nil

INTERPRETATION OF BREAK-EVEN

When interpreting break-even, it is all too easy to concentrate solely on the break-even point. The graph, for example, tells us much more than this: it also shows the profit or loss at any level of output/sales revenue contained within the graph. To find this, simply measure the gap between sales revenue and total costs at a chosen number of units, and read the money amounts off on the vertical axis (above break-even point it is a profit; below, it is a loss). For example, the graph in the Case Study above shows a profit or loss at:

- 700 units = £2,000 profit
- 200 units = £3,000 loss

Break-even analysis, whether by calculation, by table, or by graph, can be used by all types of businesses and organisations. For example, a shop will wish to know the sales it has to make each week to meet costs; a sports centre will wish to know the ticket sales that have to be made to meet costs; a club or society might wish to know how many raffle tickets it needs to sell to meet the costs of prizes and of printing tickets.

Once the break-even point has been reached, the **additional** contribution forms the profit. For example, if the business considered in the Case Study above was selling 650 toys each month, it would have a total contribution of 650 x £10 = £6,500; of this the first £5,000 will be used to meet fixed costs, and the remaining £1,500 represents the profit (which can be read off the break-even graph). This can be shown by means of a statement of profit or loss as follows:

		£
	Sales revenue (650 units at £20 each)	13,000
less	Variable costs (650 units at £10 each)	6,500
equals	Contribution (to fixed costs and profit)	6,500
less	Monthly fixed costs	5,000
equals	PROFIT FOR MONTH	1,500

BREAK-EVEN: MARGIN OF SAFETY

The margin of safety is the amount by which sales exceed the break-even point. Margin of safety can be expressed as:

- a number of units
- a sales revenue amount
- a percentage, using the following formula

$$\frac{\textit{current output} - \textit{break-even output}}{\textit{current output}} \times \frac{100}{1} = \textit{percentage margin of safety}$$

worked example – margin of safety

In the Case Study earlier in this chapter, Fluffy Toys Limited, (pages 219-222), if current output is 700 units, while the break-even point is 500 units, the margin of safety is:

- 200 units (ie 700 – 500)
- £4,000 of sales revenue (ie 200 units at £20 each)
- 29 per cent, ie $\frac{700 - 500}{700} \times \frac{100}{1}$

In interpreting this margin of safety we can say that production/sales can fall by these values before the business reaches break-even point and ceases to make a profit.

Margin of safety is especially important in times of recession as it expresses to management the amount of the 'cushion' which current production/revenue gives beyond the break-even point. Where there is a comparison to be made between two or more products, each with different margins of safety, the product with the highest margin of safety is looked on favourably; however, margin of safety is only one factor in decision-making.

BREAK-EVEN: TARGET PROFIT

A further analysis of break-even is to calculate the production and sales revenue in order to give a certain amount of profit – the **target profit.** This is calculated as:

$$\frac{\textit{fixed costs (£) + target profit (£)}}{\textit{contribution per unit (£)}} = \textit{number of units of output}$$

The sales revenue to achieve the target profit is calculated as:

number of units of output x sales revenue per unit (£) = target sales revenue (£)

Thus, if Fluffy Toys Limited (see the Case Study on pages 219-222) required a profit of £2,000 per month, the calculation is:

$$\frac{£5{,}000 + £2{,}000}{£10} = \textit{700 units of output, with a sales revenue of £14,000*}$$

* 700 units x £20 each = £14,000

This target profit can then be shown by means of a statement of profit or loss as follows:

		£
	Sales revenue (700 units at £20 each)	14,000
less	Variable costs (700 units at £10 each)	7,000
equals	Contribution (to fixed costs and profit)	7,000
less	Monthly fixed costs	5,000
equals	TARGET PROFIT FOR MONTH	2,000

Target profit can also be calculated by making use of the profit-volume (contribution-sales) ratio (see next page).

BREAK-EVEN: PROFIT-VOLUME ANALYSIS

The profit-volume (PV) ratio analyses the relationship between the amount of contribution and the amount of the value of sales. It is often referred to as the contribution-sales (CS) ratio. PV ratio is calculated as:

$$\frac{\text{contribution (£)}}{\text{selling price (£)}} = \text{profit-volume ratio}$$

The ratio, or percentage, can be calculated on the basis of a single unit of production or for the whole business. Note that the higher the PV ratio, the better for the business.

In break-even analysis, if fixed costs are known, we can use the PV ratio to find the sales revenue at which the business breaks-even, or the sales revenue to give a target profit.

worked example – profit-volume analysis

Referring back to the Case Study (Fluffy Toys Limited), the PV ratio (on a per unit basis) is:

$$\frac{\text{contribution (£)}}{\text{selling price (£)}} = \frac{£10^{*}}{£20} = 0.5 \text{ or } 50\%$$

* selling price (£20) – variable costs (£10) = contribution £10

Fixed costs are £5,000 per month, so the sales revenue needed to break-even is:

$$\frac{\text{fixed costs (£)}}{\text{PV ratio}} = \frac{£5{,}000}{0.5 \text{ (see above)}} = \underline{£10{,}000}$$

As the selling price is £20 per toy, we can get back to the break-even in units of output as follows: £10,000 ÷ £20 = 500 units

If the directors of Fluffy Toys Limited wish to know the sales revenue that must be made to achieve a target profit of £2,000 per month, the PV ratio is used as follows:

$$\frac{\text{fixed costs + target profit}}{\text{PV ratio}} = \text{required level of sales}$$

$$\frac{£5{,}000 + £2{,}000}{0.5} = \underline{£14{,}000}$$

As the selling price is £20 per toy, we can get to the units of output as follows:

£14,000 ÷ £20 = 700 units to achieve a target profit of £2,000.

WHEN TO USE BREAK-EVEN ANALYSIS

Break-even analysis is often used:

before starting a new business

The calculation of break-even point is important in order to see the sales revenue needed by the new business in order to cover costs, or to make a particular level of profit. The feasibility of achieving the level can then be considered by the owner of the business, and other parties such as the Bank Manager.

when making changes

The costs of a major change will need to be considered by the owners and/or managers. For example, a large increase in production will, most likely, affect the balance between fixed and variable costs. Break-even analysis will be used as part of the planning process to ensure that the business remains profitable.

to measure profits and losses

Within the limitations of break-even analysis, profits and losses can be estimated at different levels of output from current production. Remember that this can be done only where the new output is close to current levels and where there is no major change to the structure of costs.

to answer 'what if?' questions

Questions such as 'what if sales revenue falls by 10 per cent?' and 'what if fixed costs increase by £1,000?' can be answered – in part at least – by break-even analysis. The effect on the profitability of the business can be seen, subject to the limitations noted earlier. A question such as 'what if sales revenue increases by 300 per cent?' is such a fundamental change that it can only be answered by examining the effect on the nature of the fixed and variable costs and then re-calculating the break-even point.

to evaluate alternative viewpoints

There are often different ways of production; this is particularly true of a manufacturing business. For example, a product could be made:

- either, by using a labour-intensive process, with a large number of employees supported by basic machinery
- or, by using expensive machinery in an automated process with very few employees

In the first case, the cost structure will be high variable costs (labour) and low fixed costs (depreciation of machinery). In the second case, there will be low variable costs and high fixed costs. Break-even analysis can be used to examine the relationship between the costs which are likely to show a low break-even point in the first case, and a high break-even point in the second. In this way, the management of the business is guided by break-even analysis; management will also need to know the likely sales revenues, and the availability of money with which to buy the machinery.

LIMITING FACTORS

Limiting factors (or scarce resources) are those aspects of a business which restrict output.

Examples of limiting factors include:

- availability of materials
- availability of skilled labour
- availability of machine hours
- finance
- the quantity of the output which can be sold – whether a manufactured product or a service

At any one time there is usually one main limiting factor. It is essential to minimise its effect by optimising resources and maximising profit. After one limiting factor has been dealt with, another one then affects the business – for example, once a shortage of materials has been resolved, the limiting factor might well become a lack of skilled labour.

Where a business sells more than one product, under normal circumstances it will be best to switch output to the product that gives the highest contribution in relation to sales revenue (the contribution sales ratio). For example, a company makes two products, X and Y, with the following costs and revenues:

	Product	**X** £	**Y** £
	Selling price per unit	100	200
less	Variable costs per unit	60	140
equals	Contribution per unit	40	60

With no limiting factors, the company should concentrate on making and selling product X. The reason for this is that the contribution sales ratio is 40 per cent (£40 ÷ £100) when compared with product Y, where it is 30 per cent (£60 ÷ £200).

Where there is a limiting factor, for example the availability of skilled labour, a business will switch production to the product which gives the highest contribution from each unit of the limiting factor (eg contribution per direct labour hour). Thus the key to dealing with limiting factors is to:

maximise the contribution per unit of limiting factor

Following this rule will always maximise profits. Where there is a maximum level of output for the selected product, this product should be produced to the full if possible, and any units of limiting factors which remain unused should be 'spilled over' to the next best product. This is illustrated in the Case Study which follows.

Case Study

SOUND SYSTEMS LIMITED: LIMITING FACTORS

situation

Sound Systems Limited is a small company which makes reproduction radios to 1930s' designs (but with year 21st century sound quality). Two models are made – the 'Windsor' and the 'Buckingham'. Both products require skilled direct labour which cannot be increased in the short term. Demand for the company's products is increasing rapidly and, while the company is taking steps to train new employees, the Managing Director is unsure of the 'mix' of products that should be produced each week.

Costs and revenues are as follows:

	Product	**Windsor** £	**Buckingham** £
	Selling price per unit	50	100
less	Variable costs per unit	30	70
equals	Contribution per unit	20	30

- each radio takes two direct labour hours to make
- the number of direct labour hours available each week is 260
- the weekly fixed costs of the business are £2,000
- demand for the Windsor model is currently 100 radios per week, and for the Buckingham it is 80 radios per week

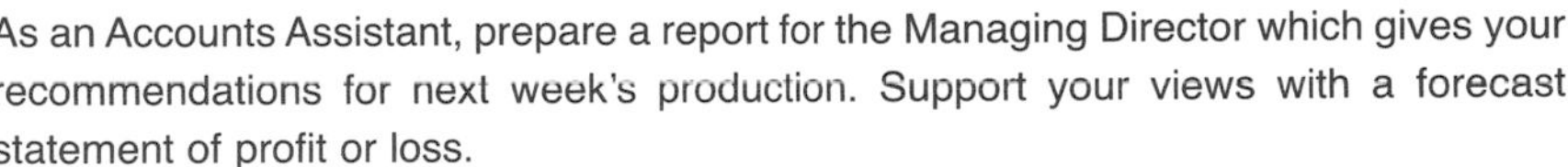

As an Accounts Assistant, prepare a report for the Managing Director which gives your recommendations for next week's production. Support your views with a forecast statement of profit or loss.

solution

Without taking into account the limiting factor of direct labour, the better model for the company to produce is the Windsor, because this gives a higher contribution sales ratio:

- Windsor: £20 contribution on £50 of sales = CS ratio of 40 per cent
- Buckingham: £30 contribution on £100 of sales = CS ratio of 30 per cent

However, as direct labour is the limiting factor, the company should maximise the contribution from each hour of direct labour:

- Windsor: contribution per direct labour hour £20 ÷ 2 hours = £10
- Buckingham: contribution per direct labour hour £30 ÷ 2 hours = £15

To make best use of the limiting factor, the company should produce all of the Buckingham model that can be sold, ie 80 per week. This will utilise 160 direct labour hours (80 units x 2 hours per unit). The remaining 100 direct labour hours (260 hours less 160 hours) will be used to produce 50 of the Windsor model (50 units x 2 hours per unit).

Report for Managing Director:

REPORT

To: Managing Director

From: Accounts Assistant

Date: Today

Production of Windsor and Buckingham models

Introduction

- You asked for my recommendations for next week's production.
- Until we have completed the training of new employees, the company has insufficient skilled labour to enable us to manufacture both models to meet customer demand. We therefore need to use our skilled labour to the best advantage of the company.

Findings

- With insufficient skilled labour we have a limiting factor (or a scarce resource). To make best use of this limiting factor to produce profits for the company, we must maximise the contribution (selling price – variable costs) from each hour of skilled labour.
- The contribution from producing each Windsor radio is £20. As this product requires two hours of skilled labour, the contribution per hour is £20 ÷ 2 hours = £10.

- The contribution from producing each Buckingham radio is £30. As this product also requires two hours of skilled labour, the contribution per hour is £30 ÷ 2 hours = £15. This is the higher contribution per labour hour.
- To make best use of the limiting factor of skilled labour, the company should produce all of the Buckingham model that can be sold, ie 80 per week. This will take 160 hours of skilled labour (80 radios x 2 hours each) and will leave 100 hours available to produce 50 of the Windsor model (50 radios x 2 hours each).
- Please note that, if this production plan is followed, insufficient Windsor models will be produced to meet demand. This may make it difficult to re-establish the Windsor in the market when full production of this model can be resumed following the completion of training of new employees.

Conclusion

- Based on the concept of maximising the contribution from each hour of skilled labour (the limiting factor), I recommend that the production for next week should be:

  80 Buckingham radios

  50 Windsor radios
- This will give a forecast statement of profit or loss for next week as follows:

		Windsor	Buckingham	Total
		£	£	£
	Sales revenue:			
	50 Windsor at £50 per unit	2,500		2,500
	80 Buckingham at £100 per unit		8,000	8,000
		2,500	8,000	10,500
less	Variable costs:			
	50 Windsor at £30 per unit	1,500		1,500
	80 Buckingham at £70 per unit		5,600	5,600
equals	Contribution	1,000	2,400	3,400
less	Fixed overheads			2,000
equals	PROFIT			1,400

Summary

The procedures for decision-making with limiting factors are:

- calculate the *contribution per unit of limiting factor* to make the decision as to which product to manufacture – the one with the higher contribution per unit of limiting factor will maximise profits
- prepare the statement of profit or loss using the *number of units of output* (and not the number of units of limiting factor)

- where there is a maximum level of output for the selected product, use as much of the limiting factor as possible, and then 'spill over' any unused limiting factor to the next best product (as in the Case Study)

Note that, where there are limiting factors, fewer of one or more products will be produced causing a shortfall in the market. It may be difficult to re-establish these products when full production can be resumed after the limiting factor has been resolved. The problem is that often customers want availability of all products and, if one isn't fully available, they won't buy the others (think of a store closing its carpet department and the effect on sales in the furniture department).

'SPECIAL ORDER' PRICING

'Special order' pricing is where a business uses spare capacity to make extra sales of its product at a lower price than its normal selling price.

'Special order' pricing, which makes use of marginal costing techniques, is normally used once the business is profitable at its current level of output, ie it has reached break-even. Additional sales – at 'special order' prices – can be made at a selling price above marginal cost, but below absorption cost. In this way, profits can be increased, provided that the additional sales are spare capacity. The key to increasing profit from additional sales is to ensure that a contribution to profit is made from the special order: the Case Study below illustrates this principle.

WYVERN BIKE COMPANY: SPECIAL ORDERS

situation

The Wyvern Bike Company produces 100 bikes a week, and sells them for £200 each. Its costs are as follows:

Weekly costs for producing 100 bikes

	£
Direct materials (£40 per bike)	4,000
Direct labour (£50 per bike)	5,000
Production overheads (fixed)	5,000
Total cost	14,000

The owner of the company has been approached by an internet sales company which wishes to buy:

- *either* 50 bikes each week at a price of £120 per bike
- *or* 100 bikes each week at a price of £80 per bike

The bikes can be produced in addition to existing production, with no increase in overheads. The special order is not expected to affect the company's existing sales. How would you advise the owner?

solution

The *absorption cost* of producing one bike is £140 (£14,000 ÷ 100 bikes). The internet sales company is offering either £120 or £80 per bike. On the face of it, with an absorption cost of £140, both orders should be rejected. However, as there will be no increase in production overheads, we can use *marginal costing* to help with decision-making.

The *marginal cost* per bike is £90 (direct materials £40 + direct labour £50), and so any contribution, ie selling price less marginal cost, will be profit:

- ***50 bikes at £120 each***

  Although below absorption cost, the offer price of £120 is above the marginal cost of £90 and increases profit by the amount of the £30 extra contribution, ie (£120 – £90) x 50 bikes = £1,500 extra profit.

- ***100 bikes at £80 each***

  This offer price is below absorption cost of £140 and marginal cost of £90; therefore there will be a fall in profit if this order is undertaken of (£80 – £90) x 100 bikes = £1,000 reduced profit.

Weekly statements of profit or loss

	Existing production of 100 units	**Existing production + 50 units @ £120 each**	**Existing production + 100 units @ £80 each**
	£	£	£
Sales revenue (per week):			
100 bikes at £200 each	20,000	20,000	20,000
50 bikes at £120 each	–	6,000	–
100 bikes at £80 each	–	–	8,000
	20,000	26,000	28,000
Less production costs:			
Direct materials (£40 per unit)	4,000	6,000	8,000
Direct labour (£50 per unit)	5,000	7,500	10,000
Production overheads (fixed)	5,000	5,000	5,000
PROFIT	6,000	7,500	5,000

The conclusion is that the first special order from the internet sales company should be accepted, and the second declined. The general rule is that, once the fixed overheads have been recovered (ie break-even has been reached), provided additional units can be sold at a price above marginal cost, then profits will increase.

COST AND REVENUE PLANNING

The principles of marginal costing can also be used to establish the effect of changes in costs and revenues on the profit of the business. Such changes include

- a reduction in selling prices in order to sell a greater number of units of output and to increase profits
- an increase in selling prices (which may cause a reduction in the number of units sold) in order to increase profits

Any change in selling prices and output will have an effect on sales revenues and on variable costs; there may also be an effect on fixed costs. The best way to show such changes is to use a columnar layout which shows costs and revenues as they are at present and then – in further columns – how they will be affected by any proposed changes. This method is used in the Case Study which follows.

Case Study

BROOKES AND COMPANY: COST AND REVENUE PLANNING

situation

Brookes and Company produces tool kits for bikes. The company produces 100,000 tool kits each year and the costs per unit of output are:

	£
Direct materials	2.20
Direct labour	2.00
Variable production overheads	0.80
Fixed production overheads	0.40
Fixed non-production overheads	0.60
	6.00

The selling price per tool kit is £10.00

The Managing Director of the business has been thinking about how to increase profits for next year. He has asked you, as an Accounts Assistant, to look at the following two proposals from a cost accounting viewpoint.

Proposal 1

To reduce the selling price of each tool kit to £9.00. This is expected to increase sales by 20,000 kits each year to a total of 120,000 kits. Apart from changes in variable costs, there would be no change in fixed costs.

Proposal 2

To increase the selling price of each tool kit to £12.00. This is expected to reduce sales by 20,000 kits each year to a total of 80,000 kits. Apart from changes in variable costs, there would be a reduction of £5,000 in fixed production overheads.

You are to write a report to the Managing Director stating your advice, giving reasons and workings. Each of the two proposals is to be considered on its own merits without reference to the other proposal.

solution

The following calculations, presented in columnar format, will form an appendix to the report to the Managing Director. Note that the three money columns deal with the existing production level, and then the two proposals.

BROOKES AND COMPANY

Cost and revenue planning for next year

	existing output (100,000 units) £	proposal 1 (120,000 units) £	proposal 2 (80,000 units) £
Sales revenue:			
100,000 units at £10.00 per unit	1,000,000		
120,000 units at £9.00 per unit		1,080,000	
80,000 units at £12.00 per unit			960,000
TOTAL REVENUE	1,000,000	1,080,000	960,000
Direct materials at £2.20 per unit	220,000	264,000	176,000
Direct labour at £2.00 per unit	200,000	240,000	160,000
Variable production overhead at £0.80 per unit	80,000	96,000	64,000
Fixed production overhead	40,000	40,000	35,000
Fixed non-production overhead	60,000	60,000	60,000
TOTAL COSTS	600,000	700,000	495,000
PROFIT	400,000	380,000	465,000

Tutorial notes:

- fixed production overheads: 100,000 units at £0.40 per unit (note £5,000 reduction under proposal 2)
- fixed non-production overheads: 100,000 units at £0.60 per unit

REPORT

To: Managing Director

From: Accounts Assistant

Date: Today

Cost and revenue planning for next year

Introduction

- You asked for my comments on the proposals for next year's production.
- I have looked at the expected profits if
  - we continue to sell 100,000 units each year at a selling price of £10.00 each
  - selling price is reduced to £9.00 per unit, with sales volume expected to increase to 120,000 units each year
  - selling price is increased to £12.00 per unit, with sales volume expected to decrease to 80,000 units each year

Report

- Please refer to the calculations sheet.
- At existing levels of production, the contribution (selling price – variable costs) per unit is:

  £10.00 – (£2.20 + £2.00 + £0.80) = £5.00 per unit x 100,000 units = £500,000

  Fixed costs total £100,000.

  Therefore profit is £400,000.
- For proposal 1, the contribution per unit is:

  £9.00 – (£2.20 + £2.00 + £0.80) = £4.00 per unit x 120,000 units = £480,000

  Fixed costs total £100,000.

  Therefore profit is £380,000.
- For proposal 2, the contribution per unit is:

  £12.00 – (£2.20 + £2.00 + £0.80) = £7.00 per unit x 80,000 units = £560,000

  Fixed costs total £95,000.

  Therefore profit is £465,000.

Conclusion

- Proposal 2 maximises the contribution from each unit of output.
- Although we expect to sell fewer units, the total contribution is greater.
- There is a small reduction in fixed costs under this proposal.
- Before proposal 2 is adopted, we would need to be sure of the accuracy of the expected fall in sales volume.

MARGINAL COSTING IN DECISION-MAKING

We have seen how marginal costing principles can be useful in short-term decision-making. Nevertheless, there are a number of points that must be borne in mind:

- **fixed period costs must be covered**

  A balance needs to be struck between the output that is sold at above marginal cost and the output that is sold at absorption cost. The overall contribution from output must cover the fixed period costs of the business and provide a profit. Overall output should be sold at a high enough price to provide a contribution equal to or greater than fixed costs.

- **separate markets for marginal cost**

  It is sensible business practice to separate out the markets where marginal cost is used. For example, a business would not quote a price based on absorption cost to retailer A and a price based on marginal cost to retailer B, when A and B are both in the same town! It would be better to seek new markets – perhaps abroad – with prices based on marginal cost.

- **effect on customers**

  One of the problems of using marginal cost pricing to attract new business is that it is difficult to persuade the customer to pay closer to, or above, absorption cost later on. Thus one of the dangers of using marginal cost is that profits can be squeezed quite dramatically if the technique is used too widely.

- **problems of product launch on marginal cost basis**

  There is great temptation to launch a new product at the keenest possible price – below absorption cost (but above marginal cost). If the product is highly successful, it could well alter the cost structure of the business. However, it could also lead to the collapse of sales of older products so that most sales are derived from output priced on the marginal cost basis – it may then be difficult to increase up prices to above absorption cost levels.

- **special edition products**

  Many businesses use marginal costing techniques to sell off older products at a keen price. For example, car manufacturers with a new model due in a few months' time will package the old model with 'special edition' features and sell it at a low price (but above marginal cost).

Chapter Summary

- Short-term decisions are those actions which will affect the costs and revenues over the next few weeks and months.

- Break-even analysis distinguishes between fixed period costs and variable product costs.

- The relationship between sales revenue, fixed costs and variable costs is used to ascertain the break-even point, by means of a calculation, a table, or a graph.

- Break-even analysis can show:
  - break-even point in units of production
  - break-even point in sales revenue
  - profit or loss at given levels of production and sales revenue

- Limiting factors (or scarce resources) are those aspects of a business which restrict output, eg availability of materials, skilled labour, machine hours. The key to dealing with limiting factors is to **maximise the contribution per unit of limiting factor**.

- 'Special order' pricing is where a business uses spare capacity to make extra sales of its product at a lower price than normal. In order to increase profits the special order selling price must be above marginal cost.

- Marginal costing principles are used in short-term decision-making for break-even, limiting factors, and 'special order' pricing.

Key Terms

relevant costs — those costs that are changed by a decision

irrelevant costs — those costs that are not affected by a decision

sunk costs — past costs which are irrelevant to decision-making

professional competence — ethical principle requiring accounting staff to maintain their professional knowledge and skill

cost behaviour — the way in which costs behave in different ways as the volume of output or activity changes

contribution selling price less variable cost

cost, volume, profit (CVP) analysis of the costs of output, the volume of output, and the profit made

break even the point at which neither a profit nor a loss is made, calculated in units of output as follows:

$$\frac{\textit{fixed costs (£)}}{\textit{contribution per unit (£)}}$$

margin of safety (%) the amount by which sales exceed the break-even point; calculated as a percentage as follows:

$$\frac{\textit{current output} - \textit{break-even output}}{\textit{current output}} \times \frac{100}{1}$$

target profit (units) the output that needs to be sold to give a certain amount of profit, calculated in number of units of output as follows:

$$\frac{\textit{fixed costs (£)} + \textit{target profit (£)}}{\textit{contribution per unit}}$$

profit-volume (PV) analysis ratio which expresses the amount of contribution in relation to the amount of the value of sales:

$$\frac{\textit{contribution (£)}}{\textit{selling price (£)}}$$

PV ratio is used to calculate the sales revenue needed to break-even as follows:

$$\frac{\textit{fixed costs (£)}}{\textit{PV ratio}}$$

limiting factor (or scarce resources) those aspects of a business which restrict output

marginal cost the cost of producing one extra unit of output

8.1 Mike Etherton, a manufacturer of cricket bats, has the following monthly costs:

Material cost	£8 per bat
Labour cost	£12 per bat
Selling price	£35 per bat
Fixed overheads	£12,000

You are to:

(a) Read from the graph (below) the profit or loss if 200 bats, and 1,200 bats are sold each month.

(b) Prepare a table showing costs, sales revenue, and profit or loss for production of bats in multiples of 100 up to 1,200. Does the table confirm your answer to (a)?

(c) If production is currently 1,000 bats per month, what is the margin of safety, expressed as a percentage and in units?

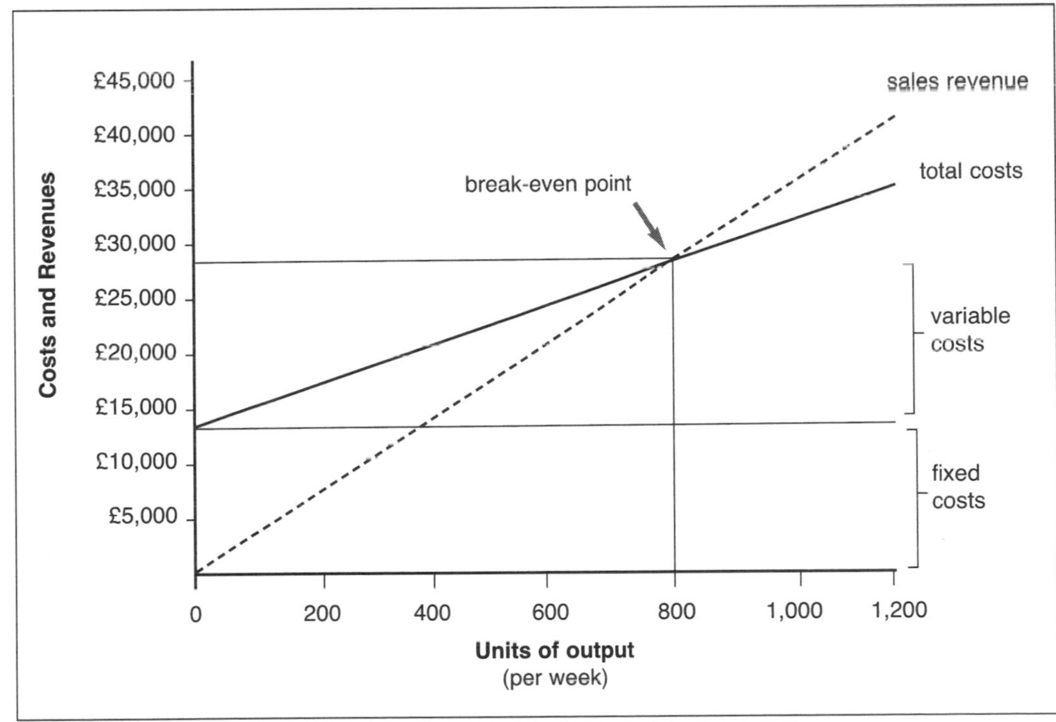

8.2 Wyvern Limited makes a product which is numbered WV5. The selling price of product WV5 is £28 per unit and the total variable cost is £16 per unit. Wyvern Limited estimates that the fixed costs per quarter associated with this product are £24,000.

(a) Calculate the budgeted breakeven, in units per quarter, for product WV5.

[ ] units

(b) Calculate the budgeted breakeven revenue, in £ per quarter, for product WV5.

£ [ ]

(c) Complete the table below to show the budgeted margin of safety in units, and the margin of safety percentage if Wyvern Limited sells 2,500 units or 4,000 units of product WV5 per quarter.

Units of WV5 sold per quarter	**2,500**	**4,000**
Margin of safety (units)		
Margin of safety percentage		

(d) If Wyvern Limited wishes to make a profit of £18,000 per quarter, how many units of WV5 must it sell?

[ ] units

(e) If Wyvern Limited reduces the selling price of WV5 by £1, what will be the impact on the breakeven point and the margin of safety per quarter, assuming no change in the number of units sold?

(a) The breakeven point will decrease and the margin of safety will increase	
(b) The breakeven point will stay the same but the margin of safety will decrease	
(c) The breakeven point will decrease and the margin of safety will stay the same	
(d) The breakeven point will increase and the margin of safety will decrease	

8.3 Riley Limited has made the following estimates for next month:

Selling price	£25 per unit
Variable cost	£10 per unit
Fixed costs for the month	£300,000
Forecast output	30,000 units
Maximum output	40,000 units

As an Accounts Assistant, you are to carry out the following tasks:

Task 1

Calculate:

- the profit-volume ratio
- the break-even point in units next month
- the break-even point in sales revenue next month
- the margin of safety in units and sales revenue at the forecast output for next month
- the number of units to generate a profit of £100,000 next month

Task 2

Calculate the profit for next month at:

- the forecast output
- the maximum output

Task 3

One of the managers has suggested that, if the selling price were reduced to £20 per unit, then sales would be increased to the maximum output.

- For this new strategy, you are to calculate:
  - the profit-volume ratio
  - the break-even point in units
  - the break-even point in sales revenue
  - the margin of safety in units and sales revenue
  - the forecast profit
- Write a report to the General Manager advising whether you believe that the new strategy should be implemented. (Use a copy of the report form in the Appendix.)

8.4 Sesame Shoes Limited manufactures shoes at its factory in Wyvern. It has three shoe ranges – the 'Madrid', the 'Paris', and the 'Rome'. The expected monthly costs and sales information for each range is as follows:

Product	'Madrid'	'Paris'	'Rome'
Sales and production units*	5,000	3,000	500
Machine hours per month	2,500	1,200	375
Total sales revenue	£150,000	£120,000	£30,000
Total direct materials	£50,000	£45,000	£10,000
Total direct labour	£25,000	£24,000	£6,000
Total variable overheads	£10,000	£9,000	£1,250

* note: a unit is a pair of shoes

The total expected monthly fixed costs relating to the production of all shoes are £72,800.

As an Accounts Assistant at Sesame Shoes Limited, you are to carry out the following tasks.

Task 1

Complete the table below to show for each product range the expected contribution per unit.

Product	'Madrid' £	'Paris' £	'Rome' £
Selling price per unit			
Less: Unit variable costs			
Direct materials			
Direct labour			
Variable overheads			
Contribution per unit			

Task 2

If the company only manufactures the 'Madrid' range, calculate the number of units it would need to make and sell each month to cover the fixed costs of £72,800.

Task 3

The breakdown of a machine used in the manufacture of shoes has reduced available machine time from 4,075 to 3,000 hours. The Finance Director asks you to calculate the contribution of each unit (pair of shoes) per machine hour.

Using the data from Task 1, complete the table below.

Product	**'Madrid'**	**'Paris'**	**'Rome'**
Contribution per unit			
Machine hours per unit			
Contribution per machine hour			

Task 4

Using the data from Task 3, calculate how many units of each of product ranges 'Madrid', 'Paris', and 'Rome' the company should make and sell in order to maximise its profits using 3,000 machine hours.

8.5 Dean Limited makes two products – A and B. Both products are made from the same type of direct materials. These materials are currently in short supply. At present the company can obtain only 500 kilos of the direct materials each week. The Production Manager seeks your guidance as to the 'mix' of products that should be produced each week. The information available is:

	Product	**A**	**B**
	Selling price per unit	£150	£200
less	Unit variable costs	£120	£150
equals	Contribution per unit	£30	£50
	Kilos of direct materials per unit	2	4
	Demand per week (in units)	200	150

The weekly fixed overheads of the business are £4,000.

As an Accounts Assistant, you are to write a report to the Production Manager giving your recommendations for next week's production. Support your views with a forecast statement of profit or loss. (Use a copy of the report form in the Appendix.)

8.6 You are an Accounts Assistant at Durning Foods Limited. The company produces ready meals which are sold in supermarkets and convenience stores. You have just received the following email from the General Manager:

EMAIL

From: General Manager

To: Accounts Assistant

Subject: Production line of Indian meals

Date: 8 October 20-8

Please prepare a cost and revenue plan for the Indian meals production line for November.

We plan to sell 36,000 meals in November and will base our projection on the cost and revenue behaviour patterns experienced during July to September.

The cost accounting records show the following for July, August and September:

DURNING FOODS LIMITED: Production line for Indian meals

Actual results for July to September 20-8

	July	**August**	**September**
Number of meals sold	33,500	31,000	34,700
	£	£	£
Direct materials	25,125	23,250	26,025
Direct labour	15,075	13,950	15,615
Direct expenses	6,700	6,200	6,940
Overheads for Indian meals production line	12,525	12,150	12,705
Other production overheads	4,000	4,000	4,000
Total cost	63,425	59,550	65,285
Sales revenue	67,000	62,000	69,400
Profit	3,575	2,450	4,115

Task 1

- Use the above information to identify the cost and revenue projections to be used in your projections.
- Use the identified cost and revenue behaviour patterns to complete the projection for November 20-8.

Task 2

After you have completed Task 1, the General Manager sends you the following email:

EMAIL

From	General Manager
To	Accounts Assistant
Subject	Production line of Indian meals
Date	14 October 20-8

Thank you for your work on the cost and revenue projections for November.

Our Buying Department has found an alternative supplier of materials – meat, rice and sauces. The buyers say that the quality is better than we use at the moment and the price is 20 per cent cheaper. However, we will need to buy in larger quantities to get such good prices. To allow for this, I would like to increase production and sales to 40,000 meals in November.

Could you please recalculate the cost and revenue projections for November 20-8 based on the increased activity and taking advantage of the cheaper prices?

Also, please calculate the break-even point in terms of the number of meals to be sold in November if we make this change. Please include a note of the margin of safety we will have.

- Use your identified cost and revenue behaviour patterns to adjust for the change in material costs and to prepare a revised projection for November 20-8 based on sales of 40,000 meals.
- Calculate the break-even point in terms of meals to be sold in November if the lower priced materials are used.
- Calculate the margin of safety, expressed as a percentage of the increased planned activity for November.

8.7 Westfield Limited makes 2,000 units of product Exe each month. The company's costs are:

Monthly costs for making 2,000 units of Exe

	£
direct materials	6,000
direct labour	4,000
production overheads (fixed)	8,000
total cost	18,000

Each unit of Exe is sold for £12.

The management of the company has been approached by a buyer who wishes to purchase:

- *either* 200 units of Exe each month at a price of £6 per unit
- *or* 500 units of Exe each month at a price of £4 per unit

The extra units can be produced in addition to existing production, with no increase in overheads. The special order is not expected to affect the company's existing sales. How would you advise the management?

8.8 Popcan Limited manufactures and sells a soft drink which the company sells at 25p per can. Currently output is 150,000 cans per month, which represents 75 per cent of production capacity. The company has an opportunity to use the spare capacity by producing the product for a supermarket chain which will sell it under their own label. The supermarket chain is willing to pay 18p per can.

Use the following information to advise the management of Popcan Limited if the offer from the supermarket should be accepted:

POPCAN LIMITED

Costs per can

	pence
Direct materials	5
Direct labour	5
Production overheads (variable)	4
Production overheads (*fixed)	6

* fixed production overheads are apportioned on the basis of current output

8.9 What is meant by the principle of professional competence?

(a)	An accounting qualification is always proof of professional competence	
(b)	The Accounts Supervisor is the person who ensures compliance with ethical principles	
(c)	Anyone with an accounting qualification can report to clients on all aspects of decision-making	
(d)	Accounting staff are required to maintain their knowledge and skills to provide a competent service	

9 Long-term decisions

this chapter covers...

In this chapter we see how cost accounting information is used to help a business to make long-term decisions. In particular, we focus on capital investment projects. For example, if we need a new photocopier for the office, shall we buy a Toshiba or a Canon model?

The main methods of capital investment appraisal are:

- *payback period*
- *discounted cash flow, also known as net present value*

We look at what capital investment appraisal involves, and then study these two methods by means of a Case Study, and make comparisons between them. Towards the end of the chapter, we look at a further capital investment appraisal method called internal rate of return.

For capital investment appraisal remember to distinguish between:

- *capital expenditure – expenditure incurred on the purchase, alteration or improvement of non-current assets, such as purchase of premises, vehicles, machinery, legal costs of buying property, delivery, installation and setting-up of a machine*
- *revenue expenditure – expenditure incurred on running costs, such as fuel for vehicles, repairs to premises, labour costs of running the business*

WHAT IS CAPITAL INVESTMENT APPRAISAL?

Capital investment appraisal enables a business to make decisions as to whether or not to invest in a particular capital investment project and, where there are alternatives, to assist in deciding in which to invest.

You will readily appreciate that, whether at home or at work, resources are limited in supply and, as a result, there is a need to use them in such a way as to obtain the maximum benefits from them. To do this it is necessary to choose between various financial alternatives available; for example, on a personal level, we have to make decisions such as:

Should I save my spare cash in a bank's instant access account, or should I deposit it for a fixed term?

Should I save up for a car, or should I buy on hire purchase?

Which make of car, within my price range, should I buy?

Should I rent a house or should I buy, taking out a mortgage?

While these decisions are personal choices, the management of businesses of all sizes are faced with making choices, as are other organisations such as local authorities and central government.

The management of any business is constantly having to make decisions on *what* goods or services to produce, *where* to produce, *how* to produce, and *how much* to produce. For each major choice to be made, some method of appraisal has to be applied to ensure that, whatever decisions are taken, they are consistent with the objectives of the organisation. This means that it is necessary to look at all the alternatives available and to choose the one that is going to give the most benefit. For example, a business may have to decide whether to replace its existing machinery with new, more up-to-date machinery. If it decides on new machinery, it then has to choose between different makes of machine and different models, each having a different cost and each capable of affecting output in a different way. The decision will affect the performance of the business – its profit or loss and its cash flow.

WHAT IS A CAPITAL INVESTMENT PROJECT?

A capital investment project is the spending of money now in order to receive benefits (or reduce costs) in future years; it is illustrated in the diagram on the next page.

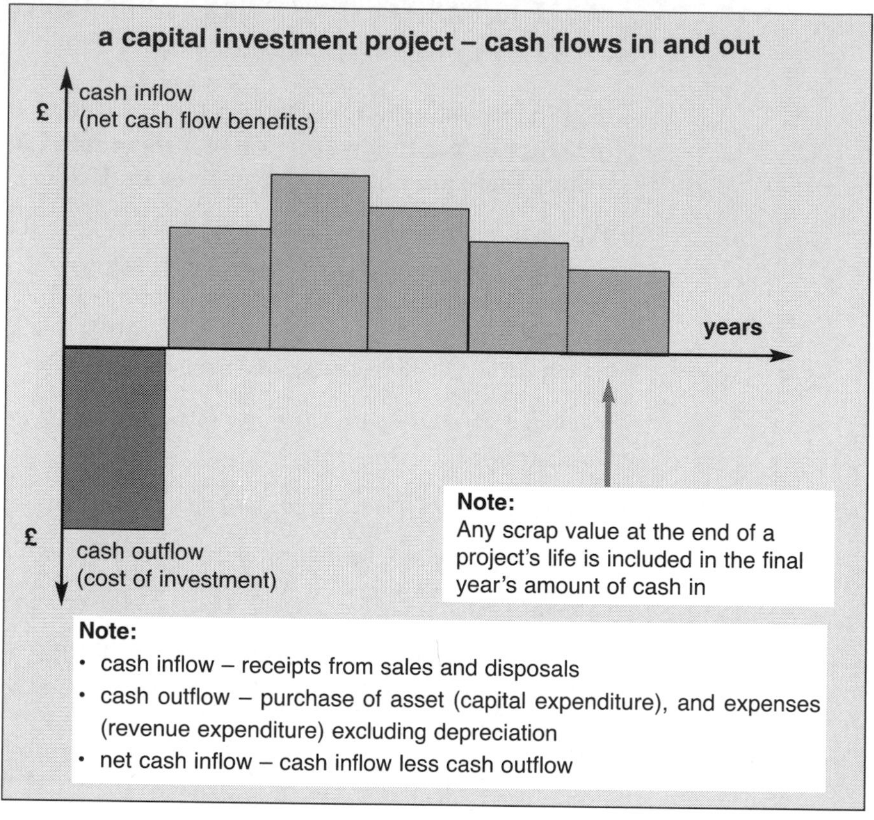

Here, the cost of the investment, or capital expenditure, is being spent at the start – either at the very beginning of the project (often stated as 'year 0'), or during the first year. The difference between these two is illustrated by the following:

- bought a new photocopier is a cash outflow at the beginning of the project
- the installation of a new production line may well incur cash outflows during the first year

The cost of the investment brings benefits in future years for as long as the project lasts. Businesses and organisations need to apply capital investment appraisal methods to ensure that the long-term decisions they make are the correct choices.

INVESTMENT APPRAISAL IN CONTEXT

As well as the cash inflows and outflows for a capital investment project, a number of other factors need to be considered before a long-term decision is made. These factors include:

- **Source of finance**. Where is the money coming from to finance the project? Is it from a cash surplus, an existing or new bank overdraft, or loans? A limited company may decide on a share or debenture (loan) issue to raise the finance for a large project. Assets such as machinery, equipment and vehicles are often financed using hire purchase and leasing.
- **Cost of capital.** All finance has a cost – invariably expressed as a rate of return. The rate of return will be different for each source of finance – from the interest foregone on cash surpluses, to that which must be paid on bank overdrafts and loans. With ordinary shares, the cost of capital is the dividend that shareholders expect to receive. Hire purchase and leasing payments include the interest cost. Note that, with variable interest rates, cost of capital may well vary during the life of a project.
- **Total estimated cost of project.** It is important to forecast accurately the total capital expenditure cost of projects. Historically, the cost of large-scale projects has often been under-estimated and the final actual cost has been much higher than anticipated, leading to financial difficulties.
- **Taxation implications.** A project will usually include both tax allowances and payments. The allowances occur when new assets – such as machinery, equipment and vehicles – are purchased; called writing down allowances, these reduce the amount of tax to be paid. However, the cost savings or increasing profits of the investment project will increase overall profitability of the business and will lead to more tax being paid.
- **Working capital requirements.** Most projects will also require an investment in working capital – inventories, receivables and payables. Thus an amount of working capital is needed at the start, and throughout the project's life. It will only be recovered at the end of the project.
- **Audit of project**. It is important to keep a regular check on costs to ensure that they are in line with the estimates. There are three separate phases that should be audited:

  – costs of bringing the project into commission ready for use

  – operational costs

  – decommissioning costs
- **Other considerations**

  Economic climate – recession or period of growth.

  Political implications – a possible change of government may affect investment decisions.

  Commissioning – the length of time that it will take for the project to be up and running.

  Training – the costs and implications of staff training.

Location – where the project is to be located, and subsequent effects on the culture of the organisation.

Capacity – effect on overall output of the organisation.

Product life cycle – the implications on the project of the stage of the company's output in the product life cycle.

Case Study

AYE OR BEE: WHICH PROJECT? MAKING THE DECISION

situation

A business is investing in a new project and has to make the choice between Project Aye and Project Bee. The initial cost and the net cash flow (cash inflow, less cash outflow, excluding depreciation) to the business have been calculated over five years for each project as follows:

	Project Aye	**Project Bee**
Initial cost at the beginning of the project	£20,000	£28,000
Net cash inflow:		
Year 1	£8,000	£10,000
Year 2	£12,000	£10,000
Year 3	£5,000	£8,000
Year 4	£4,000	£9,000
Year 5	£2,000	£9,000

- At the end of year 5, both projects will have a scrap value of £1,000; this amount is already included in the year 5 cash inflows.
- Only one project can be undertaken.
- The business requires an annual rate of return of 10 per cent on new projects.

Which project should be chosen?

solution

The two methods commonly used to appraise a capital investment project such as this are:

- payback period
- discounted cash flow

These methods will be considered in this chapter in order to help the business to make its decision. At the end of the chapter we will also look at how the internal rate of return (or discounted cash flow yield) is used in order to make a direct comparison between projects which have different amounts of capital investment at the start.

PAYBACK PERIOD

Payback is the period of time it takes for the initial cost of capital investment to be repaid from net cash inflows.

From the Case Study of Projects Aye and Bee, the cash flows and the cumulative cash flows (ie net cash flows to date) are shown in the table below. From this information it can be seen that project Aye costs £20,000 (paid out at the beginning of the project) and it is expected that the net cash flow over the first two years will equal the cost. The payback period for Project Aye is, therefore, two years, while that for Project Bee is three years. So, using payback, Project Aye is preferable because it has the shorter payback period.

	PROJECT AYE		PROJECT BEE	
Year	**Cash Flow**	**Cumulative Cash Flow**	**Cash Flow**	**Cumulative Cash Flow**
	£	£	£	£
0	–20,000	–20,000	–28,000	–28,000
1	8,000	–12,000	10,000	–18,000
2	12,000	–	10,000	–8,000
3	5,000	5,000	8,000	–
4	4,000	9,000	9,000	9,000
5	2,000	11,000	9,000	18,000

The payback period is indicated by the shading

Although these payback periods work out to exact years, they rarely do so in practice – be prepared to calculate part years in Assessments. For example, if Project Aye had an initial cost of £22,000, the payback would require £2,000 of the £5,000 cash flow in year 3. The payback period would then be 2 years + (£2,000/£5,000 x 12 months) = 2 years and 5 months (rounded up to the next month). Note that, in calculating part years, we are making the assumption that cash flows occur at an even rate throughout the year – this may not be the case for all projects – revenues (and costs) may be higher at certain times: for example, retailers are likely to have high revenues in the pre-Christmas shopping period.

The shorter the payback period the better, particularly where high technology or fashion projects are concerned – they may be out-of-date before they reach the end of their useful lives. Earlier cash flows are likely to prove more accurate estimates than later cash flows. Thus, if two projects have the same payback, the one with the greater cash flow in the early years is preferred. For example, consider two projects with a payback period of two years from the following cash flows:

	Wye	Zed
Year 1	£8,000	£12,000
Year 2	£12,000	£8,000

While both projects have the same payback period of two years, Zed is the preferred project under the payback method because of earlier cash flows.

DISCOUNTED CASH FLOW

Discounted cash flow (DCF) is a method of capital investment appraisal which recognises that money has a time value – it compares net cash flows, at their present values, with the initial cost of the capital investment to give a net present value of the capital project.

A quick example of a discounted cash flow decision is where a friend asks you to lend her £1 and offers to repay you either tomorrow, or in one year's time, which will you choose? The answer is clear: you would want the money back sooner rather than later because, if you don't intend to spend it, you can always save it in a bank where it will earn interest. Thus the rate of interest represents the time value of money.

Using £1 as an example, if it is invested with a bank at an interest rate of 10 per cent per year, it will increase as follows:

original investment	£1.00
interest at 10% on £1	£0.10
value at end of first year	£1.10
interest at 10% on £1.10	£0.11
value at end of second year	£1.21

This uses the technique of compound interest. So, with interest rates of 10 per cent per year, we can say that the future value of £1 will be £1.10 at the end of year one, £1.21 at the end of year two, and so on; thus £1 set aside now will gain in value so that, at some time in the future, we will have access to a larger sum of money. However, supposing that we were to receive £1 at the end of year one, what is it worth to us now? To find the answer to this, we need to carry out the following calculation:

$$£1 \times \frac{100}{110^*} = £0.91$$

* 100 per cent, plus the rate of interest (in this example, 10 per cent).

Therefore, if we had £0.91 now and invested it at 10 per cent per year, we would have £1 at the end of year one. We can say that the **present value** of £1 receivable in one year's time is £0.91. In the same way, £1 receivable in two years' time is £0.83, calculated as follows:

$$£1 \times \frac{100}{110} \times \frac{100}{110} = £0.83$$

We can build up a **table of present value (PV) factors** (for 10 per cent interest rate) as shown below:

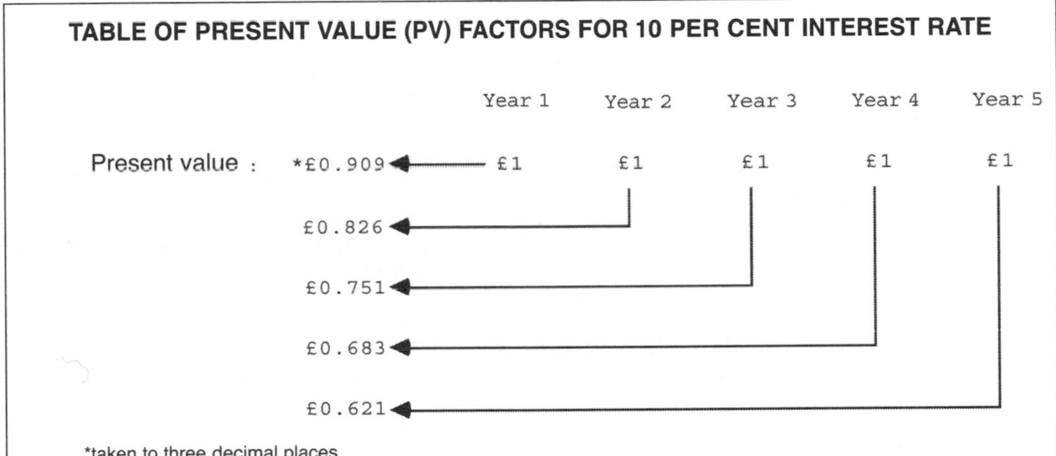

Tutorial note: there is no need to learn how to calculate present value factors – the correct factors for the interest rate used will always be given to you in Assessments; this table shows factors to three decimal places – some AAT Assessments use four decimal places for greater accuracy.

The table of factors reminds us of the basic principle that **money has a time value** and, from this, the further into the future that we expect to receive money, then the lower is its **present value.** Thus the present value (or discount) factors relate to interest rates which represent the cost of capital (ie the rate of return that the business or organisation expects on its money, or the rate of interest it has to pay when borrowing).

Let us now return to the problem of the business which has to choose between Projects Aye and Bee. We will look at this assuming, firstly, a cost of capital – or rate of return – of 10 per cent. For each project, the expected net cash flows are multiplied by the relevant factor to give the **discounted cash flow**; the difference between total discounted cash flow and the initial cost is the **net present value** of the project.

worked example – discounted cash flow calculations

Project Aye

	Cash Flow		Discount Factor		Discounted Cash Flow
	£				£
Year 0*	–20,000	x	1.000	=	–20,000
Year 1	8,000	x	0.909	=	7,272
Year 2	12,000	x	0.826	=	9,912
Year 3	5,000	x	0.751	=	3,755
Year 4	4,000	x	0.683	=	2,732
Year 5	2,000	x	0.621	=	1,242
			Net Present Value (NPV)	=	4,913

* Year 0 is the beginning of the project when the initial cost is paid. Some projects such as the installation of a new production line – may well incur cash outflows during the first year.

Notes:

- The initial cost is shown as a negative because it is a cost, whereas the net cash inflows are positive amounts. Net Present Value (NPV) is the net sum of all the discounted cash inflows and outflows.
- When using discount factors, the assumption is made that cash flows occur at the end of each year – apart, that is, from the Year 0 initial cash flow.

Project Bee

	Cash Flow		Discount Factor		Discounted Cash Flow
	£				£
Year 0	–28,000	x	1.000	=	–28,000
Year 1	10,000	x	0.909	=	9,090
Year 2	10,000	x	0.826	=	8,260
Year 3	8,000	x	0.751	=	6,008
Year 4	9,000	x	0.683	=	6,147
Year 5	9,000	x	0.621	=	5,589
			Net Present Value (NPV)	=	7,094

Here, with a cost of capital – or rate of return – of 10 per cent, Project Bee is better, producing a considerably higher net present value than Aye. Note that both projects give a positive net present value at 10 per cent: this means that either project will be of benefit to the organisation but Bee is preferable; a negative NPV would indicate that a project should not go ahead.

Thus, using a discounted cash flow method, future cash flows are brought to their value now; this means that, the further on in time that cash flows are receivable, the lower is the net present value.

INTERNAL RATE OF RETURN

The principles of discounted cash flow can be developed further in order to calculate the capital investment appraisal method of **internal rate of return** (IRR) – this method is also known as **DCF (Discounted Cash Flow) yield**.

The internal rate of return is the rate of cost of capital at which the present value of the cash inflows exactly balances the initial investment.

In other words, it shows the cost of capital, or rate of return, percentage at which the investment 'breaks-even', ie income equals expenditure, but still applying discounted cash flow principles. The table below is an illustration of the principle of IRR.

We start with a cost of capital which gives a positive net present value – using the example of Projects Aye and Bee we saw on the previous page, a 10 per cent cost of capital for Project Aye gives a NPV of £4,913. We increase the cost of capital by one or two percentage points each time, and repeat the NPV calculation (workings not shown here) until, eventually, it becomes negative. This is shown as follows (note that net present value is calculated from column A minus column B):

PROJECT AYE			
Cost of Capital*	**Present Value of Cash Flow**	**Capital Investment**	**Net Present Value**
* *or rate of return*	£	£	£
	A	B	A – B
10%	24,913	–20,000	4,913
12%	23,946	–20,000	3,946
14%	23,025	–20,000	3,025
16%	22,177	–20,000	2,177
18%	21,375	–20,000	1,375
20%	20,619	–20,000	619
22%	19,915	–20,000	–85
24%	19,242	–20,000	–758

For Project Aye, the net present value that balances the present value of cash flow with the initial investment lies between 20% and 22% – closer to 22% than 20%, so we can call it approximately 22% (an answer to the nearest one or two percentage points is acceptable for most long-term decisions).

For Project Bee, the calculations are as follows, starting with the net present value of £7,094 at a 10 per cent cost of capital – seen earlier on page 256.

PROJECT BEE			
Cost of Capital* ** or rate of return*	**Present Value of Cash Flow** £	**Capital Investment** £	**Net Present Value** £
	A	B	A – B
10%	35,094	–28,000	7,094
12%	33,423	–28,000	5,423
14%	31,859	–28,000	3,859
16%	30,430	–28,000	2,430
18%	29,099	–28,000	1,099
20%	27,848	–28,000	–152
22%	26,717	–28,000	–1,283
24%	25,628	–28,000	–2,372

For Project Bee, the net present value that balances the present value of cash flow with the initial investment lies between 18% and 20% – closer to 20% than 18%, so we can call it approximately 20%.

commenting on internal rate of return

Returning to the two projects, Aye and Bee, the tables show that the IRR for Aye is approximately 22%, and for Bee's approximately 20%. Thus, Aye gives a higher IRR – this is the preferred capital investment. The reason for this is that Aye requires a lower capital expenditure than Bee, and the timing of its cash flows is weighted towards the earlier years.

The decision-making criteria when using IRR is to:

- accept the higher IRR, where there is a choice between different capital investments
- accept projects with an IRR greater than either the cost of borrowing (the cost of capital), or the rate of return specified by the business or organisation

Thus, while IRR can be compared between two (or more) different capital investments, it can also be applied to cost of capital. In the example we have followed in this chapter, the cost of capital is 10%. The business could have gone ahead with either investment. However, if the cost of capital had been 20%, Project Bee would have been rejected and Project Aye accepted – although the 2% margin above the cost of capital is very tight.

basic internal rate of return calculations

Calculating the internal rate of return from given data can be carried out:

- by applying discount factors to net cash flows, or
- by using the technique of interpolation, or
- by assessing net cash flows against internal rate of return percentages

By **applying discount factors** we must rework the discounted cash flow calculations at various cost of capital percentages until we find the percentage where net present value is closest to zero: this percentage is the internal rate of return. This technique is shown in the table on the previous page.

Interpolation is a technique which estimates a value between two known values, for example:

- a low cost of capital percentage, which gives a positive net present value figure
- a high cost of capital percentage, which gives a negative net present value figure

The interpolation formula allows us to estimate the cost of capital percentage – between the two percentages given – at which net present value is zero: this is the internal rate of return.

The formula for interpolation uses the two known values as follows:

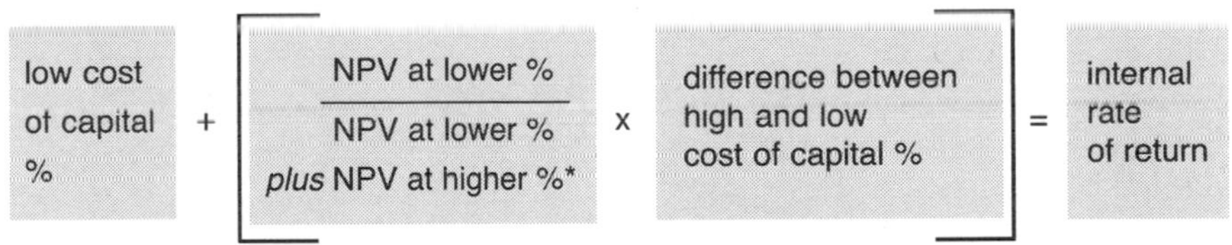

*ignore negative signs

For example:

- at 10% cost of capital, net present value is £4,913
- at 24% cost of capital, net present value is –£758

Inserting these figures into the formula:

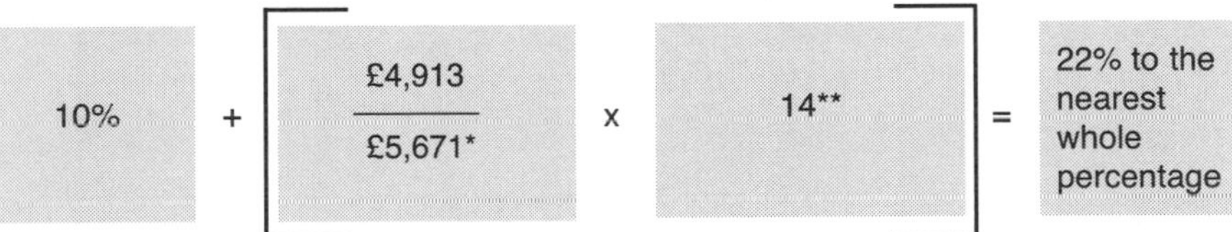

*£4,913 + £758, ie the total amount of the change from positive to negative

**24 – 10 = 14

Note that here, by using two percentages quite far apart, ie 10% and 24%, the answer is slightly less accurate than if we had used closer percentages, eg 20% and 22%. As a result, the IRR is slightly increased – in practice, the small difference is unlikely to affect the investment appraisal decision.

When assessing **net cash flows** against given percentages we can use discount factors, if they are available, for the given percentages. As an alternative we can calculate compound interest factors for each percentage. Each year's factor is divided into the cash flow for that year and the resultant amounts (which are the same as from using discount factors) are used to rework the net cash flow in order to give a net amount. The net amount for each percentage will be zero, or positive, or negative. The percentage with the net amount closest to zero is the internal rate of return. The use of compound interest factors is demonstrated in the Case Study below.

All IRR estimates are based on discounted cash flow techniques – both discount factors and compound interest factors apply the same techniques to the cash flows.

Case Study

CALCULATING THE INTERNAL RATE OF RETURN

situation

Magnus Limited has the following net cash flows for a project:

Year 0 *£000*	**Year 1** *£000*	**Year 2** *£000*	**Year 3** *£000*
–360	100	150	250

The directors of Magnus Limited ask you to assess the approximate internal rate of return (IRR) against the following percentages.

10%
15%
20%

solution

When assessing net cash flows (which are undiscounted) against given IRR percentages the technique to be followed is:

1. Calculate* a compound interest table (here to two decimal places) for each given percentage:

	10%	**15%**	**20%**
Year 0	1.00	1.00	1.00
Year 1	1.10	1.15	1.20
Year 2	1.21	1.32	1.44
Year 3	1.33	1.52	1.73

*eg, for 10%, 1.00 x 1.10 = (year 1) x 1.10 = 1.21 (year 2) x 1.10 = 1.33 (year 3)

Note that the use of discount factors is an alternative way to the compound interest method – both methods apply the same techniques to the cash flows.

2. Apply the factors from the table into the net cash flows (in £000s) as follows:

10%

$$\frac{-360}{1} + \frac{100}{1.1} + \frac{150}{1.21} + \frac{250}{1.33}$$

$$= -360 + 90.91 + 123.97 + 187.97 = \underline{42.85 \text{ net present value}}$$

15%

$$\frac{-360}{1} + \frac{100}{1.15} + \frac{150}{1.32} + \frac{250}{1.52}$$

$$= -360 + 86.96 + 113.64 + 164.47 = \underline{5.07 \text{ net present value}}$$

20%

$$\frac{-360}{1} + \frac{100}{1.20} + \frac{150}{1.44} + \frac{250}{1.73}$$

$$= -360 + 83.33 + 104.17 + 144.51 = \underline{-27.99 \text{ net present value}}$$

3. *Conclusion*

The given percentage which is closest to the internal rate of return for this project is 15%, ie the percentage at which the project 'breaks even' (ie NPV is closest to zero). The exact percentage is just a little higher than 15% but for most purposes 15% is close enough. Provided the cost of borrowing for Magnus Limited is lower than 15%, then the project – on the basis of the IRR calculations – is worthwhile.

Neither 10%, which gives a positive NPV, nor 20%, which gives a negative NPV, are close to the IRR of this project.

CAPITAL INVESTMENT APPRAISAL: COMPARISON

It is unlikely that a business will rely on one investment appraisal method only, instead two or three methods might need to be satisfied before a capital project is given the go-ahead.

Let us suppose that the business, having to choose between projects Aye and Bee applied the following criteria:

- a payback of two-and-a-half years maximum
- a positive net present value at a 10 per cent cost of capital
- an internal rate of return that exceeds a 10 per cent cost of capital

How do the two projects compare? A comparison table summarises the results:

Appraisal method	Notes	Company policy	Project Aye	Project Bee
Payback period	-	2.5 years maximum	2 years ✓	3 years ×
Net present value (NPV)	Discount at 10% cost of capital	Accept if positive	£4,913 ✓	£7,094 ✓
Internal rate of return (IRR)	Discount at 10% cost of capital	Must exceed cost of capital	22% ✓	20% ✓

Overall, the table shows that Project Aye is to be preferred as it meets all of the investment criteria.

REPORTING DECISIONS

Capital investment appraisal decisions often have to be reported to managers, or other appropriate people, with professional competence, in a clear and concise way. The information should include recommendations which are supported by well-presented reasoning.

To conclude, we include a written report addressed to the General Manager on Projects Aye and Bee, which we have looked at in this chapter. The company has the following criteria: projects must have a pay-back period not exceeding two-and-a-half years, must have a positive net present value at a 10 per cent cost of capital, and must have an internal rate of return that exceeds a 10 per cent cost of capital.

REPORT

To: General Manager

From: Accounts Assistant

Date: Today

Projects Aye and Bee

Introduction

- This report applies capital investment appraisal methods to these two projects.
- In this appraisal, the cash inflows and outflows used are those that have been given.

Report

- Please refer to the calculation sheets *(tutorial note: see page 253 and page 256, summarised on page 262).*
- Both projects are acceptable from a financial viewpoint because they each return a positive net present value (NPV) at a discount rate of 10%, as follows: Project Aye £4,913; Project B £7,094. These calculations assume that net cash inflows occur at the end of each year.
- The payback periods are: Project Aye, 2 years; Project B, 3 years.
- The internal rates of return (IRR) for the projects are: Project Aye, 22%; Project B, 20%. Both of these are well above the required rate of return of 10 per cent.

Conclusion

- Project A meets both the company requirements of payback within two-and-a-half years, and a positive NPV at a 10 per cent rate of return. It also has a higher IRR than Project B.
- Project B does not meet the payback requirement, but does have a positive NPV at a 10 per cent rate of return. It has a lower IRR than Project A.
- Project A has a lower NPV than Project B. While A's initial cost is lower, so is the total discounted cash inflow – the combination of these gives a lower NPV for Project A. However, using the IRR calculation, shows Project A to be better.
- On balance, Project A is recommended:
  - lower initial cost
  - high cash inflows in the first two years
  - quick payback
  - positive NPV
  - higher IRR in relation to the company's required rate of return

Case Study

PREPARING FOR ASSESSMENT: CAPITAL INVESTMENT APPRAISAL

situation

You are an Accounts Assistant at Wyvern Limited, a company which manufactures kitchenware such as baking trays, saucepans, etc.

One of the machines in the cutting department is nearing the end of its useful life and Wyvern Ltd is considering purchasing a replacement machine.

Estimates have been made for the initial capital cost, sales revenue and operating costs of the replacement machine, which is expected to have a useful life of three years, at the end of which it will be sold for £10,000.

	Year 0 *£000*	Year 1 *£000*	Year 2 *£000*	Year 3 *£000*
Capital expenditure	50			
Disposal				10
Other cash flows:				
Sales revenue		45	65	50
Operating costs		25	30	30

The company appraises capital investment projects using a 10% cost of capital.

You have been asked to:

- complete the table below (shown in the solution) and to calculate the net present value of the proposed replacement machine (to the nearest £000)
- state whether the net present value is positive or negative
- calculate the payback period of the proposed replacement machine in years and months (partial months must be rounded up to the next month)

solution

You complete the table as follows (remember to show negative signs where appropriate, and to round money amounts to nearest £000):

	Year 0 *£000*	Year 1 *£000*	Year 2 *£000*	Year 3 *£000*
Capital expenditure	–50			
Disposal				10
Sales revenue		45	65	50
Operating costs		–25	–30	–30
Net cash flows	–50	20	35	30
PV factors	1.0000	0.9091	0.8264	0.7513
Discounted cash flows	–50	18	29	23
Net present value	20			

Tutorial note: AAT Assessments usually give the PV (present value) factors to four decimal places for greater accuracy.

- The net present value is positive.
- The payback is 1 year and 11 months (rounded up to the next month)

ie year 1 £20,000 + (year 2 £30,000/£35,000 x 12), using net cash flows.

(When calculating payback, take care to use the **net cash flows** and not the discounted cash flows.)

OTHER CONSIDERATIONS

As well as the numerical techniques that can be used for capital investment appraisal, a business must consider a number of other factors before making the final decision. These include:

- **Total implications**. The effect of the project on the business as a whole will include implications for
  - sales, with possible increases in output
  - output, with changes in techniques, eg a switch from labour-intensive to machine-intensive output
  - staff, with possible redundancies, training needs, pay structure
  - working capital required for the project
  - needs, such as premises, transport, materials
- **Cost of finance**. Possible changes in the cost of capital will have a direct effect on the viability of the project. For example, an increase in the general level of interest rates will reduce the project's overall profitability. Projects are often financed through fixed interest rate loans, or through hire purchase and leasing, thus establishing some part of the finance at fixed rates; however, invariably working capital is financed by a bank overdraft at variable rates.
- **Taxation considerations**. The project will include the implications of both tax allowances and charges. However, a change in the level of taxation will affect the viability of the project.
- **Forecasting techniques**. These can be used to answer 'what if?' questions: for example, "what if sales increase by 25 per cent?" or "what if materials costs fall by 5 per cent?" In this way, a business can see how the project is affected by changes to any of the data used in the appraisal.
- **Size of the investment**. A major project could lead to financial difficulties for a small business if cash inflows prove to be lower than expected.

Chapter Summary

- Capital investment appraisal uses a number of methods to help in management decision-making.
- The main methods are payback period and discounted cash flow.
- Internal rate of return (also known as DCF yield) is used to rank projects, while still applying the principles of discounted cash flow.
- Businesses often use a combination of appraisal methods before making long-term decisions about major projects.
- Before authorising a capital project, other considerations include:
  - total implications for the organisation
  - cost of finance, and effect of changes
  - taxation
  - forecasting techniques to answer 'what if?' questions
  - size of the investment relative to the size of the business

Key Terms

capital expenditure	expenditure incurred on the purchase, alteration or improvement of non-current assets
revenue expenditure	expenditure incurred on running costs
capital investment appraisal	enables a business to make decisions as to whether or not to invest in a particular capital investment project and, where there are alternatives, to help to assist in deciding in which to invest
cash inflow	receipts from sales and disposals
cash outflow	purchase of asset and expenses, excluding depreciation
net cash inflow	cash inflow, less cash outflow, excluding depreciation
cost of capital	the percentage cost of financing an investment – either the rate of return that the business expects on its money, or the rate of interest it has to pay when borrowing
payback period	period of time it takes for the initial cost of the capital investment to be repaid from net cash inflows
discounted cash flow	capital investment appraisal method that uses cash flows and recognises the time value of money
net present value (NPV)	the value of cash outflows and inflows for a project discounted to present-day amounts
internal rate of return (IRR)	the rate of return at which the net present value of cash inflows equals the cost of the initial investment

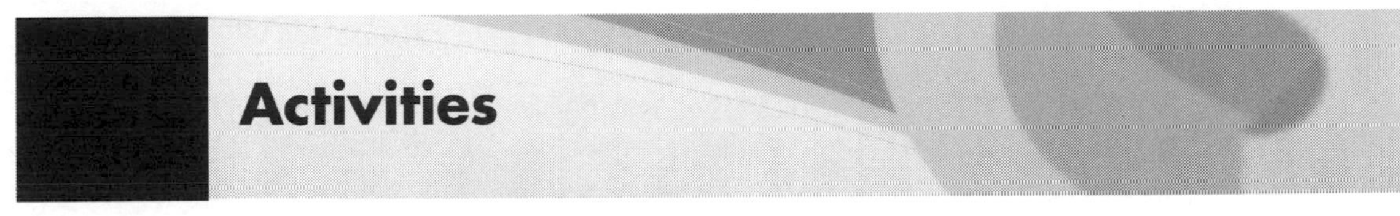

Activities

TABLE OF DISCOUNTED CASH FLOW FACTORS (to three decimal places)

Cost of capital/ rate of return	**10%**	**12%**	**14%**	**16%**	**18%**	**20%**	**22%**	**24%**
Year 1	0.909	0.893	0.877	0.862	0.847	0.833	0.820	0.806
Year 2	0.826	0.797	0.769	0.743	0.718	0.694	0.672	0.650
Year 3	0.751	0.712	0.675	0.641	0.609	0.579	0.551	0.524
Year 4	0.683	0.636	0.592	0.552	0.516	0.482	0.451	0.423
Year 5	0.621	0.567	0.519	0.476	0.437	0.402	0.370	0.341
Year 6	0.564	0.507	0.456	0.410	0.370	0.335	0.303	0.275

Tutorial note: In Assessments you will always be given the appropriate factors.

9.1 Robert Smith is considering two major capital investment projects for his company. Only one project can be chosen and the following information is available:

		Project Exe	**Project Wye**
		£	£
Initial cost at the beginning of the project		80,000	100,000
Net cash inflows, year:	1	40,000	20,000
	2	40,000	30,000
	3	20,000	50,000
	4	10,000	40,000
	5	10,000	30,000

The initial cost occurs at the beginning of the project and you may assume that the net cash inflows will arise at the end of each year. Smith requires an annual rate of return of 12 per cent, and a maximum payback period of two-and-a-half years. Neither project will have any residual value at the end of five years.

To help Robert Smith make his decision, as Accounts Assistant you are to:

- Produce numerical assessments of the two projects based on the following capital investment appraisal methods:

  (a) the payback period

  (b) the net present value

- Complete the comparison table (on the next page) and indicate whether or not each project meets the company's investment criteria.

- Advise, in a sentence, which capital investment, if either, should be undertaken, and why.

Appraisal method	**Notes**	**Company policy**	**Project Exe**	**Project Wye**
Payback period	-	2.5 years maximum		
Net present value (NPV)	Discount at 12% cost of capital	Accept if positive		
Advice to Robert Smith:				

9.2 Sesame Shoes Limited manufactures shoes at its factory in Wyvern. The company requires an annual rate of return of 10% on any new project. The Managing Director has asked you to appraise the financial effects of developing a new range of shoes. You are given the following information relating to this project.

	Year 0 *£000*	**Year 1** *£000*	**Year 2** *£000*	**Year 3** *£000*	**Year 4** *£000*	**Year 5** *£000*
Design costs	–	95	–	–	–	–
Sales revenue	–	–	60	80	100	50
Variable costs	–	–	30	40	50	23
10% Present value factor	1.000	0.909	0.826	0.751	0.683	0.621
20% Present value factor	1.000	0.833	0.694	0.579	0.482	0.402

Task 1

Calculate for the new project:

(a) The payback period.

(b) The net present value using the 10% present value factors.

Task 2

A few days after submitting your calculations to the Managing Director, she says to you:

"I have calculated the internal rate of return on the new project to be almost 20 per cent. What I don't understand is whether this is good or bad in relation to the 10 per cent return we require on new projects."

(a) Rework the calculations from Task 1(b) using the 20% present value factors. Do these show that the internal rate of return is approximately 20%?

(b) Explain the significance of the internal rate of return in relation to the return required on new projects.

9.3 What is meant by the internal rate of return (IRR) of a project?

(a) The discount factor that results in a net present value of zero	
(b) The discount factor that results in a positive net present value	
(c) The discount factor that results in a negative net present value	
(d) The discount factor that is closest to bank overdraft rates	

9.4 You are an Accounts Assistant at Durning Foods Limited. The company produces ready meals which are sold in supermarkets and convenience stores. You have just received the following email from the General Manager:

EMAIL

From: General Manager
To: Accounts Assistant
Subject: Purchase of new vehicles
Date: 10 November 20-4

We are considering the purchase and operation of our own fleet of delivery vehicles at the end of this year.

The Distribution Manager tells me that we will be able to cancel our current delivery contract and, as a result, there will be cash savings of £28,300 each year from 20-5 onwards, after taking account of the vehicle operating costs.

The vehicles will cost us £80,000 and will have a resale value of £10,000 when they are sold at the end of 20-8.

Please appraise this proposal from a financial viewpoint. I need to know the payback period and the net present value. As you know, the maximum required payback period is three years and, for net present value, we require a return of 12 per cent.

Task 1

Use the working paper on the next page to calculate the payback period and the net present value of the proposed investment. Ignore inflation and calculate all money amounts to the nearest £.

Task 2

Write a report, dated 12 November 20-4, to the General Manager evaluating the proposal from a financial viewpoint. State any assumptions you have made in your analysis. (Use a copy of the report form in the Appendix.)

DURNING FOODS LIMITED

Working paper for the financial appraisal of purchase of delivery vehicles

PAYBACK PERIOD

Year	Cash Flow	Cumulative Cash Flow
	£	£
20-4	________	________
20-5	________	________
20-6	________	________
20-7	________	________
20-8	________	________

Payback period = ______________________________
(round up to the next month)

DISCOUNTED CASH FLOW

Year	Cash Flow	Discount Factor at 12%	Discounted Cash Flow
	£		£
20-4	________	1.000	________
20-5	________	0.893	________
20-6	________	0.797	________
20-7	________	0.712	________
20-8	________	0.636	________
Net Present Value (NPV)			________

9.5 The Wyvern Bike Company is planning to introduce a new range of bikes in addition to its existing range. The company requires an annual rate of return of 12 per cent on any new project. The Managing Director has asked you, the Accounts Assistant, to appraise the financial effects of introducing the new range. You are given the following information relating to this project (see next page).

	Year 0 £000	Year 1 £000	Year 2 £000	Year 3 £000	Year 4 £000	Year 5 £000
Development costs	40	60	–	–	–	–
Sales revenue	–	–	75	90	150	100
Variable costs	–	–	30	36	60	40
12% Present value factor	1.000	0.893	0.797	0.712	0.636	0.567

Task 1

Calculate for the new project:

(a) The payback period (round up to the next month).

(b) The net present value.

Task 2

Use the data from Task 1 to prepare a report to the Managing Director on the new bike project. Your report should be based on the format shown in this chapter and will:

(a) Identify *two* additional items of information relevant to appraising this project.

(b) Make a recommendation to accept or reject the project based on its net present value.

9.6 Printpront Limited is a printing company. It needs to replace a printing press that is nearing the end of its working life.

Estimates have been made for the initial capital cost, sales income and operating costs of the replacement printing press, which is expected to have a useful life of three years, at the end of which it will be sold for £20,000.

	Year 0 £000	Year 1 £000	Year 2 £000	Year 3 £000
Capital expenditure	90			
Disposal				20
Other cash flows:				
Sales revenue		55	70	60
Operating costs		12	15	19

The company appraises capital investment projects using a 15% cost of capital.

(a) Complete the table below and calculate the net present value of the proposed replacement printing press (to the nearest £000).

	Year 0 *£000*	Year 1 *£000*	Year 2 *£000*	Year 3 *£000*
Capital expenditure				
Disposal				
Sales revenue				
Operating costs				
Net cash flows				
PV factors	1.0000	0.8696	0.7561	0.6575
Discounted cash flows				
Net present value				

Tick to show if the net present value is

	positive	
or	negative	

(b) Calculate the payback period of the proposed replacement printing press in years and months. Partial months must be rounded up to the next month.

The payback period is [ ] year(s) and [ ] months.

9.7 Marquez Limited has the following net cash flows for a project:

Year 0 *£000*	Year 1 *£000*	Year 2 *£000*	Year 3 *£000*
–900	220	350	590

The directors of Marquez Limited ask you to assess the approximate internal rate of return (IRR) against the following percentages:

4%
8%
12%

You are to use compound interest calculations, rounded to **two** decimal places, to show the internal rate of return of this project.

9.8 Excalibur Limited, a manufacturing business, has estimated the net cash flows of a project it is considering undertaking as below. The cost of capital is 10%.

(a) Complete the table below to calculate the net present value of the project (to the nearest £000). You must enter minus signs where appropriate, and round to **two** decimal places.

	Year 0 *£000*	**Year 1** *£000*	**Year 2** *£000*	**Year 3** *£000*
Net cash flows	–635	200	300	450
PV factors	1.0000	0.9091	0.8264	0.7513
Discounted cash flows				
Net present value				

(b) Based on the net present value calculated in part (a), should Excalibur accept the project?

(a) Excalibur should accept the project because the net present value is positive	
(b) Excalibur should not accept the project because the net present value is positive	
(c) Excalibur should accept the project because the net present value is negative	
(d) Excalibur should not accept the project because the net present value is negative	

(c) Complete the table below to show the net cash flows, as per part (a), and the cumulative cash flows for the project, and calculate the payback period in years and months. You must enter minus signs where appropriate in order to obtain full marks and enter whole numbers only. Partial months must be rounded up to the next month.

	Year 0 *£000*	**Year 1** *£000*	**Year 2** *£000*	**Year 3** *£000*
Net cash flows				
Cumulative cash flows				

The payback period is [ ] years and [ ] months.

continued

Excalibur requires projects to pay back within 2.0 years.

(d) Based on the payback period calculated in part (c), should Excalibur accept the project?

(a) Excalibur should accept the project because the payback period exceeds 2.0 years	
(b) Excalibur should not accept the project because the payback period exceeds 2.0 years	
(c) Excalibur should accept the project because the payback period is less than 2.0 years	
(d) Excalibur should not accept the project because the payback period is less than 2.0 years	

(e) Calculate the approximate internal rate of return (IRR) of the project in part (a).

(a) 5%	
(b) 10%	
(c) 15%	
(d) 20%	

9.9 The directors of Amit Ltd ask you to calculate the internal rate of return for a project they are planning to undertake.

The following information is available to you:

- at a cost of capital of 12%, the project gives a positive net present value of £13,870
- at a cost of capital of 24%, the project gives a negative net present value of £3,640

You are to use interpolation to calculate the internal rate of return of the project (to the nearest whole percentage).

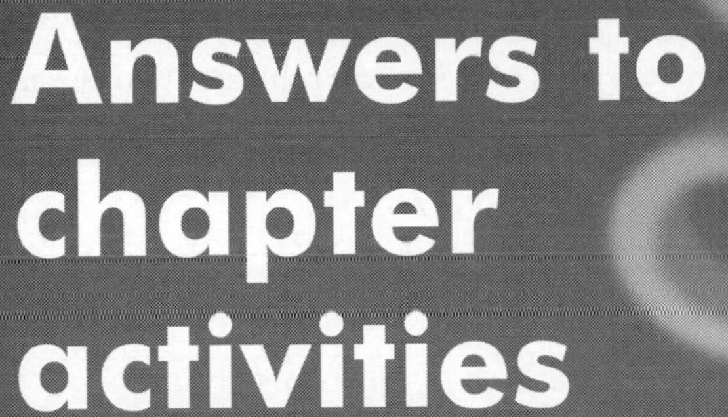

Answers to chapter activities

CHAPTER 1: AN INTRODUCTION TO COST ACCOUNTING

1.1 (d) Preparation of cost accounting information in a straightforward and honest way

1.2 **(a)**

- cost centres – segment of a business to which costs can be charged
- profit centre – segment of a business to which costs can be charged, revenue can be identified, and profit can be calculated
- investment centre – segment of a business where profit is compared with the amount of money invested in the centre
- revenue centre – segment of a business where sales revenue from the product sold or service provided is measured

(b)

Responsibility centre	**Criteria**	**Department Cee**	**Department Dee**
Cost centre	Low cost	£10,000 ✔	£12,000 X
Profit centre	High profit	£5,000 ✔	£4,000 X
Investment centre	High %	20% ✔	15% X
Revenue centre	High sales	£55,000 ✔	£35,000 X

Advice to the owner: Department Cee is performing better than Department Dee for all four of the criteria. However, both sections are earning profits which contribute to the overheads of the business, so both should continue to trade.

1.3

REPORT

To: Finance Director
From: Accounts Assistant
Date: today

Costs and revenue for last year

I report on the details of the costs and revenue for last year of each segment of the business. Details are as follows:

	Newspapers and magazines	**Books**	**Stationery**
Cost Centre	*£000*	*£000*	*£000*
• materials	155	246	122
• labour	65	93	58
• expenses	27	35	25
• total	247	374	205
Profit Centre			
Revenue	352	544	230
less Costs (see above)	247	374	205
Profit	105	170	25
Investment Centre			
Profit (see above)	105	170	25
Investment	420	850	250
Expressed as a percentage	25%	20%	10%
Revenue Centre	352	544	230

1.4 **(a)** See text, pages 16-17

(b)
- raw materials: variable
- factory rent: fixed
- telephone: semi-variable
- direct labour: variable
- indirect labour: fixed
- commission to sales staff: variable

Classifying costs by behaviour identifies them as being fixed, or semi-variable, or variable. This helps with decision making – the business might be able to alter the balance between fixed and variable costs in order to increase profits.For example, a furniture manufacturing business will have to make decisions on whether to use direct labour (variable cost) or machinery (fixed cost) for many of the production processes. The decision will be based very much on the expected level of sales, ie for lower sales it is likely to make greater use of direct labour, while for higher sales a more machine-intensive method of production might be used.

1.5

	Fixed	**Semi-variable**	**Variable**
(a) Rates of business premises	✔		
(b) Royalty paid to designer for each unit of output			✔
(c) Car hire with fixed rental and charge per mile		✔	
(d) Employees paid on piecework basis			✔
(e) Straight-line depreciation	✔		
(f) Units of output depreciation			✔
(g) Direct materials			✔
(h) Telephone bill with fixed rental and a charge for each call made		✔	
(i) Office salaries	✔		

1.6

Tubular steel	direct materials
Factory supervisor's salary	indirect labour
Wages of employee operating moulding machine	direct labour
Works canteen assistant's wages	indirect labour
Rates of factory	indirect expenses
Power to operate machines	indirect expenses*
Factory heating and lighting	indirect expenses
Plastic for making chair seats	direct materials
Hire of special machinery for one particular order	direct expenses
Grease for the moulding machine	indirect materials
Depreciation of factory machinery	indirect expenses
Depreciation of office equipment	indirect expenses

* Note: the cost of power to operate machines has been classified above as an indirect expense. This is often the case because it is not worthwhile analysing the cost of power for each unit of production. An industry that uses a lot of power will often have meters fitted to each machine so that costs may be identified and allocated to production as a direct expense. Other, lesser users of power, are unlikely to calculate the separate cost and will consider power to be an indirect expense. Whichever treatment is used, it is important that it is applied consistently.

1.7

COST ITEM	CLASSIFICATION
Dressings	direct materials
Disposable scalpels	direct materials
Surgeon's salary	direct labour
Floor cleaning materials	indirect materials
Laundry	indirect expenses*
Depreciation of staff drinks machine	indirect expenses*
Theatre heat and light	indirect expenses*
Porter's wages	indirect labour
Anaesthetic gas	direct materials
Depreciation of theatre equipment	indirect expenses
Maintenance of theatre equipment	indirect expenses
CDs for music in theatre	indirect expenses
Anaesthetist's salary	direct labour

* These items have been classified as indirect expenses – this is the most likely classification. If the money amount of any item was large, it would be worthwhile looking at the costing system to see if the item could be identified as a direct expense.

1.8

Cost item	**Total cost** £	**Prime cost** £	**Production overheads** £	**Admin costs** £	**Selling and distribution costs** £
Wages of employees working on the bottling line	6,025	6,025			
Wages of employees in the stores department	2,750		2,750		
Bottles	4,050	4,050			
Safety goggles for bottling line employees	240		240		
Advertisement for new employees	125			125	
Depreciation of bottling machinery	500		500		
Depreciation of sales staff's cars	1,000				1,000
Royalty paid to local farmer	750	750			
Trade exhibition fees	1,500				1,500
Computer stationery	210			210	
Sales staff salaries	4,095				4,095
TOTALS	21,245	10,825	3,490	335	6,595

1.9 (b) Salaries of maintenance staff

1.10 (d) Cost of paper

1.11 (a) Production overheads

1.12 (c) Administration costs

1.13 (c) A product cost is included in inventory valuation

CHAPTER 2: MATERIALS COSTS

2.1 ***Stock item D***

- maximum space = 350 units; average usage = 95 days x 3 units per day = 285 units; therefore maximum inventory is 285 units
- inventory buffer = 10 days x 3 units per day = 30 units
- re-order level = (7 days x 3 units per day) + 30 units = 51 units
- maximum order quantity = 285 units – 30 units = 255 units

Stock item E

- maximum space = 350 units; average usage = 95 days x 4 units per day = 380; therefore maximum inventory is 350 units
- inventory buffer = 10 days x 4 units per day = 40 units
- re-order level = (7 days x 4 units per day) + 40 units = 68 units
- maximum order quantity = 350 units – 40 units = 310 units

2.2 **Economic Order Quantity (EOQ)** $= \sqrt{\dfrac{2 \times 72{,}000 \times 20}{£2}}$

$$= \sqrt{\frac{2{,}880{,}000}{£2}}$$

$$= \sqrt{1{,}440{,}000}$$

$$= \underline{1{,}200 \text{ kg}}$$

2.3 (a) FIFO

INVENTORY RECORD

Date	Receipts			Issues			Balance		
	Quantity (units)	Cost per unit	Total Cost	Quantity (units)	Cost per unit	Total Cost	Quantity (units)	Cost per unit	Total Cost
20-4		£	£		£	£		£	£
January	20	3.00	60.00				20	3.00	60.00
February	10	3.60	36.00				20 10 30	3.00 3.60	60.00 36.00 96.00
March				8	3.00	24.00	12 10 22	3.00 3.60	36.00 36.00 72.00
April	10	4.00	40.00				12 10 10 32	3.00 3.60 4.00	36.00 36.00 40.00 112.00
May				12 4 16	3.00 3.60	36.00 14.40 50.40	6 10 16	3.60 4.00	21.60 40.00 61.60

(b) LIFO

INVENTORY RECORD

Date	Receipts			Issues			Balance		
	Quantity (units)	Cost per unit	Total Cost	Quantity (units)	Cost per unit	Total Cost	Quantity (units)	Cost per unit	Total Cost
20-4		£	£		£	£		£	£
January	20	3.00	60.00				20	3.00	60.00
February	10	3.60	36.00				20 10 30	3.00 3.60	60.00 36.00 96.00
March				8	3.60	28.80	20 2 22	3.00 3.60	60.00 7.20 67.20
April	10	4.00	40.00				20 2 10 32	3.00 3.60 4.00	60.00 7.20 40.00 107.20
May				10 2 4 16	4.00 3.60 3.00	40.00 7.20 12.00 59.20	16	3.00	48.00

(c) AVCO

INVENTORY RECORD

Date	Receipts			Issues			Balance		
	Quantity (units)	Cost per unit	Total Cost	Quantity (units)	Cost per unit	Total Cost	Quantity (units)	Cost per unit	Total Cost
20-4		£	£		£	£		£	£
January	20	3.00	60.00				20	3.00	60.00
February	10	3.60	36.00				20	3.00	60.00
							10	3.60	36.00
							30	3.20	96.00
March				8	3.20	25.60	22	3.20	70.40
April	10	4.00	40.00				22	3.20	70.40
							10	4.00	40.00
							32	3.45	110.40
May				16	3.45	55.20	16	3.45	55.20

2.4

(a) FIFO

INVENTORY RECORD: TYPE X

Date	Receipts			Issues			Balance		
	Quantity (units)	Cost per unit	Total Cost	Quantity (units)	Cost per unit	Total Cost	Quantity (units)	Cost per unit	Total Cost
20-4		£	£		£	£		£	£
January	100	4.00	400.00				100	4.00	400.00
February				80	4.00	320.00	20	4.00	80.00
March	140	4.20	588.00				20	4.00	80.00
							140	4.20	588.00
							160		668.00
April	100	3.80	380.00				20	4.00	80.00
							140	4.20	588.00
							100	3.80	380.00
							260		1,048.00
May				20	4.00	80.00			
				120	4.20	504.00	20	4.20	84.00
				140		584.00	100	3.80	380.00
							120		464.00
June	80	4.50	360.00				20	4.20	84.00
							100	3.80	380.00
							80	4.50	360.00
							200		824.00

(b) LIFO

INVENTORY RECORD: TYPE X

Date	**Receipts**			**Issues**			**Balance**		
	Quantity (units)	Cost per unit	Total Cost	Quantity (units)	Cost per unit	Total Cost	Quantity (units)	Cost per unit	Total Cost
20-4		£	£		£	£		£	£
January	100	4.00	400.00				100	4.00	400.00
February				80	4.00	320.00	20	4.00	80.00
March	140	4.20	588.00				20	4.00	80.00
							140	4.20	588.00
							160		668.00
April	100	3.80	380.00				20	4.00	80.00
							140	4.20	588.00
							100	3.80	380.00
							260		1,048.00
May				100	3.80	380.00	20	4.00	80.00
				40	4.20	168.00	100	4.20	420.00
				140		548.00	120		500.00
June	80	4.50	360.00				20	4.00	80.00
							100	4.20	420.00
							80	4.50	360.00
							200		860.00

(c) AVCO

INVENTORY RECORD: TYPE X

Date	**Receipts**			**Issues**			**Balance**		
	Quantity (units)	Cost per unit	Total Cost	Quantity (units)	Cost per unit	Total Cost	Quantity (units)	Cost per unit	Total Cost
20-4		£	£		£	£		£	£
January	100	4.00	400.00				100	4.00	400.00
February				80	4.00	320.00	20	4.00	80.00
March	140	4.20	588.00				20	4.00	80.00
							140	4.20	588.00
							160	4.17	668.00
April	100	3.80	380.00				160	4.17	668.00
							100	3.80	380.00
							260	4.03	1,048.00
May				140	4.03	564.20	120	4.03	483.80
June	80	4.50	360.00				120	4.03	483.80
							80	4.50	360.00
							200	4.22	843.80

Note: The cost per unit is calculated to two decimal places and is used to work out the issue costs. The total cost balance is the difference between the previous total cost balance and the issues. In assessments you should be careful to note how you should round when using AVCO.

(a) FIFO

INVENTORY RECORD: TYPE Y

Date	Receipts			Issues			Balance		
	Quantity (units)	Cost per unit	Total Cost	Quantity (units)	Cost per unit	Total Cost	Quantity (units)	Cost per unit	Total Cost
20-4		£	£		£	£		£	£
January	200	10.00	2,000.00				200	10.00	2,000.00
February	100	9.50	950.00				200	10.00	2,000.00
							100	9.50	950.00
							300		2,950.00
March				200	10.00	2,000.00			
				40	9.50	380.00			
				240		2,380.00	60	9.50	570.00
April	100	10.50	1,050.00				60	9.50	570.00
							100	10.50	1,050.00
							160		1,620.00
May	140	10.00	1,400.00				60	9.50	570.00
							100	10.50	1,050.00
							140	10.00	1,400.00
							300		3,020.00
June				60	9.50	570.00			
				40	10.50	420.00	60	10.50	630.00
				100		990.00	140	10.00	1,400.00
							200		2,030.00

(b) LIFO

INVENTORY RECORD: TYPE Y

Date	Receipts			Issues			Balance		
	Quantity (units)	Cost per unit	Total Cost	Quantity (units)	Cost per unit	Total Cost	Quantity (units)	Cost per unit	Total Cost
20-4		£	£		£	£		£	£
January	200	10.00	2,000.00				200	10.00	2,000.00
February	100	9.50	950.00				200	10.00	2,000.00
							100	9.50	950.00
							300		2,950.00
March				100	9.50	950.00			
				140	10.00	1,400.00	60	10.00	600.00
				240		2,350.00			
April	100	10.50	1,050.00				60	10.00	600.00
							100	10.50	1,050.00
							160		1,650.00
May	140	10.00	1,400.00				60	10.00	600.00
							100	10.50	1,050.00
							140	10.00	1,400.00
							300		3,050.00
June				100	10.00	1,000.00	60	10.00	600.00
							100	10.50	1,050.00
							40	10.00	400.00
							200		2,050.00

(c) AVCO

INVENTORY RECORD: TYPE Y

Date	Receipts			Issues			Balance		
	Quantity (units)	Cost per unit	Total Cost	Quantity (units)	Cost per unit	Total Cost	Quantity (units)	Cost per unit	Total Cost
20-4		£	£		£	£		£	£
January	200	10.00	2,000.00				200	10.00	2,000.00
February	100	9.50	950.00				200	10.00	2,000.00
							100	9.50	950.00
							300	9.83	2,950.00
March				240	9.83	2,360.00	60	9.83	590.00
April	100	10.50	1,050.00				60	9.83	590.00
							100	10.50	1,050.00
							160	10.25	1,640.00
May	140	10.00	1,400.00				160	10.25	1,640.00
							140	10.00	1,400.00
							300	10.13	3,040.00
June				100	10.13	1,013.00	200	10.13	2,027.00

Note: The cost per unit is calculated to two decimal places and is used to work out the issue costs. The total cost balance is the difference between the previous total cost balance and the issues. In assessments you should be careful to note how you should round when using AVCO.

2.5 Task 1

INVENTORY RECORD

Product: Wholewheat flour

Date	Receipts			Issues			Balance	
	Quantity (kgs)	Cost per kg	Total Cost	Quantity (kgs)	Cost per kg	Total Cost	Quantity (kgs)	Total Cost
20-4		£	£		£	£		£
Balance at 1 May							10,000	2,500
6 May	20,000	0.30	6,000				30,000	8,500
10 May				10,000 10,000 20,000	0.25 0.30	2,500 3,000 5,500	10,000	3,000
17 May	10,000	0.35	3,500				10,000 10,000 20,000	3,000 3,500 6,500
20 May				10,000 5,000 15,000	0.30 0.35	3,000 1,750 4,750	5,000	1,750

Task 2

20-4	**Code number**	**Debit £**	**Credit £**
6 May	3000	£6,000	
6 May	5000		£6,000
10 May	3300	£5,500*	
10 May	3000		£5,500
17 May	3000	£3,500	
17 May	5000		£3,500
20 May	3300	£4,750**	
20 May	3000		£4,750

* £2,500 + £3,000   ** £3,000 + £1,750

2.6 **(a)**

Economic Order Quantity (EOQ) $= \sqrt{\dfrac{2 \times 57{,}600 \text{ kg} \times £25}{£2}}$

$= \sqrt{\dfrac{2{,}880{,}000}{£2}}$

$= \sqrt{1{,}440{,}000}$

$= \underline{1{,}200 \text{ kg}}$

(b) and **(c)**

Inventory record for plastic grade P5

Date	Receipts			Issues			Balance	
	Quantity (kg)	Cost per kg	Total Cost	Quantity (kg)	Cost per kg	Total Cost	Quantity (kg)	Total Cost
		£	£		£	£		£
Balance as at 22 June							4,400	10,560
23 June	1,200	2.634	3,161				5,600	13,721
25 June				1,000	2.450	2,450	4,600	11,271
26 June	1,200	2.745	3,294				5,800	14,565
29 June				1,500	2.511	3,767	4,300	10,798

2.7

	Transaction	Account debited	Account credited
1	Receipt of materials into inventory, paying on credit	Inventory	Trade payables control
2	Issue of materials from inventory to production	Production	Inventory
3	Receipt of materials into inventory, paying immediately by BACS	Inventory	Bank
4	Return of materials from production to inventory	Inventory	Production

2.8 (d) Valuing inventory in order to maximise profit

CHAPTER 3: LABOUR COSTS

3.1 N Ball: 35 hours x £11.00 per hour = £385.00 (no bonus)
T Smith: 37 hours x £9.00 per hour = £333.00 + bonus £9.00 = £342.00
L Lewis: 38 hours x £10.00 per hour = £380.00 + bonus £15.00 = £395.00
M Wilson: 36 hours x £12.00 per hour = £432.00 + bonus £12.00 = £444.00

3.2

- L Fry: £400.00 (time rate)
- R Williams: £450.00 (piecework rate)
- P Grant: £362.50 (piecework rate)

3.3 Gross wages

		£
• Steve Kurtin:	35 hours at £10.50 per hour =	367.50
	4 hours overtime at £14.00 per hour =	56.00
	production bonus 45 x 50p =	22.50
		446.00
• Pete Singh:	35 hours at £12.00 per hour =	420.00
	3 hours overtime at £16.00 per hour =	48.00
	4 hours overtime at £18.00 per hour =	72.00
	production bonus 57 x 50p =	28.50
		568.50

Piecework rate for Steve Kurtin
£446.00 ÷ 45 = £9.91 per 1,000 copies printed

3.4

	MOULDING	FINISHING
• Time saved	–	500
• Bonus (£)	–	2,525*
• Total labour cost (£)	41,160	47,975

* £45,450 ÷ 4,500 hours = £10.10 x 500 hours = £5,050 x 50% = £2,525

3.5 **(a)** Week 1: 400 hours at £10.20 per hour = £4,080

50 hours at 1.5 x £10.20 = 50 x £15.30 = £765

Total gross earnings for Week 1 = £4,080 + £765 = £4,845

Week 2: 400 hours at £10.20 per hour = £4,080 = Total gross earnings

(b) Week 1: Normally treated as indirect labour cost would be overtime premium on 50 hours, ie 50 x 0.5 x £10.20 = £255

Week 2: Normally treated as indirect labour cost would be 20 hours of non-production work at basic pay, ie 20 x £10.20 = £204

3.6 **Employee's weekly time sheet for week ending 15 April 20-6**

Employee: T Mantle			Profit Centre: Finishing			
Employee number: 170			Basic pay per hour: £14.00			
	Hours spent on production	Hours worked on indirect work	Notes	Basic pay £	Overtime premium £	Total pay £
Monday	6	0		84	0	84
Tuesday	5	2	8am-10am maintenance	98	7	105
Wednesday	7	0		98	7	105
Thursday	6	3	9am-12 noon training	126	21	147
Friday	8	0		112	14	126
Saturday	5	0		70	28	98
Sunday	0	0		0	0	0
Total	37	5		588	77	665

3.7 **Task 1**

Dr	Wages Control Account		Cr
	£		£
Cash/bank (net wages)	7,500	Production (direct labour)	6,500
HM Revenue & Customs (income tax & NIC)	1,450	Production overheads (indirect labour)	2,700
Pension contributions	750	Non-production overheads (administration)	500
	9,700		9,700

Task 2

20-4	Code number	Debit £	Credit £
26 March	3300	£6,500	
26 March	5200		£6,500
26 March	3500	£2,700	
26 March	5200		£2,700
26 March	3700	£500	
26 March	5200		£500

3.8 Total cost of direct labour for October:

			£
14,400 hours	x £10 per hour	=	144,000
1,600 hours	x £15 (£10 + £5) per hour	=	24,000
16,000 hours			168,000

Cost bookkeeping entries:

	Debit	Credit
	£	£
• production – 'Mulligan' clubs (1500)	168,000	
• wages control (5000)		168,000

3.9

(a) £645, ie 43 standard hours at £15

(b) £675, ie Monday £120, Tuesday £120, Wednesday £150, Thursday £165, Friday £120

(c) £650, ie above the standard hours produced

(d) £735, ie 44 actual hours at £15, plus flat-rate bonus of £75 for the week

3.10 (a)

Labour cost	**Hours**	£
Basic pay	416	4,160
Overtime rate 1	30	375
Overtime rate 2	15	225
Total cost before team bonus	461	4,760
Bonus payment		1,000
Total cost including team bonus		5,760

(b) The direct labour cost per equivalent unit for March is **£0.48**.

(c) The equivalent units of production with regard to labour for April will be **11,000** and the bonus payable will be **£530**.

CHAPTER 4: OVERHEADS AND EXPENSES

4.1 (a)

OVERHEAD ANALYSIS SHEET		
	MOULDING	FINISHING
Budgeted total overheads (£)	9,338	3,298
Budgeted machine hours	1,450	680
Budgeted overhead absorption rate (£)	6.44*	4.85**

* £9,338 ÷ 1,450 hours

** £3,298 ÷ 680 hours

(b)

JOB OVERHEAD ANALYSIS SHEET		
	MOULDING	FINISHING
Job machine hours	412	154
Budgeted overhead absorption rate (£)	6.44	4.85
Overhead absorbed by job (£)	2,653.28*	746.90**

* 412 hours x £6.44 per hour

** 154 hours x £4.85 per hour

(c) Direct labour hour

- With this method, production overhead is absorbed on the basis of the number of direct labour hours worked.
- While this is a commonly-used method, it is inappropriate where some output is worked on by hand while other output passes quickly through a machinery process and requires little direct labour time.
- This method may be appropriate for Wyvern Fabrication; however, much depends on the balance between direct labour hours and machine hours in the two production departments.

4.2 **(a)**

Budgeted overheads	**Basis of apportionment**	**Total**	**Dept A**	**Dept B**	**Dept C**
		£	£	£	£
Rent and rates	Floor space	7,210	3,090	1,545	2,575
Depn. of machinery	Value of machinery	10,800	5,400	3,240	2,160
Supervisor's salary	Production-line employees	12,750	6,800	3,400	2,550
Machinery insurance	Value of machinery	750	375	225	150
		31,510	15,665	8,410	7,435

(b) 37 hours x 48 weeks = 1,776 direct labour hours per employee

Dept A: 8 employees = 14,208 hours = £1.10 per direct labour hour

Dept B: 4 employees = 7,104 hours = £1.18 per direct labour hour

Dept C: 3 employees = 5,328 hours = £1.40 per direct labour hour

4.3 **(a)**

Budgeted overheads	**Basis of apportionment**	**Total**	**Machining**	**Finishing**	**Maintenance**
		£	£	£	£
Rent and rates	Floor space	5,520	2,760	1,840	920
Buildings insurance	Floor space	1,320	660	440	220
Machinery insurance	Value of machinery	1,650	1,200	450	–
Lighting and heating	Floor space	3,720	1,860	1,240	620
Depn of machinery	Value of machinery	11,000	8,000	3,000	–
Supervisory salaries	No. of employees	30,000	18,000	9,000	3,000
Maintenance dept salary	Allocation	16,000	–	–	16,000
Factory cleaning	Floor space	4,800	2,400	1,600	800
		74,010	34,880	17,570	21,560
Re-apportionment of maintenance dept	Value of machinery	–	15,680	5,880	(21,560)
		74,010	50,560	23,450	–

(b) 35 hours x 47 weeks = 1,645 direct labour hours per employee
Machining Dept: 6 employees = 9,870 hours = £5.12 per direct labour hour
Finishing Dept: 3 employees = 4,935 hours = £4.75 per direct labour hour

(c) Depending on the method and type of production, the company is most likely to use overhead absorption rates based on:

- direct labour hour, or
- machine hour

These are discussed in the text (pages 138-139). Alternative methods include direct labour percentage add-on, and miles travelled.

4.4

Budgeted overheads	**Total**	**Business studies**	**General studies**	**Administration**	**Technical support**
		£	£	£	£
Overheads	81,600	40,000	20,000	9,600	12,000
Technical support	–	6,000	3,000	3,000	(12,000)
				12,600	–
Administration	–	8,400	4,200	(12,600)	–
	81,600	54,400	27,200	–	–

4.5 **(a)** $\frac{\text{total overheads}}{\text{total hours}} = \frac{\text{£59,900 (total of all overhead costs)}}{\text{3,290 (35 hours x 47 weeks x 2 partners)}} =$ £18.21 per partner hour

(b) $\frac{\text{£59,900 + £60,000}}{\text{3,290}}$ = £36.44 per partner hour

(c) 2 hours x 47 weeks x £18.21 = £1,711.74 per partner (ie £3,423.48 in total)

4.6 **(a)** Direct labour hour: (3 hours x 80 seats) + (3.5 hours x 40 seats)
= 380 direct labour hours per month = £2.63 per hour.

Machine hour: (1 hour x 80 seats) + (2.5 hours x 40 seats)
= 180 machine hours per month = £5.56 per hour.

Alternative methods could be based on a percentage of certain costs, eg direct labour.

(b) **Direct labour hour**

'Standard'	£36.50 + £7.89 (3 x £2.63)	=	£44.39
'De Luxe'	£55.00 + £9.21 (3.5 x £2.63)	=	£64.21

Machine hour

'Standard'	£36.50 + £5.56	=	£42.06
'De Luxe'	£55.00 + £13.89	=	£68.89

Note: some figures have been rounded to the nearest penny

(c) See text page 106. The machine hour rate charges most to 'de luxe' model. On balance, direct labour hours may be the best method to use because the products are more labour-intensive than machine-intensive.

4.7 Task 1

Budgeted fixed overheads for November 20-1	**Basis**	**Total** £	**Warehouse** £	**Manufacturing** £	**Sales** £	**Administration** £
Depreciation	Net book value*	9,150	1,830	6,100	305	915
Rent	Floor space	11,000	1,650	6,600	1,100	1,650
Other property overheads	Floor space	6,200	930	3,720	620	930
Administration overheads	Allocated	13,450				13,450
Staff costs	Allocated	27,370	3,600	9,180	8,650	5,940
		67,170	8,010	25,600	10,675	22,885

* carrying amount

Task 2

Budgeted fixed overhead absorption rate for the manufacturing department:

£25,600 ÷ 10,000 hours = £2.56 per machine hour

4.8 Task 1

Budgeted fixed overheads for August 20-3	Basis	Total £	Accommodation £	Restaurant £	Bar £	Kitchen £	Administration £
Bedroom repairs	Allocated	3,200	3,200				
Electricity	Metered	1,700	550	250	150	700	50
Rent	Floor space	9,000	5,850	1,350	900	450	450
Kitchen repairs	Allocated	1,025				1,025	
Staff costs	Allocated	23,595	4,550	6,740	3,045	2,310	6,950
Other property overheads	Floor space	4,000	2,600	600	400	200	200
		42,520	16,750	8,940	4,495	4,685	7,650
Administration			4,590	1,530	765	765	(7,650)
		42,520	21,340	10,470	5,260	5,450	–

Task 2

Budgeted fixed overhead absorption rate for the kitchen:

£5,450 ÷ 1,000 hours = £5.45 per labour hour

4.9

Budgeted overheads	**Basis of apportionment**	**Moulding** £	**Finishing** £	**Maintenance** £	**Stores** £	**Admin** £	**Totals** £
Depreciation charge for machinery	Carrying amount of machinery	1,200	750				1,950
Power for production machinery	Power usage	1,736	868				2,604
Rent and rates of premises	Floor space	1,425	760	570	665	855	4,275
Light and heat for premises	Floor space	975	520	390	455	585	2,925
Indirect labour	Allocated			32,200	17,150	28,450	77,800
Totals		5,336	2,898	33,160	18,270	29,890	89,554
Re-apportion Maintenance		24,870	8,290	(33,160)			
Re-apportion Stores		10,962	7,308		(18,270)		
Re-apportion Administration		14,945	14,945			(29,890)	
Total overheads to production centres		56,113	33,441				89,554

4.10 **(a)** (d) cutting £20 per hour; assembly £75 per hour

(b) (a) cutting £9 per hour; assembly £25 per hour

(c) (b) cutting-over absorbed £7,400; assembly under-absorbed £3,500

4.11

Dr Production Overheads Account: Moulding Department (3400) Cr

	£		£
Bank (overheads incurred)	5,000	Production	4,800
		Statement of profit or loss (under-absorption)	200
	5,000		5,000

Dr Production Overheads Account: Finishing Department (3500) Cr

	£		£
Bank (overheads incurred)	7,000	Production	7,500
Statement of profit or loss (over-absorption)	500		
	7,500		7,500

20-6	Code number	Debit £	Credit £
26 May	3000	4,800	
26 May	3400		4,800
26 May	3000	7,500	
26 May	3500		7,500
26 May	6000	200	
26 May	3400		200
26 May	3500	500	
26 May	6000		500

4.12

Dr	**Production Overheads Account: Baking Department (2600)**		Cr
	£		£
Bank (overheads incurred)	11,500	Production	12,000
Statement of profit or loss (over-absorption)	500		
	12,000		12,000

Dr	**Production Overheads Account: Finishing Department (2800)**		Cr
	£		£
Bank (overheads incurred)	5,000	Production	4,800
		Statement of profit or loss (under-absorption)	200
	5,000		5,000

20-6	**Code number**	**Debit £**	**Credit £**
11 March	2000	12,000	
11 March	2600		12,000
11 March	2000	4,800	
11 March	2800		4,800
11 March	2600	500	
11 March	5000		500
11 March	5000	200	
11 March	2800		200

CHAPTER 5: METHODS OF COSTING

5.1 The method of costing for each business should be justified; however, the following are the most likely methods:

- *accountant* – job costing, because each job will take a different length of time and is likely to involve a number of staff, each with different skill levels
- *bus company* – service costing, where the object is to find the cost per unit of service, eg passenger mile; job costing used for 'one-offs', eg quoting for the transport for a trip to the seaside for an old people's home
- *baker* – batch costing, where identical units are produced in batches, eg loaves; job costing could be used for 'one-off' items, eg a wedding cake
- *sports centre* – service costing, or job costing for 'one-off', eg hire of the main sports hall for an exhibition
- *hotel* – different methods of costing are likely to be used, eg service costing for the rooms, batch costing in the restaurant, and job costing for special events

5.2

			£	£
	Direct materials:	100m x £7.50	750.00	
		75m x £4.00	300.00	
				1,050.00
	Direct labour:	35 hours x £10.00		350.00
	Variable overheads:	35 hours x £8.50		297.50
(a)	TOTAL COST			1,697.50
	Profit (20% of total cost)			339.50
(b)	SELLING PRICE			2,037.00

5.3

JOB COST SHEET **Replacement Cylinder Head**		£
Direct materials		1,000.00
100 kg of high-strength steel at £10 per kg		
Direct Labour		
Foundry:	10 hours at £10.00 per hour	100.00
Finishing:	15 hours at £12.00 per hour	180.00
Overheads		
Foundry:	80% of direct labour cost	80.00
Finishing:	12 machine hours x £20 per hour	240.00
TOTAL COST		1,000.00
Profit (25% of total cost)		400.00
SELLING PRICE		2,000.00

5.4 **Total costs:**

	£
Depreciation of diesel trains £60,000* x 6 trains	360,000
Leasing charges for track	1,000,000
Maintenance charges for trains	910,000
Fuel for trains	210,000
Wages of drivers and conductors	480,000
Administration	520,000
	3,480,000

* (£1,300,000 – £100,000) ÷ 20 years = £60,000 per train per year

Total cost per passenger mile:

$\frac{\text{£3,480,000}}{\text{2.5m journeys x 5 miles}}$ = £0.28 total cost per passenger mile

5.5

Cost element	Costs	Completed units	Work-in-progress			Total equivalent units	Cost per unit	WIP valuation
			Units	% complete	Equivalent units			
	A	B	C	D	E	F	G	H
					C x D	B + E	A ÷ F	E x G
	£						£	£
Direct materials	11,500	20,000	5,000	100	5,000	25,000	0.46	2,300
Direct labour	9,000	20,000	5,000	50	2,500	22,500	0.40	1,000
Variable production overheads	18,000	20,000	5,000	50	2,500	22,500	0.80	2,000
Total	38,500						1.66	5,300

- Cost per toy is £1.66 each
- Work-in-progress valuation is £5,300

5.6 **(a)** (**Note:** normal loss, with scrap sales)

Dr		Process Account					Cr
	Quantity (litres)	Unit cost	Total cost		Quantity (litres)	Unit cost	Total cost
		£	£			£	£
Materials	22,000	0.25	5,500	Normal loss	2,000	0.20	400
Labour		0.15	3,300	Finished goods	20,000	0.53	10,600
Overheads		0.10	2,200				
	22,000		11,000		22,000		11,000

Tutorial note:

The cost per unit of the expected output is:

$$\frac{£11,000 - £400}{20,000 \text{ litres}} = £0.53 \text{ per litre}$$

(b)

	Debit £	**Credit £**
Normal loss account	400	

5.7 (**Note:** abnormal loss, with scrap sales)

Dr			Process Account				Cr
	Quantity (kg)	Unit cost	Total cost		Quantity (kg)	Unit cost	Total cost
		£	£			£	£
Materials	42,000	0.25	10,500	Normal loss	2,000	0.20	400
Labour		0.10	4,200	Finished goods	39,500	0.41	16,195
Overheads		0.05	2,100	Abnormal loss	500	0.41	205
	42,000		16,800		42,000		16,800

Tutorial note:

The cost per unit of the expected output is:

$$\frac{£16,800 - £400}{40,000 \text{ kilos}} = £0.41 \text{ per kg}$$

Dr	Normal Loss Account		Cr
	£		£
Process account	400	Bank/trade receivables	400

Dr	Abnormal Loss Account		Cr
	£		£
Process account	205	Bank/ trade receivables (500 kg x 20p)	100

5.8 (**Note:** normal loss, with scrap sales)

Dr			Process 1 Account				Cr
	Quantity (litres)	Unit cost	Total cost		Quantity (litres)	Unit cost	Total cost
		£	£			£	£
Materials	10,000	0.50	5,000	Normal loss (10%)	1,000	0.40	400
Labour		0.40	4,000	Transfer to			
Overheads		0.20	2,000	process 2	9,000	1.18	10,600
	10,000		11,000		10,000		11,000

(**Note:** abnormal loss, with scrap sales)

Dr	Process 2 Account						Cr
	Quantity (litres)	Unit cost	Total cost		Quantity (litres)	Unit cost	Total cost
		£	£			£	£
Transfer from process 1	9,000	1.18	10,600	Normal loss (5%)	450	0.50	225
Labour		0.20	1,800	Finished goods	8,300	1.58	13,130
Overheads		0.15	1,350	Abnormal loss	250	1.58	395
	9,000		13,750		9,000		13,750

Tutorial notes:

- In process 1, the cost per unit of the expected output is:

  $\frac{£11,000 - £400}{9,000 \text{ litres}}$ = £1.18 per litre (to the nearest penny, but note that £1.1778 is used to calculate total cost)

- In process 2, the cost per unit of the expected output is:

  $\frac{£13,750 - £225}{8,550 \text{ litres}}$ = £1.58 per litre (to the nearest penny, but note that £1.5819 is used to calculate total cost)

5.9 (**Note:** abnormal gain)

Dr	Process Account						Cr
	Quantity (litres)	Unit cost	Total cost		Quantity (litres)	Unit cost	Total cost
		£	£			£	£
Materials	11,000	0.50	5,500	Normal loss	1,000	0.30	300
Labour		0.35	3,850	Finished goods	10,200	1.18	12,036
Overheads		0.25	2,750				
			12,100				
Abnormal gain	200	1.18	236				
	11,200		12,336		11,200		12,336

Tutorial note:

The cost per unit of the expected output is:

$\frac{£12,100 - £300}{10,000 \text{ litres}}$ = £1.18 per litre

Dr	Abnormal Gain Account		Cr
	£		£
Normal loss account	*60	Process account	236

Dr	Normal Loss Account		Cr
	£		£
Process account	300	Bank/trade receivables	*240
		Abnormal gain account	**60
	300		300

*(1,000 litres – 200 litres) at 30p per litre. **200 litres at 30p per litre

5.10 (a)

Description	kg	Unit cost £	Total cost £	Description	kg	Unit cost £	Total cost £
Material AB4	500	1.50	750	Normal loss	100	0.80	80
Material AC5	200	2.20	440	Output	900	*16.60	14,940
Material AD6	300	4.10	1,230				
Labour			4,200				
Overheads			8,400				
	1,000		15,020		1,000		15,020

$$*\frac{£15,020 - £80}{900 \text{ kg}}$$

(b)

	Debit	Credit
Abnormal loss		✓
Abnormal gain	✓	

5.11

(a) £ 0.61 (£8,400 + £6,240) ÷ 24,000 units

(b) £ 0.95 (£25,680 – £2,880) ÷ 24,000 units

(c) £ 0.80 (£8,400 + £6,240 + £4,560) ÷ 24,000 units

(d) £ 19,200 £8,400 + £6,240 + £4,560

(e) £ 22,800 £25,680 – £2,880

CHAPTER 6: MARGINAL, ABSORPTION AND ACTIVITY BASED COSTING

6.1 **(a)**

Marginal cost per coffee machine	£
Direct materials	25.00
Direct labour	20.00
MARGINAL COST	45.00

(b)

Absorption cost per coffee machine	£
Direct materials	25.00
Direct labour	20.00
Fixed production overheads £270,000 ÷ 15,000 machines	18.00
ABSORPTION COST	63.00

(c)

COFFEEWORKS LIMITED

Statement of profit or loss: 15,000 coffee machines

	£	£
Sales revenue (15,000 x £80)		1,200,000
Direct materials (15,000 x £25)	375,000	
Direct labour (15,000 x £20)	300,000	
Fixed production overheads	270,000	
TOTAL COST		945,000
GROSS PROFIT		255,000
Less non-production overheads		200,000
NET PROFIT		55,000

6.2 **(a)**

Marginal cost per barbecue	£
Direct materials	30.00
Direct labour	25.00
MARGINAL COST	55.00

(b)

Absorption cost per barbecue	£
Direct materials	30.00
Direct labour	25.00
Fixed production overheads 150,000 ÷ 10,000 barbecues	15.00
ABSORPTION COST	70.00

(c)

COOK-IT LIMITED
Statement of profit or loss: 10,000 barbecues

	£	£
Sales revenue (10,000 x £90)		900,000
Direct materials (10,000 x £30)	300,000	
Direct labour (10,000 x £25)	250,000	
Fixed production overheads	150,000	
TOTAL COST		700,000
GROSS PROFIT		200,000
Less non-production overheads		125,000
NET PROFIT		75,000

6.3

MAXXA LIMITED
Statement of profit or loss for the month ended 31 January 20-7

	MARGINAL COSTING		ABSORPTION COSTING	
	£	£	£	£
Sales revenue 3,000 units at £8 each		24,000		24,000
Variable costs				
Direct materials at £1.25 each	5,000		5,000	
Direct labour at £2.25 each	9,000		9,000	
	14,000			
Less Closing inventory (marginal cost*)				
1,000 units at £3.50 each	3,500			
	10,500			
Fixed production overheads	6,000		6,000	
			20,000	
Less Closing inventory (absorption cost*)				
1,000 units at £5 each			5,000	
Less Cost of sales		16,500		15,000
Gross profit		7,500		9,000
Less non-production overheads		4,000		4,000
Net profit		3,500		5,000

* Closing inventory is calculated on the basis of this year's costs:

marginal costing, variable costs only, ie £1.25 + £2.25 = £3.50 per unit

absorption costing, variable and fixed costs, ie £20,000 ÷ 4,000 units = £5 per unit

The difference in the profit is caused only by the closing inventory figures: £3,500 under marginal costing, and £5,000 under absorption costing. With marginal costing, the full amount of the fixed production overheads has been charged in this year's statement of profit or loss; by contrast, with absorption costing, part of the fixed production overheads (here £6,000 x 25%* = £1,500) has been carried forward in the inventory valuation.

* 1,000 units in stock out of 4,000 units manufactured

6.4 (a)

ACTIVTOYS LIMITED

Statement of profit or loss for the year ended 31 December 20-1

	MARGINAL COSTING		**ABSORPTION COSTING**	
	£	£	£	£
Sales revenue at £125 each		162,500		162,500
Variable costs				
Direct materials at £25 each	37,500		37,500	
Direct labour at £30 each	45,000		45,000	
	82,500			
Less Closing inventory (marginal cost*)				
200 frames at £55 each	11,000			
	71,500			
Fixed production overheads	82,500		82,500	
			165,000	
Less Closing inventory (absorption cost*)				
200 frames at £110 each			22,000	
Less Cost of sales		154,000		143,000
Gross profit		8,500		19,500
Less non-production overheads		8,000		8,000
Net profit		500		11,500

* Closing inventory is calculated on the basis of this year's costs:
marginal costing, variable costs only, ie £25 + £30 = £55 per frame x 200 frames = £11,000
absorption costing, variable and fixed costs,
ie £165,000 ÷ 1,500 frames = £110 per frame x 200 frames = £22,000

(b) Reasons for different profit figures:

- The difference in the profit figures is caused by the closing inventory figures: £11,000 under marginal costing and £22,000 under absorption costing – the same costs have been used, but fixed production overheads have been treated differently.
- Only fixed production overheads are dealt with differently using the techniques of marginal and absorption costing – both methods charge non-production overheads in full to the statement of profit or loss in the year to which they relate.
- With marginal costing, the full amount of the fixed production overheads has been charged in this year's statement of profit or loss; by contrast, with absorption costing,

part of the fixed production overheads (here, £11,000) has been carried forward to next year in the inventory valuation.

Comment on the directors' statement:

- A higher profit does not mean more money in the bank.
- The two costing methods simply treat fixed production overheads differently and, in a year when there is no closing inventory, total profits to date are exactly the same – but they occur differently over the years.
- For financial statements, Activtoys Limited must use the absorption cost inventory valuation of £22,000 in order to comply with IAS 2, *Inventories*.
- For accounting staff, ethical considerations must apply – profit statements must be prepared without manipulation or bias.

6.5 **(a)** Activity based costing is a costing method which charges overheads to production on the basis of activities. The cost per unit of a product can be calculated based on its use of activities.

(b) A cost driver is an activity which causes costs to be incurred

6.6 Benefits of activity based costing (ABC) over absorption costing:

- more accurate – it identifies what causes overheads to be incurred for a particular activity
- more objective – overheads are charged to production on the basis of activities
- selling prices – more accurate because overheads are analysed to the products which use the activities
- appropriate for capital-intensive industries where overheads are high and complex in nature

6.7 (c) Agreeing with the business owner to use absorption costing for the closing inventory

CHAPTER 7: ASPECTS OF BUDGETING

7.1

	high output	15,000 units	£65,000
less	low output	10,000 units	£50,000
equals	difference	5,000 units	£15,000

- amount of variable cost per unit:

  $$\frac{£15,000}{5,000} = £3 \text{ variable cost per unit}$$

- at 10,000 units of output the cost structure is:

	total cost	£50,000
less	variable costs (10,000 units x £3 per unit)	£30,000
equals	fixed costs	£20,000

- check at 15,000 units of output when the cost structure is:

	variable costs (15,000 units x £3 per unit)	£45,000
add	fixed costs (as above)	£20,000
equals	total costs	£65,000

- therefore fixed costs, at these levels of output, are £20,000

7.2

Batches produced and sold	**1,000**	**1,200**	**2,000**
	£	£	£
Sales revenue	35,000	42,000	70,000
Variable costs:			
• Direct materials	7,500	9,000	15,000
• Direct labour	10,500	12,600	21,000
• Overheads	6,000	7,200	12,000
Semi-variable costs:	4,500		
• Variable element		1,800	3,000
• Fixed element		3,000	3,000
Total cost	28,500	33,600	54,000
Total profit	6,500	8,400	16,000
Profit per batch (to two decimal places)	6.50	7.00	8.00

7.3 (c) direct labour variance £1,400 adverse; direct materials variance £250 favourable

7.4 (d) direct labour variance £1,100 favourable; direct materials variance £450 adverse

7.5 (a) direct materials £19,575; direct labour £14,175

7.6

Flexed budget	**True**	**False**
Fixed overheads are shown in the flexed budget at a cost of £24,240		✓
Fixed overheads are shown in the flexed budget at a cost of £21,000		✓
Fixed overheads are shown in the flexed budget at a cost of £20,200	✓	
There is a fixed overheads variance of £800 adverse	✓	
There is a fixed overheads variance of £2,040 adverse		✓
There is no fixed overheads variance		✓

7.7

Cause of variance	**Adverse**	**Favourable**
Increase in material prices	✓	
Fewer materials are wasted		✓
Cheaper materials are used		✓
Theft of materials	✓	
An increase in direct labour pay	✓	
More efficient use of direct labour		✓
Overtime is paid to direct labour	✓	
A cheaper electricity supplier is used for the fixed overhead		✓
Selling prices are increased		✓
An increase in the number of units sold		✓

7.8 (a)

	Original budget	**Flexed budget**	**Actual**	**Variance**
Output level	100%	90%	90%	
	£	£	£	£
Direct materials	4,700	4,230	5,200	–970
Direct labour	10,800	9,720	8,900	820
Fixed overheads	4,100	4,100	4,500	–400
Total	19,600	18,050	18,600	–550

(b) (a) An increase in material prices

7.9 (a)

	Original budget	Flexed budget	Actual	Variance
Units sold	30,000	27,000	27,000	
	£000	*£000*	*£000*	*£000*
Sales revenue	1,800	1,620	1,650	30
Less costs:				
Direct materials	550	495	500	–5
Direct labour	340	306	297	9
Fixed overheads	650	650	645	5
Profit from operations	260	169	208	39

(b) (a) Sales revenue

7.10 (a)

	Original budget	Flexed budget	Actual	Variance
Units sold	22,000	27,500	27,500	
	£000	*£000*	*£000*	*£000*
Sales revenue	1,400	1,750	1,875	125
Less costs:				
Direct materials and direct labour	300	375	360	15
Variable overheads	500	625	645	–20
Fixed overheads	420	420	480	–60
Profit from operations	180	330	390	60

(b) (b) More efficient use of direct labour

7.11

	EX27 *(£)*	**EX45** *(£)*	**EX67** *(£)*	**Total** *(£)*
Selling price per unit	6.40	7.80	5.40	
Less: variable costs per unit				
Direct materials	2.25	3.45	2.85	
Direct labour	1.95	1.65	1.25	
Contribution per unit	2.20	2.70	1.30	
Sales volume (units)	9,000	12,000	15,000	
Total contribution	19,800	32,400	19,500	71,700
Less: fixed overheads				33,845
Budgeted profit/~~loss~~				37,855

7.12 (a)

	Original budget	**Flexed budget**	**Actual**	**Variance**
Units sold	10,000	11,200	11,200	
	£	£	£	£
Raw material A1	3,200	3,584	3,925	–341
Raw material A4	1,250	1,400	1,325	75
Skilled labour	4,850	5,432	5,060	372
Unskilled labour	1,225	1,372	1,440	–68
Variable overheads	4,025	4,508	4,310	198
Fixed overheads	5,740	5,740	6,140	–400
Total costs	20,290	22,036	22,200	–164

(b) (b) A reduction in employees' pay

CHAPTER 8: SHORT-TERM DECISIONS

8.1 **(a)** 200 bats = £9,000 loss; 1,200 bats = £6,000 profit

(b) **table**

Units of output	Fixed costs	Variable costs	Total cost	Sales revenue	Profit/(loss)*
	£	£	£	£	£
100	12,000	2,000	14,000	3,500	(10,500)
200	12,000	4,000	16,000	7,000	(9,000)
300	12,000	6,000	18,000	10,500	(7,500)
400	12,000	8,000	20,000	14,000	(6,000)
500	12,000	10,000	22,000	17,500	(4,500)
600	12,000	12,000	24,000	21,000	(3,000)
700	12,000	14,000	26,000	24,500	(1,500)
800	12,000	16,000	28,000	28,000	nil
900	12,000	18,000	30,000	31,500	1,500
1,000	12,000	20,000	32,000	35,000	3,000
1,100	12,000	22,000	34,000	38,500	4,500
1,200	12,000	24,000	36,000	42,000	6,000

* brackets indicate a loss

(c) **margin of safety**

$$\frac{\text{current output} - \text{break-even output}}{\text{current output}} \times \frac{100}{1} = \frac{1{,}000 - 800}{1{,}000} \times \frac{100}{1} = \underline{20\%}$$

margin of safety units = 1,000 – 800 = 200 units

8.2 (a) **2,000 units** per quarter

Contribution: £28 – £16 = £12 per unit

Fixed costs: £24,000

Break-even: £24,000 ÷ £12

(b) **£56,000** per quarter

2,000 units x £28

(c)

Units of WV5 sold per quarter	**2,500**	**4,000**
Margin of safety (units)	500*	2,000**
Margin of safety percentage	20%*	50%**

* 2,500 units ÷ 2,000 units to break-even

500 units ÷ 2,500 units of output x 100

** 4,000 units – 2,000 units to break-even

2,000 units ÷ 4,000 units of output x 100

(d) **3,500 units** per quarter

Fixed costs £24,000 + target profit £18,000 = £42,000

£42,000 ÷ £12

(e) (d) The breakeven point will increase and the margin of safety will decrease.

8.3 **Task 1**

- profit-volume (PV) ratio

$$\frac{\text{contribution (£)}}{\text{selling price (£)}} = \frac{\text{£15*}}{\text{£25}} = 0.6 \text{ or } 60\%$$

* selling price £25 – variable cost £10

- break-even point in units next month

$$\frac{\text{fixed costs (£)}}{\text{contribution per unit (£)}} = \frac{\text{£300,000}}{\text{£15}} = 20{,}000 \text{ units}$$

- break-even point in sales revenue next month

$$\frac{\text{fixed costs (£)}}{\text{PV ratio}} = \frac{\text{£300,000}}{0.6} = \text{£500,000}$$

check: 20,000 units x selling price £25 per unit = £500,000

- margin of safety at output of 30,000 units next month

$$\frac{\text{current output} - \text{break-even output}}{\text{current output}} = \frac{30{,}000 - 20{,}000}{30{,}000} \times \frac{100}{1}$$

= 33.3%, or 10,000 units, or £250,000 of sales revenue

- number of units to generate a target profit of £100,000 next month

$$\frac{\text{fixed costs (£) + target profit (£)}}{\text{contribution per unit (£)}} = \frac{£300{,}000 + £100{,}000}{£15} = 26{,}667 \text{ units}$$

Task 2

		Forecast output (30,000 units)	**Maximum output (40,000 units)**
		£	£
	sales revenue (at £25 each)	750,000	1,000,000
less	variable costs (at £10 each)	300,000	400,000
equals	contribution (to fixed costs and profit)	450,000	600,000
less	monthly fixed costs	300,000	300,000
equals	forecast profit for month	150,000	300,000

Task 3

- profit-volume (PV) ratio

$$\frac{£10^*}{£20} = 0.5 \text{ or } 50\%$$

* selling price £20 – variable cost £10

- break-even point in units

$$\frac{£300{,}000}{£10} = 30{,}000 \text{ units}$$

- break-even point in sales revenue

$$\frac{£300{,}000}{0.5} = £600{,}000$$

check: 30,000 units x selling price £20 per unit = £600,000

- margin of safety at maximum output of 40,000 units

$$\frac{40{,}000 - 30{,}000}{40{,}000} \times \frac{100}{1} = 25\%, \text{ or } 10{,}000 \text{ units, or } £200{,}000 \text{ of sales revenue}$$

- forecast profit at sales of 40,000 units

		£
	sales revenue (at £20 each)	800,000
less	variable costs (at £10 each)	400,000
equals	contribution (to fixed costs and profit)	400,000
less	monthly fixed costs	300,000
equals	forecast profit for month	100,000

REPORT

To: General Manager

From: Accounts Assistant

Date: Today

Proposal to reduce selling price

Introduction

- You asked me to report on the suggestion from one of the managers that the selling price for our product should be reduced from £25 per unit to £20.
- The manager has suggested that the effect of this reduction would be to increase output from the forecast of 30,000 units per month to our maximum output of 40,000 units per month.

Report

- As can be seen from the workings at current levels of output of 30,000 units per month:
  - contribution sales ratio is 60%
  - break-even point is 20,000 units
  - margin of safety is 33.3%
  - forecast profit is £150,000 per month
- If the manager's suggestion is adopted sales will increase to our maximum output of 40,000 units per month; this will give us:
  - contribution sales ratio of 50%
  - break-even point of 30,000 units
  - margin of safety of 25%
  - forecast profit of £100,000 per month

Conclusion

- From the data summarised above it can be seen that the manager's suggestion would reduce our contribution sales ratio, increase the break-even point, and reduce the margin of safety. All of these are all movements in the wrong direction.
- The main point to note is that forecast profit will fall by £50,000 per month to £100,000 per month, and the volume of output will need to be higher.
- Although we would be working at maximum output if the suggestion is adopted, this does mean that there is no scope to increase output and sales in the future without major changes to our cost structure. We would not be able to meet requests for additional sales from our existing customers, and this could cause them to seek all of their supplies from our competitors.
- For these reasons, I would recommend that the manager's suggestion is not undertaken.

8.4 Task 1

Product	**'Madrid'** £	**'Paris'** £	**'Rome'** £
Selling price per unit	30	40	60
Less: Unit variable costs			
Direct materials	10	15	20
Direct labour	5	8	12
Variable overheads	2	3	2.50
Contribution per unit	13	14	25.50

Task 2

Break-even point for the 'Madrid' range is:

$$\frac{\text{fixed costs (£)}}{\text{contribution per unit (£)}} = \frac{£72{,}800}{£13} = \underline{5{,}600 \text{ units}}$$

Task 3

Product	**'Madrid'**	**'Paris'**	**'Rome'**
Contribution per unit	£13	£14	£25.50
Machine hours per unit	0.5	0.4	0.75
Contribution per machine hour	£26	£35	£34

Task 4

- Machine hours are the limiting factor here, with only 3,000 hours available.
- To maximise profits, the company should maximise the contribution from each machine hour.
- The preferred order is 'Paris' (at £35 contribution per machine hour), 'Rome' (at £34), and 'Madrid' (at £26).
- The company's production plan will be:

'Paris', 3,000 units x 0.4 hours per unit	=	1,200 hours
'Rome', 500 units x 0.75 hours per unit	=	375 hours
'Madrid', 2,850 units x 0.5 hours per unit	=	1,425 balance of hours available
		3,000 hours

Note that this production plan does not allow for full production of the 'Madrid' range.

8.5

REPORT

To: Production Manager

From: Accounts Assistant

Date: Today

Production of products A and B

Introduction

- You asked for my recommendations for next week's production.
- Materials used in the production of both products are in short supply and we are currently only able to obtain 500 kgs each week. We therefore need to use these materials to the best advantage of the company.

Report

- With insufficient direct materials we have a limiting factor (or a scarce resource). To make best use of this limiting factor to produce profits for the company, we must maximise the contribution (selling price – variable costs) from each kg of direct material.
- The contribution from producing each unit of A is £30. As this product requires two kgs of material, the contribution per kg is £30 ÷ 2 kgs = £15 per kg.
- The contribution from producing each unit of B is £50. As this product requires four kgs of material, the contribution per kg is £50 ÷ 4 kgs = £12.50 per kg.
- To make best use of the limiting factor of direct material, the company should produce all of product A that can be sold, ie 200 per week. This will take 400 kgs of materials (200 units x 2 kgs each) and will leave 100 kgs available to produce 25 of product B (25 units x 4 kgs each).
- Please note that, if this production plan is followed, insufficient of product B will be produced to meet demand. This may make it difficult to re-establish it in the market when full production of this product can be resumed once the shortage of direct materials has been resolved.

Conclusion

- Based on the concept of maximising the contribution from each kg of material (the limiting factor), I recommend that the production for next week should be:

  200 units of product A

  25 units of product B

- This will give a forecast statement of profit or loss for next week as follows:

		Product A	Product B	Total
		£	£	£
	Sales revenue:			
	200 product A at £150 per unit	30,000		30,000
	25 product B at £200 per unit		5,000	5,000
		30,000	5,000	35,000
less	Variable costs:			
	200 product A at £120 per unit	24,000		24,000
	25 product B at £150 per unit		3,750	3,750
equals	Contribution	6,000	1,250	7,250
less	Fixed overheads			4,000
equals	Profit			3,250

8.6 Task 1

DURNING FOODS LIMITED: Production line for Indian meals

Planned results for November 20-8

Number of meals to be sold	36,000
	£
Direct materials at 75p per meal	27,000
Direct labour at 45p per meal	16,200
Direct expenses at 20p per meal	7,200
Overheads for Indian meals production line	
at £7,500 + 15p per meal	12,900
Other production overheads	4,000
Total cost	67,300
Sales revenue at £2.00 per meal	72,000
Profit	4,700

Workings (using figures for July):

- direct materials per meal = £25,125 ÷ 33,500 meals = £0.75
- direct labour per meal = £15,075 ÷ 33,500 meals = £0.45
- direct expenses per meal = £6,700 ÷ 33,500 meals = £0.20
- overheads for Indian meals production line

	Meals	£
high	34,700	12,705
low	31,000	12,150
difference	3,700	555

variable cost per meal = £555 ÷ 3,700 meals = £0.15

fixed cost = £12,525 – (£0.15 x 33,500 meals) = £7,500

- other production overheads: fixed cost = £4,000 per month
- sales revenue per meal = £67,000 ÷ 33,500 meals = £2.00

Task 2

DURNING FOODS LIMITED: Production line for Indian meals

Planned results for November 20-8: increased activity

Number of meals to be sold	40,000
	£
Direct materials at 75p – 20% = 60p per meal	24,000
Direct labour at 45p per meal	18,000
Direct expenses at 20p per meal	8,000
Overheads for Indian meals production line at £7,500 + 15p per meal	13,500
Other production overheads	4,000
Total cost	67,500
Sales revenue at £2.00 per meal	80,000
Profit	12,500

Break-even point

		£	£
Contribution per meal:			
	selling price		2.00
less	variable costs:		
	direct materials	0.60	
	direct labour	0.45	
	direct expenses	0.20	
	production line overheads	0.15	
			1.40
equals	contribution per meal		0.60
Fixed costs:			
	production line overheads		7,500
	other production overheads		4,000
			11,500

Break-even point:

$$\frac{£11{,}500}{£0.60} = 19{,}167 \text{ meals}$$

Margin of safety

$$\frac{40{,}000 - 19{,}167}{40{,}000} \times \frac{100}{1} = 52\%$$

8.7 The marginal cost per unit of Exe is £5 (direct materials £3 + direct labour £2), and so any contribution, ie selling price less marginal cost, will be profit:

- *200 units at £6 each*

The offer price of £6 is above the marginal cost of £5 and increases profit by the amount of the £1 extra contribution, ie (£6 – £5) x 200 units = £200 extra profit.

- *500 units at £4 each*

This offer price is below the marginal cost of £5; therefore there will be a fall in profit if this order is undertaken of (£4 – £5) x 500 units = £500 reduced profit.

WESTFIELD LIMITED
monthly statements of profit or loss

	Existing production of 2,000 units	Existing production + 200 units @ £6 each	Existing production + 500 units @ £4 each
	£	£	£
Sales revenue (per month):			
2,000 units at £12 each	24,000	24,000	24,000
200 units at £6 each	–	1,200	–
500 units at £4 each	–	–	2,000
	24,000	25,200	26,000
Less production costs:			
Direct materials (£3 per unit)	6,000	6,600	7,500
Direct labour (£2 per unit)	4,000	4,400	5,000
Production overheads (fixed)	8,000	8,000	8,000
PROFIT	6,000	6,200	5,500

The conclusion is that the first special order should be accepted, and the second declined.

8.8

POPCAN LIMITED
monthly statements of profit or loss

	Existing production of 150,000 cans	Existing production + 50,000 cans at 18p each
	£	£
Sales revenue (per month):		
150,000 cans at 25p each	37,500	37,500
50,000 cans at 18p each	–	9,000
	37,500	46,500
Less production costs:		
Direct materials (5p per can)	7,500	10,000
Direct labour (5p per can)	7,500	10,000
Production overheads – variable (4p per can)	6,000	8,000
– fixed*	9,000	9,000
PROFIT	7,500	9,500

* 6p x 150,000 cans = £9,000

The offer from the supermarket chain should be accepted because:

- the marginal cost of producing each can is 14p (direct materials 5p, direct labour 5p, variable production overheads 4p)
- the offer price is 18p per can, which is above marginal cost, and gives a contribution of 4p
- profits increase by the amount of the extra contribution, ie (18p – 14p) x 50,000 cans = £2,000 extra profit

8.9 (d) Accounting staff are required to maintain their knowledge and skills to provide a competent service

CHAPTER 9: LONG-TERM DECISIONS

9.1 (a) payback period

	PROJECT EXE		PROJECT WYE	
Year	**Cash Flow**	**Cumulative Cash Flow**	**Cash Flow**	**Cumulative Cash Flow**
	£000	*£000*	*£000*	*£000*
0	–80	–80	–100	–100
1	40	–40	20	–80
2	40	–	30	–50
3	20	20	50	–
4	10	30	40	40
5	10	40	30	70

As can be seen from the above table:

- Project Exe pays back after two years
- Project Wye pays back after three years

(b) net present value

		PROJECT EXE		PROJECT WYE	
Year	**Discount Factor**	**Cash Flow**	**Discounted Cash Flow**	**Cash Flow**	**Discounted Cash Flow**
	at 12%	*£000*	*£000*	*£000*	*£000*
0	1.000	–80	–80	–100	–100
1	0.893	40	35.72	20	17.86
2	0.797	40	31.88	30	23.91
3	0.712	20	14.24	50	35.60
4	0.636	10	6.36	40	25.44
5	0.567	10	5.67	30	17.01
Net Present Value (NPV)			13.87		19.82

Appraisal method	Notes	Company policy	Project Exe	Project Wye
Payback period	-	2.5 years maximum	2 years ✔	3 years **x**
Net present value (NPV)	Discount at 12% cost of capital	Accept if positive	£13,870 ✔	£19,820 ✔
Advice to Robert Smith: Project Exe is to be preferred as it meets both of the investment criteria.				

9.2 Task 1

The net cash flows are:

	£000
year 1	–95
year 2	30
year 3	40
year 4	50
year 5	27

(a) payback period

Year	Cash Flow	Cumulative Cash Flow	
	£000	*£000*	
1	–95	–95	
2	30	–65	
3	40	–25	
4	50	25	∴ £25,000 required
5	27	52	

The design costs are recovered half-way through year 4: £30,000 + £40,000 + (£25,000/£50,000 x 12 months). Thus the payback period is 3 years and 6 months from the start of the project; in terms of revenue, the payback period is 2 years and 6 months. Note that these assume even cash flows during the year.

(b) net present value

Year	Cash Flow		Discount Factor at 10%	Discounted Cash Flow
	£000			*£000*
1	–95	x	0.909	–86.36
2	30	x	0.826	24.78
3	40	x	0.751	30.04
4	50	x	0.683	34.15
5	27	x	0.621	16.77
		Net Present Value (NPV)		19.38

Task 2

(a)

Year	Cash Flow		Discount Factor at 20%	Discounted Cash Flow
	£000			*£000*
1	–95	x	0.833	–79.14
2	30	x	0.694	20.82
3	40	x	0.579	23.16
4	50	x	0.482	24.10
5	27	x	0.402	10.85
		Net Present Value (NPV)		–0.21

This shows that the internal rate of return of the project is approximately 20%

(b)

- For this new project, the IRR, of almost 20 per cent is much higher than the 10% return required on new projects.
- This means that, in financial terms, the new project is acceptable – the wider the margin of IRR above the return required, the better.

9.3 (a) The discount factor that results in a net present value of zero

9.4 Task 1

DURNING FOODS LIMITED

Working paper for the financial appraisal of purchase of delivery vehicles

PAYBACK PERIOD

Year	Cash Flow	Cumulative Cash Flow	
	£	£	
20-4	–80,000	–80,000	
20-5	28,300	–51,700	
20-6	28,300	–23,400	
20-7	28,300	4,900	£23,400* required
20-8	38,300	43,200	

* £28,300 – £4,900

Payback period = 2 years + (£23,400/£28,300) = 2 years and 10 months (rounded up to the next month)

DISCOUNTED CASH FLOW

Year	Cash Flow	Discount Factor at 12%	Discounted Cash Flow
	£		£
20-4	–80,000	1.000	–80,000
20-5	28,300	0.893	25,272
20-6	28,300	0.797	22,555
20-7	28,300	0.712	20,150
20-8	*38,300	0.636	24,359
Net Present Value (NPV)			12,336

* £28,300 + £10,000 resale value

Task 2

REPORT
To: General Manager **From:** Accounts Assistant **Date:** 12 November 20-4
<u>Purchase of delivery vehicles</u> The proposal to purchase delivery vehicles is acceptable from a financial viewpoint for the following reasons: • The payback period is during 20-7. If we assume even cash flows during the year, the payback period can be calculated as 2.8 years (or 2 years and 10 months) from the start. This is acceptable since it is shorter than the company requirement of a maximum of three years, although there is not a great deal of room for error in the cash flow calculations. • The project returns a positive net present value of £12,336 at a discount rate of 12 per cent. This calculation assumes that all cash flows occur at the end of each year.

9.5 **Task 1**

The net cash flows are:

	£000
year 0	40
year 1	–60
year 2	45
year 3	54
year 4	90
year 5	60

(a) payback period

Year	**Cash Flow**	**Cumulative Cash Flow**	
	£000	*£000*	
0	–40	–40	
1	–60	–100	
2	45	–55	
3	54	–1	
4	90	89	∴ £1,000 required
5	60	149	

The development costs are recovered in the very early part of year 4: £45,000 + £54,000 + (£1,000/£90,000 x 12 months). Thus the payback period is 3 years and 0.13 months (ie less than one week into the next year) from the start of the project; in terms of revenue, the payback period is 2 years and 1 month (rounded up to the next month). Note that these assume even cash flows during the year.

(b) net present value

Year	**Cash Flow**		**Discount Factor at 12%**	**Discounted Cash Flow**
	£000			*£000*
0	–40	x	1.000	–40
1	–60	x	0.893	–53.58
2	45	x	0.797	35.86
3	54	x	0.712	38.45
4	90	x	0.636	57.24
5	60	x	0.567	34.02
		Net Present Value (NPV)		71.99

Task 2 (a) and **(b)**

REPORT

To: Managing Director

From: Accounts Assistant

Date: Today

<u>Introduction of a new range of bikes</u>

I have carried out an appraisal on the project, based on the information provided.

The net present value technique relies on discounting relevant cash flows at an appropriate rate of return. It would be helpful to know:

1. whether there are any additional cash flows beyond year 5
2. whether the introduction of a new range of bikes will affect sales of our existing bikes

On the basis of the information provided, the project has a positive net present value of £71,990 and should be carried out.

9.6 **(a)**

	Year 0 £000	**Year 1 £000**	**Year 2 £000**	**Year 3 £000**
Capital expenditure	–90			
Disposal				20
Sales income		55	70	60
Operating costs		–12	–15	–19
Net cash flows	–90	43	55	61
PV factors	1.0000	0.8696	0.7561	0.6575
Discounted cash flows	–90	37	42	40
Net present value	29			

	positive	✓
or	negative	

(b) The payback period is 1 year and 11 months (rounded up to the next month)

ie 43 + (90 – 43 = 47/55 x 12 months), using net cash flows

9.7 Compound interest table for each given percentage:

	4%	8%	12%
Year 0	1.00	1.00	1.00
Year 1	1.04	1.08	1.12
Year 2	1.08	1.17	1.25
Year 3	1.12	1.26	1.40

Applying the factors from the table into the net cash flows (in £000s):

4%

$$\frac{-900}{1} + \frac{220}{1.04} + \frac{350}{1.08} + \frac{590}{1.12}$$

= –900 + 211.54 + 324.07 + 526.79 = <u>162.40 net present value</u>

8%

$$\frac{-900}{1} + \frac{220}{1.08} + \frac{350}{1.17} + \frac{590}{1.26}$$

= –900 + 203.70 + 299.15 + 468.25 = <u>71.10 net present value</u>

12%

$$\frac{-900}{1} + \frac{220}{1.12} + \frac{350}{1.25} + \frac{590}{1.40}$$

= –900 + 196.43 + 280.00 + 421.43 = <u>–2.14 net present value</u>

Conclusion

The given percentage which is closest to the internal rate of return for this project is 12%, ie the percentage at which the project 'breaks even' (ie NPV is closest to zero).

9.8 (a)

	Year 0 £000	**Year 1 £000**	**Year 2 £000**	**Year 3 £000**
Net cash flows	–635	200	300	450
PV factors	1.0000	0.9091	0.8264	0.7513
Discounted cash flows	–635	181.82	247.92	338.09
Net present value	132.83			

(b) (a) Excalibur should accept the project because the net present value is positive

(c)

	Year 0 £000	Year 1 £000	Year 2 £000	Year 3 £000
Net cash flows	–635	200	300	450
Cumulative cash flows	–635	–435	–135	315

The payback period is | 2 | years and | 4 | months.

(d) (b) Excalibur should not accept the project because the payback period exceeds 2.0 years

(e) (d) 20%

Workings *(all figures in £000s)*

We know from part (a) that the NPV at 10% is £132.83. This tells us that IRR will be higher than 10%.

- Applying compound interest at 15%, the factors are:

  year 0 = 1.00; year 1 = 1.15; year 2 = 1.32; year 3 = 1.52

  Calculations are:

  $$\frac{-635}{1} + \frac{200}{1.15} + \frac{300}{1.32} + \frac{450}{1.52}$$

  = –635 + 173.91 + 227.27 + 296.05 = 62.23

- Applying compound interest at 20% the factors are:

  year 0 = 1.00; year 1 = 1.20; year 2 = 1.44; year 3 = 1.73

  Calculations are:

  $$\frac{-635}{1} + \frac{200}{1.20} + \frac{300}{1.44} + \frac{450}{1.73}$$

  = –635 + 166.67 + 208.33 + 260.12 = 0.12

Conclusion: IRR is approximately 20%, because this is the cost of capital at which NPV is closest to zero.

9.9

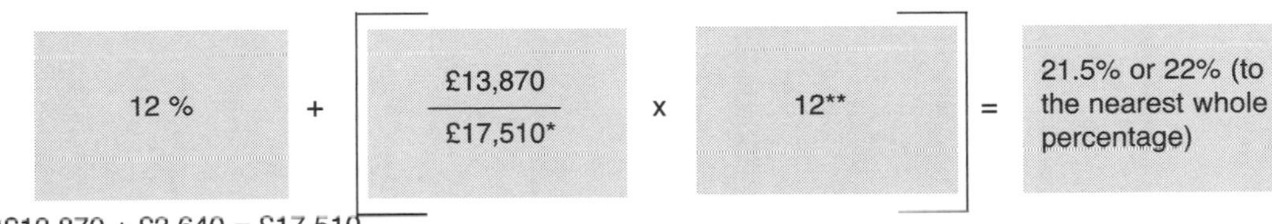

12 % + [£13,870 / £17,510* x 12**] = 21.5% or 22% (to the nearest whole percentage)

*£13,870 + £3,640 = £17,510

**24 – 12 = 12

Appendix: photocopiable resources

INVENTORY RECORD

Date	Receipts			Issues			Balance		
	Quantity (units)	Cost per unit	Total Cost	Quantity (units)	Cost per unit	Total Cost	Quantity (units)	Cost per unit	Total Cost
		£	£		£	£		£	£

EMPLOYEE'S WEEKLY TIME SHEET

Employee:			Cost/Profit/Investment Centre:			
Employee number:			Basic pay per hour:			
	Hours spent on production	Hours worked on indirect work	Notes	Basic pay £	Overtime premium £	Total pay £
Monday						
Tuesday						
Wednesday						
Thursday						
Friday						
Saturday						
Sunday						
Total						

ALLOCATION AND APPORTIONMENT TABLE

Budgeted overheads	Basis of apportionment	Profit centre £	Profit centre £	Support centre £	Support centre £	Support centre £	Totals £
Totals							
Re-apportion support centre							
Re-apportion support centre							
Re-apportion support centre							
Total overheads to production centres							

WORK-IN-PROGRESS CALCULATION

Cost element	Costs	Completed units	Work-in-progress			Total equivalent units	Cost per unit	WIP value
			Units	% complete	Equivalent units			
	A	B	C	D	E	F	G	H
					C x D	B + E	A ÷ F	E x G
	£						£	£

PROCESS COSTING ACCOUNTS

Dr			Process Account				Cr
	Quantity	Unit cost	Total cost		Quantity	Unit cost	Total cost
		£	£			£	£

Dr Abnormal Gain/Loss* Account		Cr	
	£		£

* delete as required

Dr Normal Loss Account		Cr	
	£		£

BUDGET REPORT

	Flexed budget	Actual	Variance	Favourable (F) or Adverse (A)
Volume sold				
	£000	*£000*	*£000*	
Sales revenue				
Less costs:				
Direct materials				
Direct labour				
Variable overheads				
Profit from operations				

REPORT
To: **From:** **Date:**

Index

for your notes

for your notes

for your notes

for your notes

for your notes